The Quest for Ecstatic Morality in Early China

THE QUEST FOR ECSTATIC MORALITY IN EARLY CHINA

Kenneth W. Holloway

Oxford University Press is a department of the University of Oxford.
It furthers the University's objective of excellence in research, scholarship,
and education by publishing worldwide.

Oxford   New York
Auckland   Cape Town   Dar es Salaam   Hong Kong   Karachi
Kuala Lumpur   Madrid   Melbourne   Mexico City   Nairobi
New Delhi   Shanghai   Taipei   Toronto

With offices in
Argentina   Austria   Brazil   Chile   Czech Republic   France   Greece
Guatemala   Hungary   Italy   Japan   Poland   Portugal   Singapore
South Korea   Switzerland   Thailand   Turkey   Ukraine   Vietnam

Oxford is a registered trademark of Oxford University Press
in the UK and certain other countries.

Published in the United States of America by
Oxford University Press
198 Madison Avenue, New York, NY 10016

© Oxford University Press 2013

All rights reserved. No part of this publication may be reproduced, stored in a
retrieval system, or transmitted, in any form or by any means, without the prior
permission in writing of Oxford University Press, or as expressly permitted by law,
by license, or under terms agreed with the appropriate reproduction rights organization.
Inquiries concerning reproduction outside the scope of the above should be sent to the
Rights Department, Oxford University Press, at the address above.

You must not circulate this work in any other form
and you must impose this same condition on any acquirer.

Library of Congress Cataloging-in-Publication Data
Holloway, Kenneth W., 1971-
The quest for ecstatic morality in early China / Kenneth W. Holloway.
p. cm.
Includes bibliographical references (p.) and index.
ISBN 978-0-19-994174-2 (pbk.: alk. paper)—ISBN 978-0-19-974482-4
(hardcover: alk. paper)
1. Ethics—China—History—To 1500.   2. Ecstasy—China—History—To 1500.
3. Xing zi ming chu.   I. Title.
BJ117.H6 2013
170.931—dc23   2012010937

ISBN   978-0-19-994174-2
ISBN   978-0-19-974482-4

9 8 7 6 5 4 3 2 1
Printed in the United States of America
on acid-free paper

For my father, Dr. Peter W. Holloway

CONTENTS

Preface   *ix*

Introduction   1
1. *Qing*, from Conflict to Ecstasy   9
2. The Role of Nature in a World of Friction   29
3. Having Fun with the Dao   45
4. Absolute versus Relative Morality   75
5. The Rectification of Names   89

Appendix   *113*
Notes   *125*
Bibliography   *147*
Index   *157*

PREFACE

On 08/08/08 the Olympics opened in China and each performer proudly unfurled an oversized replica of a document written on strips of bamboo. My first book analyzing exactly the same recently excavated bamboo manuscripts would be published by Oxford University Press in five months' time. The astonishment I felt was profound. I had been researching bamboo strips from the Warring States for almost a decade, and this work had been done in almost complete isolation. Seeing replicas of my bamboo strips on prime-time American TV was entirely unexpected.

I began to understand the broader connection of my work a little more clearly in the spring of 2009 when Master Hsing Yun, founder of the Fo-kuang Shan Buddhist order, asked me to present a paper at the Second World Buddhist Forum. This would be the first conference ever to begin in China and concluded in Taiwan. I presented a paper on the religious dimension of bamboo manuscripts from the end of the fourth century BCE and expected the response among Buddhist monastics to be tepid.[1] Surprisingly, every Chinese monk I spoke with was intensely interested in my paper. The opportunity to gain new insight into the early development of their own religious beliefs was something they immediately saw as important.

My research benefited immensely from a number of presentations I gave in preparation for writing this book. The first public talk I gave was at the Institutes for Advanced Studies in Humanities and Social Science at National Taiwan University, and it was organized by their dean, Dr. Huang Chun-chieh.[2] Following this, I received important feedback from talks at Carnegie Mellon, Eastern China Normal University, Fudan University, Rutgers University, and the American Academy of Religion. My last presentation on the term "Dao" was at the conference Contemporary Reflections on Epistemological Issues I was invited to at the philosophy department of National Taiwan University. I am very grateful for that opportunity, as it caused me to rethink several key parts of my project.

The challenge of writing this book was a direct result of analyzing the "Xing zi ming chu" 性自命出, a text which was lost for two thousand years. Then in the 1990s, it was suddenly found in two separate tombs in China that date from around 300 BCE. One tomb is called Guodian after the modern village that lies next to it. The other was looted and recovered on the black market in Hong Kong by the Shanghai Museum; it is referred to as the Shanghai Corpus. Excitement over these discoveries resulted in a number of scholars creating critical annotated editions of the "Xing zi ming chu," and they are cited in the appendix of this book. This wealth of research resulted in a staggering number of ways that the text could be interpreted. The characters date from before the First Emperor of China unified the script, so a large percentage of the characters can be read in two ways. Some can be read in three or four ways in Chinese, meaning that crafting an English translation was nothing less than a nightmare. The scholarship of Professor Ding Yuanzhi 丁原植 was an enormous help in writing this book. He assembled the main scholarly editions of the text, and provided copious references to numerous individual readings of every highly contested character. Naturally, Ding was not the only source I used, but it gave me a starting point for creating my own compilation of editions and the heavily annotated translation that appears as the appendix to this book.

Without the support of the Levenson family in endowing my chair in Asian Studies at Florida Atlantic University, it would be incredibly difficult to maintain the pace of my research, so I am grateful for their support. I would also like to thank my students for being an invaluable sounding board for my theories. In particular, my senior seminar class in the fall of 2009 was a huge help in working through my initial ideas for this book, which were at the time somewhat tentative. Dr. Paul R. Goldin was also extremely generous in reading an earlier draft of my translation that appears in the appendix of this book. Furthermore, his work in maintaining electronic bibliographies is a great service to the field. Dr. Steven Heine has been an important mentor during my time in South Florida, and his advice has been of great value. Alex Cheung generously allowed me to use his font for the appendix of this book. This project would not have been possible without the help of Cynthia Read, whose unwavering support has been truly fantastic.

Finally, none of this would have been conceivable without the support of my family. My wife Shuling has been incredibly patient with my many late nights working on this book. I would also like to thank my father, Dr. Peter W. Holloway. My earliest childhood memories of going with him to his lab at the biochemistry department at the University of Virginia instilled in me a love of research. It is to him that I dedicate this book.

The Quest for Ecstatic Morality
in Early China

Introduction

A recently excavated Guodian manuscript tells us that there should be times when our happiness is so great we are unable to contain ourselves. We erupt in song and our body begins to shake. This shaking builds and we cannot stop our feet and arms from spontaneously dancing. At the opposite end of the emotional spectrum, there should also be times when we are overcome with rage. When this happens, the emotion builds from anger and develops into melancholy before bursting forth with the beating of one's breast. The final expression of this emotion is jumping up and down, as is captured in the cliché "hopping mad." This is the world of the manuscript "Xing zi mingchu" 性自命出. The title is tough to translate, but it approximately is "Nature emerges from endowment."[1] Here in sections 11–12, the highs of joy are the beginning of the crash toward crying in grief.

Today we would dismiss this move from an emotional high to a crash as bipolar. In this bamboo manuscript found in the Guodian tomb and the Shanghai Corpus, understanding the common ground behind these binary opposites was called the supreme expression of *qing*情. The importance of *qing* can be seen in the secondary name scholars have assigned the "Xing zi mingchu," which is the "Xing qing lun" 性情論, or the "Discourse on nature and *qing*." Comprised of emotions, *qing* is how we start to understand the Dao.

Because the mechanism we use to understand the Dao is utterly human, scholars such as Tang Yijie 湯一介 see the Dao as the smaller, socially bound "way we do things" of Confucius.[2] This line of reasoning is taken further by Liao Mingchun, who feels that the "Xing zi mingchu" was written by Confucius's grandson Zisi, which eliminates any possibility of influence from Laozi.[3] An interesting transition is evident in Ding Sixin's 丁四新 categorization of the "Xing zi mingchu" as Confucian. He touches on heaven as a transcendent principle in the *Analects*, but this is an idea more commonly associated with Laozi. Because of this, I see Ding's analysis as beginning to shift toward a hybrid view of the "Xing zi mingchu."[4]

I will demonstrate in this book that the "Xing zi mingchu" contains elements of both the transcendence of Laozi and the immanence of Confucius. This happens in the concept of *qing*, which bridges the categories of immanent and transcendent. It is worth mentioning that these categories are contentious because both Confucius and Laozi have higher models that are to be enacted in society, giving them an element of immanence. The primary model for Confucius is heaven, and for Laozi it is Dao. What is different between the two texts is that Confucius does not develop his model outside of a human context. In contrast to this, Laozi has any number of passages where he discusses the origin or function of the Dao with zero reference to its specific relationship to humans. It is for this reason that I categorize Confucius as immanent and Laozi as transcendent. The historical significance of the "Xing zi mingchu" containing both of these ways of constructing an ethical system is that I believe it represents a missing link between the *Analects* and the *Daode jing*.

There are passages in the "Xing zi mingchu" where Confucian concepts of ritual and music are foregrounded but others, such as section 7, state, "the Dao is the Dao of all things."[5] As a universal construct, the Dao transcends the human; we are not a necessary reference point for describing it in total. The same cannot be said for *qing*, which is the utmost of joy and grief in section 11. It would be incorrect to dismiss *qing* as merely emotional. Qing serves as a conduit for understanding the Dao, so it involves much more than "emotion" connotes in English. By the same line of reasoning, it is also erroneous to shrink our definition of Dao to fit our method of discovery, *qing*. The problem of shuttering off our complete views of the "Xing zi mingchu" arises from a belief that competing schools of thought dominated early China. True, there are important areas of overlap with Confucius, but labeling it as such hides the way the text relates to Laozi.

Little effort is needed to exclude an exact match with the category Confucian. The major terms "nature" and "*qing*" each appear only twice in the *Analects*. Even attempting to find other significant ideas such as anger (*yun* 慍) comes up with only a few instances and they all have undesirable connotations. One such example is in the first passage of the text where we are told that "Is not one noble when others do not know you yet you are not angry?" 人不知而不慍, 不亦君子乎?[6] Confucius is describing a situation where we might have good reason to be angry, yet we are told to find a way to eradicate what would otherwise be a normal, healthy response. The "Xing zi mingchu" is completely different from this; it tells us that sometimes it is perfectly acceptable to be hopping mad. This is not to say that common ground is absent between the *Analects* and "Xing zi mingchu." Rather, my point is that looking for linear connections based on single terms used the same in both texts will not produce sound results.

One feature of the "Xing zi mingchu" that is particularly surprising is the way it deals with orthopraxy. In the *Analects,* we are accustomed to understanding correct behavior as context specific. We learn how to act in a manner similar to an MBA student learning from a Harvard Business School case study. When we read the *Analects* we are supposed to accumulate knowledge of what worked in a series of question-and-answer sessions between Confucius and his students. Then we can create a composite sketch of what we should do in our own situation. The key to our being able to assemble this composite sketch is that each of these individual mini case studies within the *Analects* is deemed correct. A question is asked, then answered, with usually a single action prescribed by Confucius for that person at that moment. I refer to this as absolute truth since it is possible to act correctly in an absolute sense at any single given moment. Confucius does not understand orthopraxy as being diachronically constant, but in his answer to any given question there is a certainty as to what is proper in that specific situation. The shortcoming of using the term "absolute" is it can carry the unwanted freight of absolutism, which is not an intended connotation here.

In contrast to the *Analects* notion that a person can be absolutely correct at any given moment, the "Xing zi mingchu" sees the situation as much messier. Section 16 tells us that we can be loathed when we are righteous and refuted for being humane. Moral action is conflicted. Strangely, this conflict is not a criticism of these moral tenets. The problem is not that humanity and righteousness represent deficient qualities; they are praised in the text. Instead, the issue lies in what we have or have not accomplished in our self-cultivation. It is analogous to the manner in which moral action in "The Five Aspects of Conduct" 五行 is judged not based on what you do, but by the morals formed within your body. The "Xing zi mingchu" also sees conflict as present or absent based on whether or not we are connected with the Dao.

The "Xing zi mingchu" dramatically alters our understanding of early China because its fundamental assumption about life is that moral truths have the potential to exist in conflict. This conflict is not insurmountable; it is confined to the immanent level of the text. In the "Xing zi mingchu," the presence of conflict at the immanent level prevents us from being absolutely correct because people will continue to loathe us when we act morally. Despite this, humanity and righteousness are correct ways of acting in section 16. The truth of these two terms is relative, but the Dao is absolute. In other words, when morality is explored at the transcendent level, this conflict is absent. Access to this transcendence is achieved by using our *qing* to connect to the Dao, at which point our actions become free from this conflict. The transcendent qualities of the Dao override this resistance and these passages cease to mention tension. Because of these dual standards for measuring orthopraxy, we are forced to accept that there are truths and higher truths. While this worldview is firmly rooted in recently excavated pre-Han manuscripts, it foreshadows the later Buddhist argument of *upaya*, skill in means.[7] While I want to be clear that this book is tightly focused on the "Xing zi mingchu," it is hoped that it will be of use to scholars of later religions such as Buddhism and Neo-Confucianism. In particular, there is an unavoidable connection between the focus of this book, the "Xing zi mingchu," and later developments in Chinese religion. At the forefront is new light this text can shed on our understanding of the early development of nature (性 *xing*), a term central to the development of Neo-Confucianism in the Song and Ming dynasties.

This issue of context relates to a highly controversial side of this book. I see the "Xing zi mingchu" as containing a coherent perspective on a variety of topics, such as the aforementioned Dao and *qing*. Because of this, I am in stark disagreement with the vast majority of scholars in the field. Li Tianhong describes the situation as follows:

> Presently, scholars are comparatively consistent in seeing these 67 strips [of the "Xing zi mingchu"] as divisible into a first and second part, called the first and second chapters.
>
> 目前學界比較一致的看法是，這67枚簡可分爲上下兩部分，稱之為上、下篇。[8]

Li's chapter continues with an overview of various scholars who see the text as divisible in different ways, including cutting it into three different sections. One of the favorite areas to divide the text is around strip 35 or 36 of the Guodian edition, which is the start of section 13 in the appendix of this book. My analysis will show that this majority position is incorrect by proving that the "Xing zi mingchu" is religiously and philosophically consistent. The relationship between *qing* and Dao is the focus of the "Xing zi mingchu," and these importantly interconnected terms become meaningless if the text is divided.

By attacking the coherence of the "Xing zi mingchu," scholars create an atmosphere where the text can be more easily manipulated into agreeing with various grand narratives of early China.[9] One representative proponent of this methodology is Liao Mingchun, who argues in favor of dividing the "Xing zi mingchu," and has decided that the text must have been authored by Confucius's grandson Zisi.[10] The original context in which the "Xing zi mingchu" was discovered is a Guodian context, and this is in danger of being lost. It may seem somewhat counterintuitive, but we must study the texts in an isolated manner before larger and more significant connections can be established. Because of this, I am excited by innovative scholarship that broadens the field of analysis by connecting excavated manuscripts to Neo-Confucianism and Buddhism, but am skeptical of work that narrows Guodian by assigning specific texts to Zisi.

The foundation of my analysis of the "Xing zi mingchu" began in my previous book, *Guodian: The Newly Discovered Seeds of Chinese Religious and Political Philosophy*.[11] What I discovered was that texts in the Guodian tomb share a common conceptual framework in seeing the world as able to be unified through balancing moral elements that exist as binary opposites. The specific construction of opposition and its unification is a distinctly Guodian phenomenon. The "Xing zi mingchu" is best understood as existing within the broad landscape of this tomb. Conflict between opposing options for moral behavior is so amplified in the text that it indicates a rupture would have to exist between those who were privy to the full extent of the mechanics of the ethical universe and others who would be able to understand but a small fraction.

This conflict exists on two levels, and what is confusing is that each of these levels contains several elements. Let us begin by calling the two levels lower and higher. The lower level is social, and is fraught with conflict. Above this is a higher level where these conflicts are absent. The lower level can be seen as immanent, and because of the conflict, absolute morality is unattainable. Stated somewhat differently, this means that if all we have at our disposal are the tools of morality that exist within society, we cannot hope to be completely correct at any given moment because others will continue to consider us wrong. Because we cannot be free of this criticism, all we can hope for is to be relatively correct, and the reason is our cultivation is not sufficiently advanced. It must be remembered that relativity only exists when we are unable to implement the higher-level morality of the Dao.

Regarding the higher level, it is only present in passages that discuss the Dao in "Xing zi mingchu." In such situations, the text ceases to introduce the problem of friction. A note of caution is necessary here because the Dao itself also exists on multiple levels. There are four levels to the Dao, and my analysis of these levels is in the latter part of the second chapter of this book. The short version of the analysis is that each of the four types of Dao encompasses a progressively smaller category. These four Dao are universal, material, human, and righteous. In the text, the universal Dao is simply termed Dao. This Dao, without limits, is what we connect to in the latter half of section 16. Here we gain the wisdom of the Dao and then reflect it to those above us, below us, and internally.

Further information on the internalizing of the Dao is provided in section 1 of the "Xing zi mingchu," where I read the phrase the "Dao starts with *qing*" as meaning that *qing* is the beginning of how we know about the Dao. The undifferentiated or universal Dao is free of tension in sections 1 and 16, so it contains the ability to be correct in an absolute sense. While this universal Dao includes us, it does not need humans to be defined, making it transcendent. From this we have two groups of descriptors: Immanent and relative is one group; the second is universal and absolute. The result is that in the "Xing zi mingchu" we can be absolutely correct like Confucius by connecting to a transcendent Dao, similar to Laozi.

My usage of the terms "immanent" and "transcendent" is indebted to the important advances of previous scholars. The conclusions I reach are different in certain ways because the starting point of my analysis was a strict focus on the "Xing zi mingchu." In *Thinking Through Confucius*, Hall and Ames argue that it is inappropriate and distorting to interpret any ideas of Confucius as transcendent. They argue that despite heaven (they prefer it romanized as *T'ien* 天) existing as a higher power, in Confucius it is internalized by people making it ultimately immanent. The reason is that while heaven is a standard we perceive as above us, it is not abstract. It only has meaning when we put it into practice in society.[12]

A different perspective is explored by de Bary in his study *The Trouble with Confucianism*, which is much broader in that it includes an analysis of the last two millennia. He focuses on the importance of Heaven as the consistent standard for moral conduct. Over time, the same challenge continues to vex Confucians, and that is how we can bring Heaven's standards to bear on society. In his terminology, Heaven is transcendent, but it only has value when realized in society.[13] While de Bary differs in seeing the source of the standard as transcendent, he agrees that it is ultimately inseparable from implementation in what Hall and Ames term the immanent.

In "Xing zi mingchu," we can say that Dao becomes part of us internally through our use of *qing*, so there is an immediate overlap with the immanence discussed in the above scholarship. Dao is a standard that exists above us but it becomes part of our life as a guide. The major difference I find is that sections 2–4 of the "Xing zi mingchu" construct a context that is both larger and exclusive of humans, in the same vein as the Dao of all things. This context includes cows, geese, trees, and rope, which is intentionally independent of the human, and thus transcendent. In contrast, the immanent level of the "Xing zi mingchu" is the one that if properly developed must be connected with the Dao. What this means is that while the immanent level may not exist in complete isolation, the Dao can. I do not dispute the Hall and Ames assessment as it pertains to the *Analects*, but I do find the "Xing zi mingchu" importantly different.

The question remains, what sort of person has the ability to connect to the Dao? The answer has to be assembled from several sections, but my conclusion from having gone over the various pieces of evidence is that we should refer to the group possessing this capacity as clergy. In Guodian, there are people who are morally distinct from the rest of us. Their power is religious and not political or academic. In my first book, I discussed "The Five Aspects of Conduct," where people with high moral achievement were variously characterized as having jade-like skin, a voice like a bronze bell, and a voice like a jade chime. All of these characteristics represent an embodiment of ritual norms that create a miraculous transformation of the sort befitting a member of the clergy.

"Xing zi mingchu" also has individuals that are morally distinguished by embodying *qing*.[14] Section 16 of the text describes people with *qing* having a collection of exceptional abilities. They include a variety of duties that a normal government would undertake, but they are accomplished by unusual means. For example, you are believed without speaking, and people are respectful without the need for punishment. The conclusion of the section states, "The regulation of what is inside is at ease. The regulation of what is outside needs control." 門內之治, 欲其逸也。門外之治, 欲其制也.[15] This term I translate as "regulation" could also be translated as "govern."[16] The section is describing people who act with *qing* and Dao, yet they have authority. Since this is not a political source of power, I felt that using the term "govern" would misrepresent the meaning.

Eligibility for inclusion in the clergy seems completely open. All people have *qing*, the only prerequisite for connecting to the Dao. The problem is that we have to make our *qing* beautiful, and this involves special training that few can complete. One section where this is discussed is section 8. A crucial part of our cultivation is relying on the four classics that were created by sages. These books are the the Odes詩, Documents書, Rites禮, and Music樂. When we are successfully taught this curriculum, it excites our *qing* and ritual is created. This makes the process a living tradition, and ritual in particular is something that is seen as a deep element of our lives. In a more modern context, we might dismiss ritual as formal and unable to touch us deeply. This could not be further from the way it is used in early China, and the closing line of section 8 makes the point beautifully: "Laughter is the surface of ritual; music is the depth of ritual." 笑, 禮之淺澤也. 樂, 禮之深澤也. The point here is that self-cultivation is supposed to be fun, and ritual is inseparable from music and joy. While the subsequent analysis is not lighthearted, it is important to remember that the original manuscript was intended to spread happiness.

CHAPTER 1

Qing, from Conflict to Ecstasy

The "Xing zi mingchu" tells us that sometimes when we make a mistake, we do not deserve to suffer negative consequences; at other times, we uphold morals yet encounter loathing.[1] These forms of social friction raise a question of how immanence was perceived in the text, and this is the focus of the first part of this chapter. If we did not have further context with which to judge this surprising approach to amnesty, we might imagine that avoiding repercussions for our mistakes could be an example of the compassion of others. The problem with hoping that another will be sympathetic is that in shifting the locus of approval outside each individual, our ability to exercise free will is inhibited. An alternative approach is proposed by the recently excavated manuscript "Xing zi mingchu." Here, in section 16, the answer is *qing* (情). By acting with *qing*, we can gain the power to rise to a leadership level in society, one privilege of this is absolution for some mistakes. Section 16 is describing the positive and negative repurcussions of moral cultivation, and it undergoes a change halfway through. The focus of the section shifts from *qing* to having the wisdom of the Dao. I argue that this wisdom is attainable because we already have figured out how to act with *qing*, and after establishing a connection to the Dao there is no more mention of friction.

Understanding how *qing* functions will provide an important foundation for answering the ultimate question of the source and solution to social tension. There are two ways of analyzing this question of wrong being right and right being wrong. One is to look at the negative side, which is loathing (惡), and explore the source of this judgment. The "Xing zi mingchu" will ultimately conclude that what most judge to be either attractive or repulsive is based on a partial understanding of our world. In fact, these seeming polar opposites are interlinked—they actually create each other.

While we struggle to appreciate this unification of opposites in and around ourselves in society, the Dao exists separately. In passages 5–7 where the Dao is explored, these tensions between love and hate are conspicuously absent.

In society, we remain mired in tension, and this will be the focus of this chapter. The next chapter of this book will explore the starting point for connecting to the Dao. These two sides of the text can be seen as immanent and transcendent. The key to moving between these two ways that the world can operate is *qing*, which ultimately leads us from the tensions of society to connecting with the Dao. A divide exists in society where our actions create friction with others; seeing beyond these finite problems allows us to embrace the Dao. Our own ultimate comprehension of the correctness of what we do is somewhat indirect in that it is initially filtered through *qing* prior to ultimately leading to a higher understanding of the Dao. *Qing* is something that relates directly to our lives, but Dao encompasses much more than what is simply human. In the second half of section 16, connecting to the Dao is explored and it will be shown to surpass divisions between good and bad to focus on unconditional unity. The conclusion of this chapter will be that negativity has to be seen as a partner with positivity to form a unity of binary opposites. This focus on overcoming opposites at a social level shifts to an exploration of purely interconnected unity when we are able to connect with the Dao. A unity comprised of opposites is a lower level of truth for society while binary divisions cease to remain as an important organizing concept at the higher truth level of the Dao.[2]

Social tensions and their solutions such as are noted at the start of this chapter form the immanent side of *qing* in the text. Taken in isolation, these specific passages remain entirely focused on solving human problems. Morals are defined by referencing entirely tangible concepts that exist within our life experience. At times, such as in section 20, these discussions begin to take on the air of the truisms found in the *Analects* of Confucius. "When you are happy you should want wisdom but not superfluous things" 喜欲智而無末. The reference to emotions here is important because *qing* is deeply connected to the emotions of happiness and sadness. Through understanding a range of feelings from happiness to sadness, we can transition from the immanent to the transcendent.

There are also sections of the "Xing zi mingchu" that are only concerned with transcendent principles such as the Dao. Section 16 is particularly important because it contains a transition halfway through, where it shifts from societal concerns at the beginning, to connecting to the Dao. We have to understand that the text is developing these two as separate ethical frameworks. *Qing* gives us the ability to make this transition from one framework to another and allows us to become connected to both aspects of our universe.

METHODOLOGY

Prior to tackling the question of understanding the means by which *qing* allows us to transcend the difficulties of our life, it is necessary to discuss my analytical methodology. This chapter will argue that leadership in "Xing zi mingchu" is best understood from within a religious instead of a purely rational secular context. In section 16, we have several ways that authority is manifested through examples of the sorts of benefits that such a person can bring to society. Many of the attributes of authority relate to what we would today categorize as outside the main auspices of secular government. One of the challenges with this categorization is that it remains a heuristic device; the divide between religion and state is a much more modern notion. Despite this methodological challenge, what the text indicates is that there are benefits being performed by a person who possesses *qing* that are either redundant or parallel to what is being carried out by other governmental entities. So while there is no requirement that government be secular at this time, the key element of the passage is these activities will be performed in counterintuitive ways such as getting people to work hard without reward. Another example is evident when the text states that there is an ability to attract people without being wealthy. This signifies either a challenge to the status quo from an outside group or a willingness to exist as a separate auxiliary resource for guiding people. It is in discussing leading the people from an outsider perspective that the "Xing zi mingchu" takes on strongly religious overtones.

The question then arises, what should we call a leader of this sort. "Clergy" seems to be the best term to encompass the role of leading others who are working to develop a common religious message but not serving as an officially sanctioned governing force. Faith is a necessary element of this system since we rely on these clergy to shape society through exceptional means. The term "faith" here is meant to serve as a marker for what is challenging to explain when relying purely on tangible logical reasoning. When the "Xing zi mingchu" describes morality as a sufficient enticement for getting people to work hard, there is an underlying assumption that under normal circumstances, hard work would need remuneration. This reversal of normal expectations can also be seen in the question of positive actions having negative consequences. As will be discussed, higher powers exist in the text and one of them is the Dao. Morality is connected to the full Dao, which is a moral framework that remains in some ways beyond the understanding of most people; we must simply believe in our clergy without relying on logical justification.

It is precisely this rupture between the spiritual abilities of average people and those able to understand the Dao where the argument of transcendence gains traction. The text understands Dao as a concept that we need to attain harmony, but there is no reciprocal requirement for the Dao to need humans in order for it to be complete. Part of the reason for this comes from the multiple perspectives on the Dao in the text. In section 13, for example, four levels of Dao are mentioned, but section 16 and many others only have a single Dao. When the Dao is treated as separate from humans it constitutes a higher power in the text. This higher power is one that clergy can strive to understand, but others will only experience in a muted fashion when filtered through the actions of their religious leaders. The lower truth realm is much more familiar; it elicits responses from us that are highly visceral. When we are either very happy or sad, the text describes us as unable to control our emotions, and there is no condemnation of this primal responsiveness. Our emotions simply come pouring out and we begin hopping in anger or dancing with glee to express our ecstatic response.

If it were not for exceedingly narrow definitions of what does or does not constitute religion in some scholarship, the term "clergy" would be a natural way to characterize leadership in the "Xing zi mingchu." Recent work has argued that the tendency to promote rational explanations of traditional Chinese texts is more the consequence of a manic push for modernity during the Nanjing Decade instead of anything that is either organic or dominant in the tradition.[3] The value of exploring the religious side of early China is not to simply demonstrate that a connection exists with a Western construct. Instead, there are ways that religiosity can illuminate the inner working of a text that does not always rely on logic. When faced with separate levels of truth, faith becomes an important method for explaining the text. This is particularly important in trying to understand how ecstatic emotional states can play a role in a normative system. Such practices of this period are not well documented, so there are of course major elements of this religious system that will remain uncertain.

One reason why the religious culture surrounding Guodian is important is that another practice of this time and place, the burial of bronze funerary objects, had a surprisingly tenacious hold on the society. What burial practices tell us is that religion spread with great ease, and was something worth enduring great expense to perform properly during this period of Chinese history. Lothar von Falkenhausen has shown that this religious tradition had the ability to endure long after its contemporary political and social institutions were extinct. The decision of what was placed in a tomb had the ability to traverse vast geographic expanses and even cross what we might have otherwise believed were insurmountable political divides. He has shown that the details of these practices had an amazing ability to propagate. This makes it particularly important to examine the faith side of Guodian texts. In his analysis of China's tomb culture, von Falkenhausen proposes purposefully marginalizing written texts in order to let the archaeological evidence be understood objectively. "... archaeological research is or should be to contribute to the understanding of history. But I would insist equally strongly that in order to do this effectively, archaeology must be released from the leash of text-based inquiry."[4]

Much of the material culture of Guodian was removed by looters, so I will be modifying von Falkenhausen's methodology slightly to examine textual evidence from within its specific tomb context with minimal interruption from the received tradition for the first two chapters of this book. One way this can be explained is to imagine an intellectual firewall that blocks as much infiltration as possible from the received texts to allow the coherence within and among these lost primary sources to become the first order of context. Paying attention to the elements of the Guodian texts that could pertain to religious beliefs is an excellent tool for teasing out what elements might have persistent importance in a similar way that specific styles of bronzes were able to achieve surprisingly wide acceptance as a means for expressing power and status within the society.

In taking the issue of power in the Guodian context seriously, we have to see what attributes are associated with religious leadership. Of even greater importance is paying attention to areas where the actions of clergy are likely to produce friction that could result in the loathing of others. The first potential source of dissatisfaction is with the issue of embodied morality. This relates to the question of how a group perceives itself and how it is constituted. A second source to be discussed below is the actions of the clergy that could create tension. "The Five Aspects of Conduct" describes masters of morality as having jade-like skin, and a voice like a bronze bell or a jade chime. These physical markers separate advanced practitioners from ordinary people.[5] Finding this obvious separation supports my argument that there was a group of individuals who acted in a manner akin to the notion of clergy. In that the markers that distinguish these people are aesthetic and thus subjective, it would be easy to imagine a questioning of their status. Skeptics could easily become the source of friction and actually hate these moral paragons.

An even more pressing issue that would strain relations is in the judging of a legal case in "The Five Aspects of Conduct." The identity of the religious community is reified by the stark divide between serious transgressions that are judged as requiring execution and other minor ones that should be literally covered up (ni 匿). Interestingly, harsh justice is seen as an application of righteousness and forgiving a crime is following humanity. It is valuable to remember that the person performing these judgments is distinguished by physical transformations of the body into something that resembles jade and bronze ritual implements. Although "The Five Aspects of Conduct" believes that applying these punishments will produce harmony, it is easy to see how a person whose loved one was just executed would have intense loathing for the person responsible for this "proper" action. On the other hand, if the case is minor, resulting in no punishment, the injured party could be very unhappy despite this being the correct thing to do in such a situation.[6]

A final reason why ethical behavior would produce tension can be seen in the Guodian text "Tang Yu zhidao," which describes humanity and righteousness as being connected to questions of royal succession. There are two options: hereditary transmission or selecting the next ruler based on merit. The text states that in ideal circumstances, the selection process produces harmony, but this is only achieved over time. At any particular moment, there is tension that results from one group being privileged over another. In such cases, the disenfranchised party would be a prime candidate for detesting the implementation of morality. The "Xing zi mingchu" fits this trend of exploring how a moral paragon might be seen, at least by some, in a poor light.

When we are asked to forgive errors but a dim view is held of people who follow humanity and righteousness, it forces us to reassess what we classify as normative. The first step toward elucidating what counts as an error involves clearly understanding a few key instances of *qing* in the text. In the midst of section 8 and its discussion of the Dao and ritual, we have several examples of *qing*. First among its range of meanings, the term is seen as an essential element of classical texts.[7] We should remember that these texts and this *qing* are but parts of a cosmic whole, the Dao. Although we are part of this transcendent cosmos, all we are directly able to connect with is the classics, *qing*, and ritual.

IMMANENT QING

Qing is important for its ability to connect us to the Dao and for distinguishing our leaders. However, this raises a question, is *qing* static or something that we develop. In section 8, we see an answer in a statement that *qing* can be made beautiful. While we cannot know if it is inborn or not from the section, it is significant that it appears next to other attributes that are also able to be cultivated, including morality (*yi* 義) and appearance (*rong* 容). This means that *qing* is a type of ability akin to many other moral qualities that we can either choose to develop or allow to languish. The value of this observation is that it inserts free will into the discussion of how we become leaders in "Xing zi mingchu."

The other side of finding an aesthetic transformation characterizing the development of our *qing* is that it can help explain its association with the role of a leader. We are able to observe the quality of a person's *qing*, making it a tangible attribute. Since *qing* also relates to our ability to become connected to others in the world we live in, finding it described as beautiful should also be part of its power to establish connections. This physical transformation is not superficial; it is an outward physical manifestation of our inner moral perfection.

> A noble person has beautified his or her *qing*, made venerable his or her righteousness, is good at etiquette, made the utmost of his or her appearance, enjoys the Dao, delights in teaching; thus he or she is made respectful by them.

> 君子美其情,［貴其義］善其節,好其容,樂其道,悅其教,是以敬焉。

When we cultivate morals in section 8, there is a corresponding change in our external appearance that is reminiscent of another Guodian text, "The Five Aspects of Conduct." In both of these texts, morals are an embodied manifestation of an aesthetic and ethical congruence that form the core of self-cultivation. *Qing* is the mechanism in the "Xing zi mingchu" that allows our self-cultivation to develop into something that is manifest externally, but we need to understand it as part of a Guodian trend. In the next section we will see how people with *qing* are leaders, and this is the where the ability to connect people together appears.

The external side of *qing* is clear in section 16. It begins with a discussion of the way that *qing* can protect you from the criticism of others in society.

> Of all people's *qing* it can be delighted. If you use your *qing*, although you are excessive you are not loathed; if you do not use your *qing*, although you endure hardship you will not be treated as venerable. If you have your *qing*, although you do not act, other people will believe you.
>> If you have not yet spoken and people [already] believe you, you are a person with an admirable *qing*.
>> If you have not yet taught [them] ⑤① and people are [already] enduring, you are a person whose nature is good (adept).

If you have not yet [bestowed] reward and people are [already] hard working, you are a person with concealed moral abundance. ❷❷

If you have not yet [meted out] punishments and the people are [already] respectful, you are a person with ⑤② respect in your heart.

One who is destitute but treated by the people as venerable, is due to a person having virtue.

One who is poor, but the people flock to you, is due to a person having the Dao.

One who lives alone but happy, is due to a person having inner substance.

When people loathe you but you cannot be refuted you are one who has reached righteousness.

When people refute you but you cannot be loathed you are one who is earnest in humanity.

Acting but not being excessive, is a person with wisdom of the Dao.

Hearing the Dao and reflecting it to those above, is someone who interacts with those above.

Hearing the Dao and reflecting it to those below, is someone who interacts with those below.

Hearing the Dao and reflecting it personally, is someone who cultivates his or her body.

Interacting with those above is close to serving a noble,

interacting with those below achieves closeness with engaging in politics, cultivating your body is close to achieving humanity.

Interacting with people of the same station is a person who uses the Dao.

Interacting with people of a different station [is to use the special purpose]. Interacting with people with the same happiness is a person who uses virtue.

Interacting with people with different happiness, is a person who uses planning.

The regulation of what is inside is at ease. The regulation of what is outside needs control.

凡人情為可悅也。苟以其情，雖過不惡； 不以其情，雖難不貴。苟有其情，雖未之為，斯人信之矣。

未言而信，有美情者也。
未教而民恆，性善者也。
未賞而民勸，含福者也。
未刑而民畏，有心畏者也。
賤而民貴之，有德者也。
貧而民聚焉，有道者也。

獨處而樂，有內體者也。

惡之而不可非者，達於義者也。

非之而不可惡者，篤於仁者也。

行之不過，知道者也。

聞道反上，上交者也。

聞道反下，下交者也。

聞道反己，修身者也。

上交近事君，

下交得近從政，

修身近至仁。

同方而交，以道者也。不同方而 [交以故者也。]

同悅而交，以德者也。不同悅而交，以猷者也。

門內之治，欲其逸也。門外之治，欲其制也。

This passage begins by telling us how *qing* will benefit our lives. The first benefit we enjoy is being free from the loathing of others, even when we make a mistake. At first, this line of reasoning seems to run counter to our ethical fiber. Would it not be preferable if mistakes were atoned for, if they were not it would seem to threaten to spread chaos in the world? The reason *qing* does not cause the spread of moral degeneration is that the actions in the first half of the section are but lower achievements that form a precondition for attaining a connection with the Dao in the second half. Splitting the world into two halves is seen in the three parallel sentences that describe what you can do after hearing the Dao. The first two state that you can reflect it to what is above or below you, and this is deemed a form of interaction. In the third, it says that reflecting it inside is cultivating your body. These three phrases are unidirectional in that we hear from the transcendent Dao and only then are able to reflect this wisdom in all three directions.

These three directions are then repeated in the text and here the third part is the least problematic. This third item relates to cultivating your body, which is explained as achieving humanity, a straightforward expression. If we work from this point of clarity, we can see that the Dao as a transcendent moral source provides the basis for the cultivation. The humanity that we achieve is also emanating from the Dao, and it acquires value as it is manifest as part of our embodiment of virtue. Serving a noble and engaging in politics are less clear, but there is no reason they should follow a different pattern from cultivating humanity after hearing about it from the Dao. Assuming this is the case, the knowledge of government service should also be obtained from hearing the wisdom of the Dao. In other words, this second grouping of three actions is an extension of the first group; it is clarifying how we will apply what we received from the Dao. We have gained an ability to connect to the transcendent Dao above, and this is being used to affect the immanent world below. It is the third sentence that underlines the importance of the person who is performing this networking function; such a person is reflecting this morality internally. This is related to section 8 where the *qing* of a noble is made beautiful; in both situations embodiment of morality is a core part of the process.

In order to understand more clearly the means of achieving this connection with the Dao, we need to return to the first half of section 16 and examine the subsequent series of positive attributes that are engendered by our mastery of *qing*. Among the traits it lists are several that point to a leadership role, such as causing the people to be respectful and enduring. The most compelling is the idea of being impoverished but having the power to attract people. There is an interesting permutation on personal magnetism; being partnered with other counterintuitive statements it evidently shows that at the time most people would be expected to be only attracted by material wealth. This points to an alternative value system in that it is distinguishing itself from a standard measure of prosperity. A higher calling exists and it has an ability to produce results that are beyond the norm. Connecting to the Dao distinguishes a person, and he or she can then use this alternate source of power to interact with those above or below. The divide between those of us who are able to access the Dao and the rest of the people who we are then tasked with looking after reinforces the use of the category of religion as an analytical tool. These leaders act similar to a clergy in that they follow a religious value system that ran parallel to other more secular principles.

Early in the passage a sharply contrasting situation is described where it says that despite enduring hardship, people will not perceive your value as noble. The difference between enduring a difficult encounter and being seen as a winner or a loser is *qing*. A person with *qing* is afforded a measure of protection, and there is a parallel approach in the subsequent sentences where a person can be believed without speaking. Another way to understand what is occurring here is that this person's actions are having a far more profound impact on his or her surroundings than the mere subtotal of their actions might indicate. This judgment of an action is not its result in any sort of logical manner; it is something that is based on the moral attainment of the performer of the action. Pragmatic explanations are not present here since the world operates on the faith of a religious system.

It is crucial that others are able to gain awareness of your faults at the start of section 16. The same process occurs again in an amplified manner further along in the paragraph when the issue of loathing and refutation is again raised. Both of these expressions of disapproval are sourced in other people. "When people loathe you but you cannot be refuted you are one who has reached righteousness. When people refute you but you cannot be loathed you are one who is earnest in humanity." At first blush, it would seem that this sentence represents a situation where you are the one loathing and refuting others. The motivation for exploring this alternate reading is that it is just so surprising to see bad results of good behavior. This would change the translation to "Loathing people but you cannot refute them you are one who has reached righteousness. When you refute people but you cannot loathe them you are one who is earnest in humanity." The problem with this becomes obvious immediately. It is illogical to see righteous people as being able to despise someone but not have the power to refute them.

The status of people must be unusually high if they can enjoy this sort of protection against a total descent into abhorrence by the general populace. They must be leaders of some sort. Such privilege would be difficult to account for if shared by the public at large, but it raises an important question: What sort of a leader is being described here? The second part of the section describes people whose economic status is low. Specifically, it mentions "being poor but people flock to you." The example of poverty appears with two others, being destitute and living alone. These last two examples suggest an eremitic lifestyle of the practitioner.[8] Obviously this is something admired by Zhuangzi, but it is also important in the *Analects*. Likely the most famous is 6.11 where Yan Hui 顏回 is praised for his ability to live in aching poverty.[9]

What is different in section 16 is that these three instances appear directly after examples of solving more standard governmental problems, albeit through unusual methods. "If you have not yet [bestowed] reward and people are [already] hard working, you are a person with concealed moral abundance. If you have not yet [meted out] punishments and the people are [already] respectful, you are a person with respect in your heart." It is important to note that this quote is not implying that rewards and punishments could be available as an alternative to leading through moral example. Instead, what we have is a situation where a person without governmental power is able to achieve comparable or actually superior results. This is a further reason why the passage is describing a religious system that runs parallel to the standard operation of the state.

The underlying message is that our ability to attain morality is not something that we can achieve by ourselves; we need to see and hear another person who has already mastered these abilities. The social side of moral cultivation returns us to the argument being proposed for section 16. These texts are describing leaders with powers that extend beyond their mere actions. Powers such as these are having a transformative impact on those they are encountering; one example is "You do not teach but the people are enduring." We cannot know much about the actual organization or operation of these leaders, but their actions do seem akin to what we would term "clergy" in the West.

There is an obvious tension between specific moral concepts such as humanity and righteousness that is conspicuously absent from received texts such as the *Analects* and *Mencius*. The closest we even find to a focus on individual moral tenets is when Confucius is continuously peppered with requests to explicate a single moral concept by his students. The fourth chapter of this book will examine this question in more detail in reference to *Analects* 2.5–2.6 where there are repeated identical questions about how to perform a single moral concept, acting in a filial manner. Although it remains unstated as a requirement of cultivation in the *Analects*, it is interesting that there is an observable tendency to focus on mastering morality a single concept at a time. This creates a stark divide from Guodian where self-cultivation famously involves mastering five types of morality at once in "The Five Aspects of Conduct." In "Xing zi minghchu," moral concepts also work in concert since *qing* requires the Dao to reach its full expression.

Likely, the clearest moment where we can see this contrast between single and multiple is when the rectification of names is proposed by Confucius as the single action necessary to solve the entire world's problems. Here, rectifying names has massively positive consequences that spread to include everyone in the empire in a unified whole. This issue of rectifying names will be the subject of the fourth chapter of this book, entitled The Rectification of Names. In sum, the ease by which Confucius believes this utopian unity can be attained is in striking contrast to the "Xing zi mingchu" where moral action often brings dissent.

One important difference is that while "The Five Aspects of Conduct" contains numerous instances where humanity and righteousness are paired, "Xing zi mingchu" does not follow this as closely.[10] Instead, righteousness is paired with *qing*. We see this in the first section of the text.

> When you start you are close to *qing*, when you end you are close to righteousness. Those who know *qing* can express it; those who know righteousness are able to internalize it.
>
> 始者近情，終者近義。知[情者能] 出之，知義 者能入之。

There are two sentences in the quote and the first one describes the entire scope of the process from a start with *qing* to a conclusion with righteousness. Following this, the second sentence provides further details about the operation of *qing* and righteousness within what is described in sentence one. The other possibility is that the process of self-cultivation begins with *qing* and emitting, and then ends with righteousness and internalizing. If this second possibility were accepted, it would seem to conflict with the way *qing* is described in several sections, including 9, 11, and 16. In these later sections, *qing* functions as a concept that has meaning over the duration of our lives, so limiting it to only the starting point of self-cultivation seems incorrect.

Interestingly, the order of starting with *qing* and ending with righteousness is not adhered to in section 8. Here, they appear in reverse: "...embodied the morality [of the classics] and by ordering, refined them; organized the *qing* [of the classics], expressed and internalized them. After this they can again be used for instructing." 體其義而節文之，理其情而出入之. 然後復以教. The term translated in this quote as "morality" is the same as righteousness in section 1, but the term seems to be related to a broader moral concern in this quote than the narrow term "righteousness" would be able to convey. Another term that is translated differently can be seen in the same character rendered "expressing" in section 1; that character is here translated as "emanated." The reason for the change is the textual reference in the sentence that precedes it justifies narrowing the scope of what is given off to something involving volition.

The partner concept to emanating is internalizing, and it is in the pairing of these concepts in section 9 that we can gain a degree of clarity regarding the process of moving from *qing* to righteousness. "Of all sounds, when they emanate from one's *qing*, are trusted; furthermore, after it enters and moves a person's heart it is profound." 凡聲，其出於情也信，然後其入撥人之心也夠. After introducing this third quotation into the discussion, an interesting trend appears. Although the order of *qing* before righteousness is not always followed, internalizing invariably appears after emanating.[11] The important new piece of information we gain from section 9 is that entering relates to the entering of a person's heart. Without this clarification, entering could be limited to a clarification of some sort of metaphysical activity at the transcendent level of "nature emerging from endowment." Instead, we see that entering is profound and personal. This resonates with section 8 where we are told that we embody the morality we obtain from the classics. Literally, these morals become a part of our body.

If entering is the process of receiving morals, then the question becomes where the source of teachings can be found. There is a direct source mentioned in section 9, and that is music. The section lists specific music that is believed to affect us in a positive manner, and the general category we find is that it relates to what the former kings listened to in antiquity. We must remember that music and ritual are connected in the text, so this is another source of positive influence. Less directly, the source of these morals is obtained from the Dao through the conduit of our *qing*. The process of emanating is not limited to humans, but internalizing is an action we strive to perform.

We are told "nature emerges from endowment" at the start of the text. What emerges is something positive that we are hoping to embody. This issue of emerging then becomes an important one for understanding the moral resources valued in the text. These include natural sources in the universe, but also the packaged versions of what nature has to offer that are contained in music and ritual. The text tells us that when this touches us it is profound, or more literally, the results are abundant. In other words, when we internalize we are absorbing something massive, and we are touched in a deep manner. There are many instances in the text where heightened displays of extreme happiness and sadness can be found. These displays of what we today would call a highly emotional response are not criticized. One possible explanation for the text being accepting of this type of ecstatic response is that it believes what we are attempting to internalize is truly massive. These are cosmic ideas we are embodying so excitement is to be expected.

ECSTATIC *QING*

The key to understanding how *qing* is able to serve as a bridge between the immanent and transcendent is that it is incredibly durable. This durability is exhibited in sections 11–12, where we can see *qing* not merely tolerating, but actually embracing extreme emotional friction at the immanent level. These sections show the emotions that *qing* embraces reaching an apogee. It is at this moment where the degree of expression has reached its highest point that reversion begins and the argument for ecstatic immanence takes on its full form. The world we live in is not a dystopian realm where we simply hope for a connection to the Dao for our salvation. Instead, the bipolar emotional swings we experience can be understood as interconnected and this harmonization of opposites forms the text's perspective on immanence.

Section 11

Of all utmost joy, there is the starting point of grief, crying is indeed grief; these two together are the utmost of your *qing*. Sadness, and joy they are close to our nature, for this reason they are not far from our heart. Crying's movement of the heart, in tears and isolated, you are intensely unable to bear parting, melancholy with the end. Joy's movement of the heart reaches deep and becomes giddy; if you are intense then you are tearful and in grief; leisurely in contemplation.

凡至樂必悲, 哭亦悲, 皆至其情也。哀、樂, 其性相近也, 是故其心不遠。哭之動心也, 浸殺, 其烈戀戀如也, 戚然以終。樂之動心也, 浚深鬱陶, 其烈則流如也以悲, 悠然以思。

Section 12

Of all anguished thoughts, afterwards there is grief; all musical/joyous thoughts afterwards there is delight. All thoughts use the mind deeply. Lamentation provides a method for [expressing] your thoughts. Sound changes thus [the heart follows.] When the heart changes the sound also changes this way. Chanting, reveals your sadness; "zao" chirping reveals your joy; "jiu" chirping reveals resonance, singing folk songs reveals the heart. Happy and carefree, carefree and vigorous, vigorous and singing, singing and shaking, shaking and dancing. Dancing, happiness's end result. Angry and anguished, anguished and grieving, grieving and melancholy, melancholy and beating your breast, beating your breast and hopping around. Hopping, anger's end result.

凡憂思而後悲, 凡樂思而後忻, 凡思之用心為甚。歎, 思之方也。其聲變則 [心從之矣。] 其心變則其聲亦然。吟遊哀也, 噪, 遊樂也。啾遊聲, 謳遊心也。喜斯陶, 陶斯奮, 奮斯詠, 詠斯猶, 猶斯舞。舞, 喜之終也。慍斯憂, 憂斯戚, 戚斯懟, 懟斯辟, 辟斯踊。踊, 慍之終也。

What is particularly interesting about these two sections quoted above is that aside from section 1 of the text, sections 11–12 are the only ones that contain the term "grief." In section 1 we find that grief is part of a list of a range of emotions: "The *qi* of being happy, angry, sad, and grieved are nature." 喜怒哀悲之氣, 性也. The last three emotions are negative and are only found in sections 11, 12, 14, and 20. As far as rhetorical planning, the text introduces general moral concepts through a universal context in the beginning, but in these later sections, we see how these morals relate to our everyday life. Among these later sections, 11 and 12 are excellent examples of the juxtaposition of positive and negative emotions. If we consider the juxtaposition from the perspective of attempting to convince us of the benefit that one can attain from practicing *qing*, it is surprising that the author has not softened the edges that disturb our emotional journey. There is no avoidance of the harsh realities of life, most noticeably both sadness and joy are present. *Qing* relates to the fullness of life, and is not a numbing uniformity. With this, we are asked to gain a sensitivity that appreciates the breadth of the human condition. It provides a vivid reflection of the phrase from section 1 "Likes and dislikes are nature." A similar understanding is expressed in section 11, where we see that "Of all utmost joy, there is the starting point of grief."

In these sections 11–12, binary opposites are used to represent the contrasting extremes of life, and this is celebrated. No instances exist in the text where we are told that when we attain higher knowledge, these conflicting elements will suddenly be denigrated as lowly. We can connect to a transcendent unity with the Dao, but the vibrancy of life is not subsumed into a homogenized unity. There is one phrase, which comes closest to indicating that opposites are equal. "Sadness, and joy they are close to our nature, for this reason they are not far from our heart." 哀、樂, 其性相近也, 是故其心不遠. Taken by itself the first half of the sentence seems as though it could be read, "the nature of sadness and joy are close to each other." The question comes down to what the pronoun *qi* 其 is referring to in the phrase. I take it as referring to the person who is reading the text and trying to follow its curriculum for cultivation. This is because the second half of the sentence is parallel to the first; "not far" mirrors "close" in the first half. "Nature" and "heart" are also similar terms, so the subject is not sadness and joy in isolation, but how these two concepts play a role in our lives.

When we experience these strong emotions, our reaction is not limited to our isolated selves; it is inherently a social experience. This is particularly apparent in paragraph 11 where the term "melancholy" (戚 *qi*) appears. In other contexts, the term can simply mean having a proper familial demeanor. One example is in paragraph 19 of "The Five Aspects of Conduct" where it is something we exhibit around our brothers and ultimately leads to the proper expression of intimacy. If we return this context to "Xing zi mingchu," it would imply that the melancholy produced from separation anxiety comes from not wanting to be apart from one's family. Moving earlier in the sentence, we see that the melancholy here is part of crying and being cut off from others. The unmitigated sadness is contrasted in the next sentence with joy, but both function in a similar manner by being expressed with the entire body. Our emoting includes vocalizations and all manner of body movements, indicating a high degree of agitation. Despite this, it is interesting that we do not lash out at others at any point.

The way we connect to others is through singing about our joys and our sorrows, and this is followed by others being able to see us shaking, dancing, beating our breast, and even leaping around. These reactions to joy and anguish are interesting because there is no indication that these ecstatic reactions are being seen as in error. The seeming excesses here might even be able to explain what is being expressed at the start of section 16. At that moment, going overboard is an important fault that the text specifically says we should *not* be concerned about if we are using our *qing*. This is amplified by the details provided in sections 11 and 12 where the emotions overflow into song and dance. So how do we know about the Dao? We know about it by singing, wailing, dancing, and beating our breasts. This is the human Dao, and we connect to it in an extremely human manner in the "Xing zi mingchu."

Admittedly, sections 11 and 12 are difficult to analyze because their description of life's trials and joys continues to have a strong axiomatic quality despite the massive length of time that elapsed between burial and discovery. Deep spiritual needs resonate with these outlier moments in life, and these moments connect us to the cosmos through the familiar concept of *qing*. This is no coincidence; the text is addressing a religious dimension of its intended audience, and this must include the epic moments of life. The range of emotions is part of our moral core, and it should be unfettered. One element that is most surprising from the Western perspective is the inclusion of anger in this cornucopia of sentiments.

In Greece and Rome, anger was seen as something that was dysfunctional, particularly when expressed in public. Private anger was seen as also something that led to the brutalization of others, and certainly had no positive moral attributes.[12] Medieval and early modern scholarship similarly describes a trope where civility involves a break from earlier times when anger was allowed to blossom forth to the immediate detriment of others. This created a desire to suppress anger as it was connected to the notion of sinful behavior.[13] Obviously the stifling of emotions is not part of the worldview of "Xing zi mingchu," but this contrast raises the question of why.

One major difference between emotions in the Western tradition and that of the "Xing zi mingchu" is that the latter does not see them as arbitrary. Reacting to our environment based on *qing* is not something that is dividing us from the proper decision-making methods of other humans; it is in fact seen as something shared. We have not lost our connection to a rational discourse as was imagined in Greece and Rome. Instead, we have become connected to the universal Dao by getting in touch with the extremes of emotional responses. Anger is not seen as something to repress, for it is not seen as degenerating into improper expressions of violence. Instead, when we reach such outlier moments in our lives it is an opportunity to stretch our understanding and reach a transcendent level.

When contextualizing the "Xing zi mingchu" perspective on anger, a much closer source is Zhuxi 朱熹 (1130–1200), a person who saw emotions as having the ability to connect us to the transcendent. He saw emotions as part of the process of self-cultivation because of his reading of the classic work the *Zhongyong* 中庸, a text most often dubiously translated as the *Doctrine of the Mean*. What is interesting is that this text does view emotions positively, but our goal is to keep them well regulated. It identifies pleasure, anger, sorrow, and joy as incipient tendencies that exist in a natural state of harmonious regulation.

> Prior to the start of happiness and anger, sadness and joy, we call it equilibrium. When they start and all are properly regulated, we call it harmony. Equilibrium is the great root of all under heaven and harmony is achieving the Dao of all under heaven. The highest degree of equilibrium and harmony establishes heaven and earth, and the myriad things will grow among them.
>
> 喜怒哀樂之未發謂之中發而皆中節謂之和中也者天下之大本也和也者天下之達道也致中和天地位焉萬物育焉.[14]

This is quite unlike the "Xing zi mingchu" in that it contains a strong bias against extreme passions.

Mencius is another text that Zhuxi identified as supporting his belief in the beneficial aspect of emotions. Mencius talks about compassion being an innate characteristic of humans that leads directly to moral behavior, and Zhuxi uses this as a basis for asserting that this compassion is *qing*, a positive emotional trait. In *Mencius* 6A.6, when asked if nature is ethically neutral or malleable, Mencius responds by saying that *qing* can be good. While this can explain Zhuxi's perspective, it also points to the changes that *qing* underwent between the pre-Qin period and the Song Dynasty.[15]

The most important change is that there is no mention of regulating *qing* in *Mencius*, but when this encounters the positivist tendencies of Zhuxi's general philosophy it is transformed into a belief that we will all have the ability to control our excessive passions.[16] Li Yujie 李玉潔 supports this perspective and writes about the compatibility of "Xing zi mingchu" and Neo-Confucianism by drawing connections to both Zhuxi and the Cheng brothers. Peng Guoxiang 彭國翔 takes the compatibility further by showing that it continues through the Ming Dynasty.[17] The control of passion that Zhuxi believes is of such great importance is one area we find conspicuously absent in the "Xing zi mingchu." Reintroducing this missing link in the tradition requires the grand tradition of Confucianism to be understood as even more tolerant than we might have previously imagined.

One way we can expand our understanding of the issue of control is by referencing another Guodian text, "The Five Aspects of Conduct." Here we find an exploration of punishment as an expression of our cultivation. In particular, the concepts of humanity and righteousness develop into separate ways of dealing with light or heavy crimes. Because of this, those who are the recipients of the punishment are likely people who have failed to follow the process of becoming ethical. "The Five Aspects of Conduct" believes that heavy crimes should receive capital punishment, but light ones should be forgiven. This focus on punishment is a tantalizing detail fully absent from the "Xing zi mingchu." Because there are two types of crimes in "The Five Aspects of Conduct," it is possible that the excess of section 16 is still deemed a minor crime that should simply be forgiven. Exhibiting anger and dancing with joy is certainly no crime so there is no need for punishment. The text has faith that emotions can be let loose without there being a danger of them overflowing into the larger community. This is not the world of oedipal tragedy, this is a time and place where the family sphere was seen as able to function independent of state intervention as is illustrated in the *Analects* 13.18 story of Upright Gong.

A more precise way to understand why emotions are not seen as dysfunctional in "Xing zi mingchu" is to analyze exactly what the text means by anger. In order to accomplish this we must compare the expanded discussion of sections 11 and 12 with the brief mention of the term "anger" (*nu* 怒) in section 1. The *nu* term for anger only appears twice in the text, so we have to pay attention to the terms it appears in concert with to begin to unravel its meaning. A separate character for anger (*yun* 慍) appears twice at the end of section 12, but it is not used again. This creates a difficult analytical challenge because we do not have enough instances of either character for anger to arrive at a solid consensus on the two terms.

The *yun* term for anger offers the best avenue for analysis because it appears in a parallel phrase in section 12. Here, *yun* anger is placed in opposition to happiness (*xi* 喜) as we see in the examples A and B below, which follow each other in the text.

> A: Happy and carefree, carefree and vigorous...dancing. Dancing, happiness's end result.
>
> B: Angry and anguished, anguished and grieving...hopping around. Hopping, anger's end result.
>
> A: 喜斯陶, 陶斯奮...舞。舞, 喜之終也。
>
> B: 慍斯憂, 憂斯戚...踊。踊, 慍之終也。

What is significant about this parallel is that here in section 12 the juxtaposition of happiness and anger is consistent with section 1. The term "*xi*," happiness, appears in both sections, but the character for anger is different. In the first section, the list of emotions begins with *xi* happiness, and this is followed by *nu* anger. This establishes a corollary relationship between the two graphically different characters for anger in the text. If we take this parallel seriously, then we have to understand this shift from happy to angry in both sections as providing a description of nature.

Sections 5–7 of the text mentions movement with nature, and there is certainly movement in the form of dancing and hopping in section 12. The difference is that the nature of section 5 is really just being described on the universal scale of the Dao as a whole as we saw at the end of section 6 where what grows nature is the Dao. When we contrast this with section 12, the most dramatic change is that the earlier section does not include negative elements. We know from the first section that nature includes desirable and undesirable sides, but sadness is not revisited until section 11.

Finding a holistic perspective on emotions that is inclusive of both positive and negative is pivotal for our assessment of the goal of self-cultivation in the text. The first section of "Xing zi mingchu" describes what appears to be a process that begins with simply reacting to our surroundings but concludes with cultivation producing establishment. An initial reading of this description would appear to be that of a person who mastered emotional distress and is no longer pulled erratically by the troubles of emotions. The problem with this is that at no point in the text do we find deeply emotional reactions described as negative. Quite to the contrary, there seems to be an embracing of the complete range of emotions from happiness to grief. If this is the case then we need to clarify the first line of the text where it states, "All people, despite their nature, have hearts with no stable will." This line must not be describing a problem; it is simply explaining a world where reacting in a sincere manner to the joys or tragedies we encounter is a valued achievement. The term "established" in the first instance then is describing an attribute of our heart, but the second instance is describing the state of our cultivation as not being prone to retrogression.

CHAPTER 2

The Role of Nature in a World of Friction

The previous chapter explored the tension that exists at the immanent level and the role of *qing* in ameliorating the problem. *Qing* and Dao are two opposite concepts in that one is completely personal and the other is transcendent. The text needs a third construct that exists on both levels, and nature (性) fills this void. There are sections of the "Xing zi mingchu" where nature is disconnected from our lives, but in other places it plays an active role in our moral project. The reason is that it is omnipresent.

It is important to reestablish the parameters of the problem before discussing the role nature plays in the solution. At the start of section 16 the text emphasizes our individual agency by explaining that mistakes, here resulting from excess, can be exempt from negative repercussions. The important proviso for enabling this to happen is that we must be acting with *qing*. "If you use your *qing*, although you are excessive you are not loathed" 苟以其情, 雖過不惡. In this quote, there are three ways we can understand the source of the error. The first is that the person with *qing* could be imperfect and thus a mistake is simply made. Another option is that the person with *qing* could actually be correct but others just fail to understand the situation. The third option is that it might not be possible to act in a way that is perfect in an absolute sense at any single moment, so neither the actor nor the audience is deficient. Within these three options, there is a degree of overlap in that a question is posed regarding different levels or definitions of truth. When we are acting with *qing*, it connects us to a more advanced level of cultivation that others might not understand. This third option raises the possibility that there is a judgment from a lower level based on incorrectly perceived excess; the presence of myopia might make some degree of tension unavoidable.[1] What would override this claim of inexorable tension is a construct that not only connects us to the Dao in the fashion of *qing*, but also has a firm grounding in the world around us. Nature is just such a dual construct, and it will be shown as having the potential to illuminate the tension that is such a knotty problem to understand in the text.

The first two explanations of the source of friction are similar in that they assume inadequacy on either the part of the actor or the observer. In the third instance, understanding is complete but the world does not operate in a manner that allows correctness to be achieved. The purest sense of this dystopian interpretation where the myopia of even a few is an inevitable element of the human condition is contradicted by the idealism expressed in the second half of section 16. Reaching the transcendence of the Dao is possible, but that does not deny our ability to observe our world from our earlier vantage point of mere immanence. This final description will be shown to be the most compelling, but we must remember that these binary opposites of loathing and *qing* are separated by a spectrum of gradations. Opposites are not without overlaps that result from these multiple ethical frameworks.

In the third explanation, we see that the text is describing a moment when a mistake is being made. The problem is that using *qing* connotes acting properly, and this is the conundrum. These two options are unlike the tension between good and evil where one side is deemed high and the other low. Instead, we have a mutual interdependence where praise and disdain are inseparable. We can understand the connection by observing another example where *qing* mitigates this negative social response to an error. When this occurs, it begins to establish an emotional element: It counteracts anger. Later the text underscores the emotive side of the term "Those who use *qing* to the utmost, it becomes particularly important in times of sadness and joy." 用情之至者, 哀樂為甚. Positive and negative emotions simply exist; one is not better than the other. In addition, we should be careful not to interpret the connection to emotions as an attempt to marginalize the term. Emotions are not seen as irrational, and the epic implications of this discovery will be discussed later in this chapter. For the moment, the point is that higher moral understanding includes being in touch with our emotions at their apogee. The quote here simply says sorrow and joy, but section 12 raises it to no less than an ecstatic emotional response.

Another reason we cannot dismiss *qing* as undesirable, along with the bipolar manifestations of its immanent aspect, is that in section 1 *qing* is a sublime conduit to the awesome cosmic forces of the Dao and nature. Nature is interesting in the text because there are many instances, such as the conclusion of section 2, where it is a term that is seen as having little direct connection with our personal lives. "[For people,] although there is nature, if the heart does not obtain it will not emanate." The heart is much more important, and any role that nature might play is secondary. Being secondary does not mean there are not instances where *qing* does have value, such as section 13 where we see that "Humanity is the method of nature." What is clear is that the dual views of nature as both peripheral and at times valuable in "Xing zi mingchu" are quite different from the consistent centrality of the term in Mencius.

One place where we see the importance of nature to Mencius is in 6A.1–3. In these passages, nature is the pivotal construct that drives moral cultivation. This is completely different from the passivity of "Xing zi mingchu" in section 6, which states "All that: moves nature is a material." This statement in its utter blandness does not speak strongly to any of our deep emotional responses such as those that *qing* can elicit. In stark contrast to the vibrancy of *qing*, the shift toward detachment marks the style of passages where we find nature and the Dao such as sections 5–7. This difference between *qing* and passages where nature is less connected to our lives provides one element of the claim that there is a divide between truth and higher truth. It is important to remember that there are other passages where nature connects to our lives, making it present at both the immanent and transcendent levels. The lower conflicted level exists as an arena where you must endure another person's loathing while working toward a higher harmony with the Dao.

What is evident here is that there is no such thing as absolute zero from a moral perspective. Even when we sink in the eyes of others to a point where we are loathed, therein is a measure of correctness. Similarly, we cannot dream of being completely correct since there is always a perspective from which our actions will be deemed in error. This constant conflict can be seen as existing at a lower level; from a higher perspective, this conflict is less important. Opposing sides can achieve balance in the Dao and this balance can move to the foreground in the text of the "Xing zi mingchu" to eclipse any discussion of discord. A complicating factor is this higher moral authority, which is inseparable from our internal side. The basis of ethical standards lies within us; it is immanent. In other words, the source of this higher perspective is not something external to us; it is found through a turn inward. The Dao is after all born in *qing*.

Let us return for a moment to our example of encountering opprobrium despite being correct in the later portion of section 16. "When people loathe you but you cannot be refuted you are one who has reached righteousness. When people refute you but you cannot be loathed you are one who is earnest in humanity." 惡之而不可非者, 達於義者也. 非之而不可惡者, 篤於仁者也. At first blush, humanity and righteousness seem to provide no protection from disapproval, unlike *qing* did in the earlier part of section 16. Humanity and righteousness coupled with scorn creates a false impression of amplified vulnerability to contempt. In fact when acting with humanity, righteousness, and *qing* there is no detectable difference in the potential to encounter scorn; in all cases the one who acts properly is perceived as having committed an error. If *qing* provided immunity then there would be no mention of excess. All of these instances include mistakes, so we cannot conclude that humanity and righteousness are in some way providing an inferior degree of protection than *qing*. The fact is that moral attainment does not allow one to navigate the challenges of life unscathed in the "Xing zi mingchu."

There is important common ground shared by the two quotations related to friction in section 16: They both discuss results that are opposite to what we would expect. It is surprising that acting correctly leaves a negative impression, even if the impact of this negativity can be mitigated to some degree. If moral behavior is correct then error, scorn, and loathing remain a surprising consequence. This conflict means we must embrace two distinct standards. Humanity and righteousness are just as clearly correct as being refuted and loathed are incorrect. The discrepancy is not so much a difference of point of view as much as a divergence between levels of truth.

Because of the correctness of humanity, righteousness, and *qing*, the possibility entertained earlier in this chapter that a person who acts with *qing* might lack sufficient understanding is illogical. If the world we live in contains inherent connectivity, then a person who acts with *qing* would be in touch with profound truths of the world. In such a situation, a mistake caused by a lack of complete knowledge would seem improbable. It is important to remember that *qing* is but an intermediary concept that is itself born of nature. Therefore, we must maintain the possibility that when judged from the higher perspective of nature there is no error. Contempt emanates from this group of outsiders, lacking *qing* and thus unable to comprehend what is really happening. The result of observing *qing* from a higher or a lower perspective is that the text sees the situation as one where you will always have a critic. Higher and lower truths in Guodian can relate to the selection of one form of moral conduct over another, such as applying righteousness at one point in time and humanity at another. When one truth is chosen over another, it is with an understanding that later there will be a balancing out. Prior to this balancing others will come to express dissatisfaction. In other words, humanity and righteousness do not exist in a hierarchical relationship in the way section 1 describes *qing*, nature, and the Dao. Instead, higher and lower simply refers to what is best for that moment in time without prejudice. Beyond this momentary binary tension, there is also a higher truth.

I am against dividing the "Xing zi mingchu," but we can see that the text does emphasize different aspects of the single process of self-cultivation. If we look at the first seven sections of the text, we see that they are focused on the universal or higher truth side of the process. As such, these distinctions are only present in the background. Then from sections 8 through the end of the text, we find a greater emphasis on the human aspect or lower truth. This lower truth is filled with value judgments and the dramatic emotional contrasts from crying to laughing. In examining this question of the divide between the first and second halves of the text, we will have to analyze unambiguous examples of the text's aesthetic standards. In the first section, we see: "Likes and dislikes are nature. What you like and what you dislike, are materials." 好惡, 性也. 所好所惡, 物也. The epistemological upshot of this quote is that nature is the locus and thus likely the source of the standard. Nature is separate from the object of scrutiny, materials, but these two are linked in that both relate to standards of assessment. A more literal reading of the role of materials is "That by which you like; that by which you dislike are materials." The function of the character *suo* 所 is that it serves as a mechanism for another action to take place. Based on the order of the text we can see that the potential of nature is described in the first sentence, and this goes on to be realized by the addition of materials in the second.

This relationship between nature, materials, likes, and dislikes can be clarified by borrowing terminology from Neo-Confucianism. A millennium of Chinese history passed before Neo-Confucianism was codified, but both systems share an interest in understanding how the world can be divided yet interconnected. One aspect of the world is deemed above forms, while the other is within or below forms. The goal of self-cultivation is to grasp a unity that can overcome this divide. Nature appears first in the section 1 quote, and we can see that it is above form because it is without materials. The category of below form, or possessing form, appears in the second sentence in the concept of "Materials." This means that materials are what provide the visible manifestation of this ethereal nature. This separation between the material world and the nature that shapes it supports my assertion that nature has an element of detachment in a way that is quite opposite to *qing*. In order to understand this connection to Neo-Confucianism better, we should begin by examining the relevant aspect of the "Xing zi mingchu."

By taking the question of detachment seriously, we see an indication that nature and its standards are formless because they are seen as transcending the physical world. Materials function as the mechanism that allows nature and its standards to be manifest, and therefore it can be observed in its immanence. However, the warning that subsequent debates in Neo-Confucianism sparked serve as a reminder that the transcendent modeling function should not be seen as dead.[2] Similarly, in "Xing zi mingchu," the transcendent has an intimate connection to our lives as long as we succeed in our project of moral cultivation. Nature is the term that exemplifies this connection, and it shifts in interesting ways between transcendent and imminent in that it is described differently from each of these two perspectives. This hints at the construct nature as having a similarly "living" characteristic.

This split between transcendent and immanent is evident in the first section of one of the most frequently quoted lines of the text "Nature emerges from endowment, endowment descends from heaven. ■ The Dao starts with *qing*, *qing* is born of nature." 性自命出, 命自天降. ■ 道始於情, 情生於性. This quote is explicit in section 1 that different levels operate in the universe. The black boxes in the text indicate a logical divide of some sort in the author's mind.[3] Each section contains three nouns, the second one being repeated once, creating two pairs of two nouns. The repetition of the term "nature" as the last character creates a linked form of logic known as epanaleptical sorites. In this case, it underscores the interrelatedness of the cluster of nouns and excludes the possibility of seeing a complete divide from one to the next. Each pair of nouns differs in terms of value or size but the important message is that even great things depend on lesser ones. It is this egalitarian message that attaches the cosmic to our person.

The middle point is the term "descending," which distinguishes the items in the first half of the sentence as above us and therefore transcendent. There are scholars who would use this divide to argue that the next term "Dao" is only related to the way of humans.[4] When the text wants to distinguish between the human way and the larger way it does so; in this instance it contains no such language. More precisely, such a position of rupture depends on how much of a break is understood to exist with the black box in the quote. Nature is repeated at both ends of the quotation, making a hard division between the two sides of transcendent and immanent difficult to justify. At the center of the quote, we have two universal concepts, heaven and the Dao. What it means by "starts with *qing*" is that our comprehension of the Dao, however we define it, begins to be obtained from *qing*. This is different from the next statement, which is not describing a methodology but is instead an epistemological claim. The inception of *qing* coming from nature explains why *qing* is able to serve as a conduit between our immanent emotional understanding and the higher transcendent Dao.

These two sentences are connected in that they begin and end with nature, and it is in this repetition that we can see nature related to both the transcendent and the immanent. In section 1, nature is not something that is only specific to humans; instead it is something that is inherent in all things. As such it is not always capable of contributing to our moral development. "All people, despite their nature, have hearts with no stable will." 人雖有性, 心無定志. If we read this quote in tandem with the discussion of nature that appears at the end of the same section, we find a doubling of the reinforcement behind the idea that nature has the potential to be separate from material and our lives. There is a definite divide in this quote between this force called nature and any impact on our moral lives. Nature may be something that is physically present, but its influence on us in this quote is ethereal. The distance between nature and the development of our morality marks this passage as transcendent. It is interesting that nature is playing a subordinate role to heart, which is seen as the locus of a singularly important goal, a stable will.

The heart is more relevant to our lives in that nature represents a grand uniformity inclusive of all things living and inanimate. This side of the term is explained in section 4 of the text.

> With all materials, everything is different.
>
> Of a hard tree, you get hardness.
>
> Of soft rope, you get softness.
>
> Within the four seas, our nature is the same, but we use our heart differently; teaching makes it so.
>
> 凡物無不異也者。
>
> 剛之樹也, 剛取之也。
>
> 柔之約, 柔取之也。
>
> 四海之內, 其性一也, 其用心各異, 教使然也。

The link between nature and material in section 1 makes more sense after seeing it expanded upon in this quote. The likes and dislikes that are nature in section 1 is but a list representing a range of what is included in the potential of nature. Material is what manifests this in many different forms: some that you like, others that you dislike. There is an emphatic element to the original Chinese at the start of the section; it contains a double negative that I translated "everything is different." In fact it says "nothing lacks difference," which forms a contrast with the oneness of nature. We could just as easily take the unity of nature as active instead of descriptive, which would mean that nature creates a unity in the world. The active voice is appropriate in that the text is explaining a process of cultivation we are supposed to carry out to promote cohesion.

Another link between section 4 and section 1 is the return to a binary opposite style to represent the range of manifestations that materials can acquire; this time the range is from hard to soft. The additional clarity this section brings is that it tells us how these differences are the result of the material and our judgment of such things; it is not something that is derived from nature itself. This does not mean that the differences between a tree and a piece of rope are illusory' they are real as manifest by material and perceived by our heart. The heart is unique and this is where diverse responses are created.

There is once again a dominant role ascribed to the heart in section 2. It concluded with a statement that without the mind, nature is unable to function. "[For people,] although there is nature, if the heart does not obtain it will not emanate." [□□]雖有性心, 弗取不出. At the start of the section, the mind is not mentioned but there is once again an interesting limitation of nature's abilities. "All those who make nature their master it is materials that obtains them." 凡性為主, 物取之也. In the middle of the section, an interesting figuration of the issue of limits is provided in the description of a bell that is not able to be rung unless it is struck.

Section 2 follows a consistent methodology in exploring the relationship between what is above forms and what is within forms. This relationship is comprised of three elements, each of which includes a desired result that requires a secondary factor for it to achieve fruition. The section starts with materials being a necessary ingredient before nature can be deemed master. In the middle of the section, the desired result is the sound of the bell that remains unrealized without the action of striking. There is potential for sound, but the sound remains above the form of the instrument until the striking makes it manifest. Finally, emanation is a desired result akin to sound; both are something that is given off by an object. True, we could call these different in that a bell is inanimate and we are animate, but the text understands us as having a shared relationship between transcendent and immanent. If we include the context of section 4, we see that this common ground comes from nature being the same in all things. The lesson for us is that nature by itself cannot generate results; it is separate from forms. In our lives, we rely on our heart to animate the world like the ringing of a bell.

The implication of section 2 is that a transcendent element exists that needs to be primed before it can produce results. This transcendent side exists as a latent force in the same way that a bell presents only the potential to produce sound. With the bell, force brings fruition, but for nature, it needs the more literal aspect of materials and the heart. The question this raises is if the heart is or is not a repository for *qing*. I would hate to guess blindly about this issue and lacking incontrovertible evidence, I feel that this is all we can do. Instead, a more exacting analysis would be that the two have the potential to function in corollary roles and this can be said for some instances of nature as well. Instead of positing a hierarchy where the heart is a repository for *qing* and or nature, we should simply see them as working as a group.

Qing, the heart, and nature are used as a group at the start of section 11, and this illustrates their relationship to the merging of positive and negative emotions. "Of all utmost joy, there is the starting point of grief, crying is indeed grief; these two together are the utmost of your *qing*. Sadness, and joy they are close to our nature, for this reason they are not far from our heart." 凡至樂必悲, 哭亦悲, 皆至其情也. 哀、樂, 其性相近也, 是故其心不遠. Previously, when this quote was discussed the emphasis was on the way that joy and grief are interconnected. It is at this moment when the text is showing that the full range of emotions is unified when *qing* reaches its zenith. This happens in the close proximity of our nature and our heart. When this happens, the principle of nature and the organ of our heart are activated like a bell being rung.

We are seeing nature inch slowly closer to an active role in our lives, particularly in difficult times. This is in contrast to nature's aloofness in section 4, which was not entangled in the messiness of immanence. Section 16 states, "If you do not speak and are believed, you are a person with a beautiful *qing*. If you do not teach but the people are enduring, you are a person whose nature is good (adept)." 未言而信, 有美情者也. 未教而民恆, 性善者也. *Qing* has been shown to be a concept that is always close to our lives, and nature is appearing in an exactly parallel sentence. The parallel means that *qing* and nature are in this quote fused in a manner unlike their usage elsewhere. This is a surprising shift from section 1 where nature embodies both positive and negative traits. In section 16, nature is simply good, which is opposite from section 11 where it seemed that it was an important contributor to our effort to see a unity behind opposing emotional states. There are two observations that can be made about the goodness of nature. First, when section 1 tells us that nature has potential for both good and bad, it is actualized by power. This is parallel to the statement that likes and dislikes are actualized by matter. While the potential exists in nature, it is not realized until materials and power are added to the equation. After the transcendent has become manifest with these added components there is nothing stopping it from being good, bad, liked, or disliked. The second observation we can make about section 16 is that this quote comes from the first half prior to hearing the wisdom of the Dao. In other words, this is a description of a lower level of truth, one filled with conflict and friction.

Another area where we can see nature becoming an integral part of our lives in times of difficulty is in section 13. This section begins by saying, "Of all who cultivate, seeking one's heart is difficult." 凡學者求其心為難. Obviously, this is not inaugurating a section where the idyllic harmony of transcendent understanding is going to be explored. Instead, it is firmly mired in the social friction of immanence. Further support of this characterization of the section can be found at its end where we are reminded that only the human Dao can be known. From start to finish, the section is concerned with the messiness of social forces. It is in the midst of this that we find nature linked to our moral development. "Humanity is the method of nature; nature gives birth. Loyalty is the method of faith. Faith is the method of *qing*. *Qing* emanates from nature. There are seven ways to love one's kind, only nature's love is close to humanity." 仁, 性之方也, 性或生之. 忠, 信之方也. 信, 情之方也. 情出於性. The end of this quote is reminiscent of the first section of the text where *qing* is born of nature. In both cases, nature is the source and *qing* emerges from it. What is different is the appearance of parallel statements that once again draw equivalence between *qing* and nature. This is more than an observation about origins; it goes further into our physical practice in a way strongly reminiscent of section 16.

Peng Guoxiang is particularly interested in the relationship between *qing* and nature, and he finds an important parallel in the writings of the Neo-Confucian scholar Wang Ji 王畿.[5] The process of self-cultivation is described by Wang Ji as "When *qing* returns to nature, this is the utmost of *qing*." 情歸於性, 是為至情.[6] This quote is describing a relationship between *qing* and nature that is similar to what is found in the "Xing zi mingchu," but what is more interesting is that Wang Ji was not alone in his understanding of these concepts.[7] The problem I see is that the constructs of above forms and below forms are conceived along too rigid a line in Peng's scholarship. I believe that nature in "Xing zi mingchu" straddles both above and below forms, which makes it particularly resistant to being defined too tightly. So while these analytical categories raise interesting questions, further study is needed to understand the long-term implications of these recently excavated texts.

Another area where the relationship between "Xing zi mingchu" and Neo-Confucianism could be better understood is related to the question of *ming* (命), a term that can be translated as "endowment." This term is tantalizing in that its appearance in section 1 of the "Xing zi mingchu" bears striking resemblance to the *Zhongyong*. Unfortunately, the term only appears in one sentence of the "Xing zi mingchu" so it is difficult to build much of an argument based on such anecdotal evidence. It is for this reason I feel it was wise for Michael Puett to leave "Xing zi mingchu" out of his analysis of *ming* in Early China, and instead focus on seminal texts that understand the term from a clear philosophical position.[8] The fourth chapter of this book will analyze a cognate term, *ming* 名 (name), and show how it functions as an important part of self-cultivation in the *Analects* and *Daode jing*. But, beyond this, it is difficult to provide a more robust account of endowment in the "Xing zi mingchu."

A brief recap of *qing* is as follows. Section 16 begins with a description of *qing* working to create harmony in a social context where friction is unavoidable. The second half of the section transitions to discussing the workings at a higher transcendent level where conflict is absent. The reason why *qing* can function as a bridge in 16 is explained in section 1, where it appears between universal concepts, the most important of which is nature. Dao is the primary universal concept that the text emphasizes, and this is the focus of the next chapter of this book. Prior to embarking on this focused analysis of Dao, it is important to begin to transition into this by clearing up the areas where *qing* and nature overlap with an understanding of what constitutes the Dao.

Section 8 is central to understanding this bridge to the Dao. There is a degree of overlap between how the process occurs here as in other sections, since self-cultivation is the key to establishing the connection from immanent to transcendent. The difference is the introduction of a new concept in the process, and that is ritual. Once again, *qing* is the center of this additional piece of information as we are told "Ritual is created from *qing*" 禮作於情. Because *qing* has both a connection to the cosmos and a deeply human emotional side, we can assume that these characteristics should also be part of how the text understands ritual. One way we will see this manifest is in the equivalency drawn between music and ritual at the end of section 8: "Laughter is the surface of ritual; music is the depth of ritual." 笑, 禮之淺澤也. 樂, 禮之深澤也. The emotional component of ritual is more easily imagined as a part of music, a construct that brings people together by conveying our inner feelings that are too complex for words alone. Similarly, ritual serves as a conduit for expressing *qing* by bringing out laughter. This is not people at their worst; when we embrace rituals, the text tells us we laugh with joy. Such a reaction makes sense when we understand ritual as attempting to develop our best side. As such, *qing* acts in a way akin to a handle, allowing us to gain access to universally proper attributes of the Dao and express them in society. Ritual works well with this because it is a tangible manifestation of *qing*. The chaos of society becomes mitigated by the Dao through the tools of ritual.

This returns to the question, though, what is the Dao that we are reaching in the "Xing zi mingchu"? It is interesting that section 8 describes a division within the Dao. "In the entire Dao, the heart's technique is chief. The Dao has four techniques, only the human Dao[9] can be known." 凡道, 心術為主. 道四術, 唯人道為可道也. The human Dao is a subset of a larger but unknowable entity.[10]

There is a particularly fine point that I feel it is important to make here regarding our ability to know versus be connected through *qing* or nature to the complete Dao. The character being translated as "known" at the end of the quote is a repetition of the character Dao 道. It could also be translated "be spoken of," but the point is we are looking at the verbal form of the noun Dao.[11] That verb, however we translate it, can only be used by us to interface with the human subset of the complete Dao. What this means is that the impediment is not that we cannot connect to the complete Dao; rather we can just not do as the Dao would in a direct fashion. Remember, section 16 tells us that we can know the wisdom of the Dao and hear it as well. The solution to this seeming contradiction can be found by observing the addition of a single term, *qing*, in section 16. Having gained the ability to use your *qing*, you can accomplish things that section 8 tells you are impossible.

The part of section 16 that helps us understand this is the oft-mentioned transition we find halfway through the section where it discusses the criticism of people who practice humanity and righteousness. After these two sentences, it shifts to a careful discussion of the uniformly positive results we can expect from being connected to the Dao. If we look at the way positive results are presented in the first half, we see that they are achieved as the product of a collection of trials we must overcome. Each sentence includes a challenge such as not speaking, not teaching, not rewarding, and not punishing. Some are made more problematic by the situation the person is found in, such as being destitute, poor, or living alone. These trials we face rise to a crescendo right before the midpoint when the text describes practicing humanity and righteousness but still encountering loathing and refutation.

The turning point is reached in the next sentence where we have the wisdom of the Dao. When this happens we can act without being excessive, a clear reference to having reached a higher level of cultivation than at the start of the section where you act with *qing* but are still excessive. A bridge has been crossed here; at the start we are just acting with our *qing* but at the midpoint, we are able to connect to the entire Dao. The concluding sentences provide a discussion of how we can use the Dao to interact with those above us and those below us. We also use the Dao to benefit our own cultivation. In this second half, the trials are over and unmitigated positivity dominates the discourse.

One lingering question we have about the Dao from the aforementioned section 8 is what those four divisions might mean. The end of section 13 has a similar statement "There are four Daos, only the human Dao can be known." 所為道者四, 唯人道為可道也. These two quotes highlight an important lacuna in our understanding of the text. If we do not know what these four types of Dao might be, or what these four techniques might represent, it is difficult to develop a solid analysis for anything else.[12] Identifying these components from clues within the "Xing zi mingchu" is particularly challenging, but it asks an even more pressing question: Is there a rupture that separates what we comprehend from the higher truth of the complete Dao?

We can be certain that the human Dao is one of the four, but the three others need to be identified by looking at the entire text to find potential candidates. The closest candidate appears in both of these sections, 8 and 13, and that is "the righteous Dao." In fact, the concept is found twice in section 8. The next most likely candidate for inclusion in the group is "the Dao of things," which appears at the end of section 7. Interestingly this is on the same strip as the quote regarding the four techniques. What I have translated as "the righteous Dao" could be more loosely termed "the Dao of morals." If we look at it more generally as a moral category, it can then serve as a counterpoint to the Dao of things. The material world is simply the way that phenomena appear instead of addressing their value in addressing moral questions. In other words, it is possible that there is overlap as to the subject of examination but the lens being applied sharpens either a moral or a physical side.

Identifying the fourth is much more complicated. Since we can really only be completely certain that the human Dao is one of the four, this raises the possibility that a complementary concept, the heavenly Dao, is also part of the set. Unfortunately, "Xing zi mingchu" does not mention this term. The Dao of heaven (天道) is found in the Guodian text "The Five Aspects of Conduct," and there it figures quite prominently. "The Five Aspects of Conduct" uses the Dao of heaven and the Dao of humans as a pair, which would seem to support the argument that this is the missing fourth Dao. While confining the search for this term to Guodian texts constitutes a stronger argument than turning to received texts for an answer, it is far inferior to building from the "Xing zi mingchu" itself.

A return to examine the "Xing zi mingchu" in fact uncovers a surprising fourth Dao. The term "Dao" is used as a comprehensive undifferentiated transcendent entity that encompasses the other subdivisions in a number of places, but is particularly clear in sections 8 and 13. In other words, we have Dao as a general unitary concept and three others that are divisible into the phenomenological, moral, and human. The best example of the shift the text undergoes between the unitary and divided meanings can be found in sections 6 and 7. These two sections are part of a set of parallel phrases that began in section 5. If we examine the conclusions of each of these paragraphs, it provides a clear illustration of the connection between the three. The last characters of section 5 can be translated as "some grow it." This is then copied and expanded upon to form the conclusion of section 6, "grows nature is the Dao."

The term "growing" is not repeated in section 7, but there is no indication it could be deemed a contradiction to the previous endings. Instead, we find a further elaboration on the topic that began in section 5. Section 7 concludes the set of three sections by stating, "The Dao is the Dao of all materials." What we have here are evolving permutations from just growth to the source growth being the Dao to a final narrowing of what is grown by the Dao to the category phenomenon. While somewhat unclear, it seems logical to conclude that the Dao itself cannot grow, but other constructs can. The Dao of phenomena is a subset of the unitary or undifferentiated Dao and it is broad since it includes humans. The two forms of Dao are not entirely differentiated in that they inform each other: part and whole. Humans perform righteousness or they do not, and this again forms a smaller subset of the human Dao.

Among these four types of Dao, the category of phenomena needs some further justification. The phrase where it is found states, "The Dao is the Dao of all things." 道 也者, 群物之道. There are two ways to read this quote. One way is to isolate it from the rest of its usage in the text, and the other is fully contextualized. If we look at this phrase alone it could be read as saying the Dao is nothing more than the tangible world, and as such, it seems to eliminate much of my argument about transcendence and immanence. However, this ignores the other areas of the text that says the Dao is multiple and contains more than one level. The second way to read this is to consider section 16 where we understand the Dao. Because the term "Dao" is not modified, I take it as the unitary Dao, not the Dao of righteousness of things. Within this second reading, one interesting possibility is that the four types of Dao exist in progressively smaller categories. Unitary is the largest, then materials includes all things in the world. Humans are a subset of things, and within our lives, we can divide out an even smaller unit of behavior called righteous.

The main question that we have regarding the divide between sections 5–7 and 8 is if this break in understanding corresponds to an epistemological or moral rupture. Put simply, we have to take seriously the two instances in the text where we are told that all we can know is the human Dao. These statements are emphatic; there is no qualification to tell us that there are certain exceptions to our limited knowledge. The text is also equally forceful in its statement in the first section of the text saying that the source of the Dao is *qing*. It is important that the character Dao in section 1 is not modified to limit its scope. I have already presented my argument as to why this phrase should be read as a statement that the source of our understanding of the entire Dao is *qing*. In section 1, it is impossible to dismiss the statement as relating to only the human Dao; no limitations are included. The text terms it the Dao without further restrictions. This reading gains further support from the claims of sections 8 and 13 that we can only know or speak (Dao) of the human Dao. If we were to take the claims of 8 and 13 in simple combination with section 1, it is possible that a pure contradiction would be our only available conclusion. However, the addition of other passages provides an avenue for coherently understanding these multiple Daos. We cannot know the unitary Dao directly, but we can comprehend it in a deep and substantive manner through our *qing*.

CONCLUSION

The conflict between higher and lower truths in the "Xing zi mingchu" creates a sense of tension between judgments made based on what is above forms or what is below. On several occasions, the text distinguishes between latent principles of the world that obtain their manifestation through phenomena. Section 1 has "Awaiting materials, then there is a reaction" 待物而後作, section 2 includes "Bronze and stone [instruments] having sound, [without striking they do not ring…]" 金石之有聲[也, 弗擊不鳴 □□.] and finally section 6 tells us, "All that: moves nature is a material" 凡動性者, 物也. We must understand our world as existing on two levels; there is substance that surrounds us but it is given form by transcendent principles. These two levels then correspond to the two levels where we need to develop morals. Because of the ethical charge that is applied to both levels involved, each can be seen as pertaining to a form of truth.

There is also a divide between what exists within the material world. Examples of these are ritual norms being resisted and divisions in the positive or negative reactions we have to our surroundings. These distinctions exist on a lower or mundane level. A person who embodies *qing* and nature is able to establish a connection to higher truths of the Dao where friction is absent. Nature plays a central role in bridging the connection between mundane and higher truths since it is described in both ways. As such, nature has promise as a concept that can produce a meaningful transformation of the mundane world.

What is particularly important in the structure of truths and higher truths in "Xing zi mingchu" is that negation and harmonization exist on two levels. On the level of phenomena, we have several ways that behavior is deemed correct or incorrect. Another divide is between desirable and undesirable emotional states. In both cases, these opposing concepts are understood as indivisible. These two sides create each other and are thus unable to be ranked hierarchically. This is how harmony is created on the more mundane level. Then this harmonization of opposites is understood as being itself re-negated because there are principles that exist above forms. We are able to connect to this higher truth through our *qing*. When we do establish this connection, we can hear and understand the Dao. Finally, the text tells us that this higher truth of the Dao starts in *qing*, which exists inside us. This places the source as an undiscovered inchoate trait that we learn from getting in touch with our unchecked emotions.

These wild emotional swings do indicate that at least certain sections of the text are quite comfortable with chaos, and this led me to previously characterize the text as anarchist.[13] We can see this in the first line of the text "All people, despite their nature, have hearts with no stable will." 凡人雖有性, 心無定志. One way we can read the line is that it is describing our state prior to self-cultivation. Another possibility is that stability is not valued since the bipolar highs and lows of life are part of reaching the Dao. While stability may not be part of the goal of the text, a more animated ideal such a harmony is valued. Nature is omnipresent, including positive and negative attributes. What is important is what we make of it, and this is where it can benefit our moral development.

CHAPTER 3

Having Fun with the Dao

So far, in the discussion of self-cultivation that has dominated this book, a significant amount of time has been spent on the warnings the text gives us of pitfalls we could encounter in the context of practicing *qing*. In the analysis of the challenges we face, the role of nature was explored. It was found that certain passages describe nature as unconnected to our morality while others show its relevance with great clarity. An underlying cause for this difference is a split between immanent and transcendent. The problem is that the moment in the text where this split is most obvious is in relation to the Dao, but this book has only examined the question from the perspective of *qing* and nature. Now it is time to look through the telescope from the other end and see what our world looks like from above.

One major question this chapter will answer is if the Dao in the "Xing zi mingchu" is a metaphysical construct. There are two basic models for understanding Dao in late Warring States China. In *Analects* 4.20 we see that Dao is just the sum total of the way a person acts. The passage tells us that acting in a filial manner means continuing to follow the Dao of your father for three years. The term just means "way" or "manner"; there are no metaphysical elements present. *Laozi* 42, which is found in the Mawangdui and received versions of the text, has the Dao producing all things in the universe. Clearly he sees Dao as a force in the universe beyond what is merely apparent from outward appearance.

"Xing zi mingchu" has two parts that speak to this question in an obvious fashion. The first we will analyze is sections 5–7 where a large network of meanings forms the structure of the Dao. As the text explicates these subtle structures we can begin to see that it is related to more than just our father's Dao. Understanding these structures provides a solid grounding in how the text views the world. Working forward in the text provides this chapter with a needed respite in the form of the section Music and Fun, which focusses on the role of music in section 8. Music provides our lives with a vivid means of expressing and enjoying the interconnectivity of sections 5–7. Heart-Nature-Dao is the next section, and this turns to analyze the difficult metaphysical questions of section 1. The conclusion of the chapter is Dancing with the Dao, and this describes how we are moved by the Dao both spiritually and through dance in the "Xing zi mingchu." This final section also will attempt to deliver on the promise of the chapter title, which was having fun.

As the text oscillates between metaphysical inquiry and discussions of how this touches our lives and relates to society, it can be seen as a missing link between the transcendence of Laozi and the immanence of Confucius. Part of how the text straddles these two extremes has already been touched on in passing; the seeming epistemological rupture between the human Dao and the whole Dao was found not to exist. Instead, it was argued that the "Xing zi mingchu" understands the world as existing at two levels that are in no way hopelessly divided. A better way to understand the difference is to see it as a question of truths versus higher truths. There might be friction between the two, but they share some important characteristics. This explanation works well for the latter half of the text where differences between positive and negative are more prevalent. Now it is time to explore how we reach the Dao and become free from friction.

Proceeding beyond this question of rupture, we can attain a better understanding of the process of attaining knowledge in the "Xing zi mingchu." Sections 5–9 are of particular importance for understanding the transcendent Dao. The first three sections (5–7) of this group are interesting in their parallel style; the order of the ideas discussed is transferred from one to the next with only minor alterations. The first section begins with nature and then finishes with the Dao. In its midst are exclusively positive attributes. One example is that happiness is the only emotion appearing in these sections. The importance of happiness to the process becomes steadily more obvious in sections 8–9 where we see the development of moral concepts occurring in tandem with having a good time. Joy and music are two sides of the character *yue* 樂 that are both important to the process of self-cultivation.[1] This reading is supported in these sections by accompanying discussions of both the emotion of happiness *yue* 悅 and specific types of music. Music is distinguished by geographic origin and also by the instrument used in its performance such as the zither. The point is that while the previous chapter discussed averting crisis by looking at the second half of the "Xing zi mingchu," this one will analyze the first half where the fun side of morality eclipses other concerns.

Section 8 forms an important transition between the more transcendent framing of nature and the Dao in sections 5–7 and the discussion of music in section 9. As a transitional area, section 8 straddles two sides: The first examines the tools humans have at their disposal to understand the Dao in a direct manner. These tools are classical texts that the sages put together and the core moral terms that they convey. The second is the web of interconnections that are detailed in sections 5–7; specifically they are concerned with the range of items that exist between nature and the Dao.

It is interesting in section 8 that the initial mention of the full Dao is followed by an immediate narrowing of the field down to the human side by focusing on the human way. This encapsulates the transitional moment between the previous sections where the universal side is emphasized and the more humancentric discussion that follows. We should be cautious about finding this transition to be too complete in these early lines, however. The term "heart" is used in the context of cows and wild geese in section 3, so it stands to reason that here it also should refer to all beings. The important point is that there are two levels of truth here, and the larger more encompassing one is the Dao. Below that are smaller subcategories. The Dao here is not a formless unity that lacks differentiation; elements within it such as the heart can be identified. Furthermore, there is the human Dao that appears as an important subset of the larger Dao. Since we can only directly know about the human Dao but we are still aware of moral distinctions in the world, it would make sense that there is a degree of continuity between what we are able to understand and the greater truths of the cosmos.

In order to elaborate on the question of the heart, we should see that section 3 begins by stating "All hearts have wills," and this is followed by statements about cows and geese growing and maturing. Section 2 discusses nature and the way it needs materials to be activated. It clarifies this construct through the mention of the way a bell will not sound without striking. Since sections 2 and 3 both identify the heart and nature with nonhuman constructs, then the term "heart" in section 8 should also include the hearts of animals. This makes the text very interesting because if the category "heart" in the text is always meant to include animals, then it is not that human hearts are paramount, but animal cognition is also a chief aspect of the Dao. There are certainly enough anthropomorphic discussions in early China to move such a conjecture about the importance of creatures into the realm of plausible. Zhuangzi's discussion of the joy of fishes and his dream of being a butterfly are but the most famous examples of the blurring of the lines between people and animals. The point the "Xing zi mingchu" seems to be making by including animals in its sketches of how our world functions is somewhat different; it is arguing that the difference between us and them is slight. Lacking details that provide differentiation, we are left with a message significantly unlike that of Mencius who sees dysfunctional humans as analogous to animals in a move that would create a clearly pejorative assessment of cows and geese.

Another way to consider this issue is that simply because there are forces beyond our human cognition does not mean that there is also a rupture between what we experience and the cosmos we inhabit. If the entire scope of the Dao in the text were limited to humans, it would only make sense if the term were used in a restricted sense of path, but the text is certainly interested in larger, more universal discussions such as the subject of heaven. An interesting challenge appears if we are only privy to knowledge of the one human corner of our universe: How do we know the proper way to act? This question is tied to important epistemological questions; the most pressing is what impact this has on mechanisms for understanding the Dao. This chapter will argue that the term "Dao" is simultaneously single and multiple in the "Xing zi mingchu." The single Dao is unitary and not limited to what involves humans; the multiple Dao is divided into human versus other elements as represented by the four Daos of section 13. This means that on a higher level of the unitary Dao, the four divisions cease to maintain their importance.

Before we can delve into this further we have to revisit how the term "Dao" is characterized at the start of the text. Section 1 tells us "The Dao starts with *qing*, *qing* is born of nature." *Qing* is a complex term that is transcendent in its connection to the cosmic Dao, but it also relates to us personally in the form of our emotions. The order of nature being the source of *qing*, which in turn begins the Dao, is surprising because in section 6 it tells us "what grows nature is the Dao." If the starting point of the Dao is something that is formed in nature we would seem to have stepped into the circular epistemology of M. C. Escher. The key to unraveling this is to carefully examine the structure of sections 5–7 to see what they might say about the Dao and also nature.[2]

It is significant that *qing* is not present in sections 5–7 but figures prominently in sections 8–9. These earlier sections are interesting in that they remain comparatively neutral regarding the benefits of the Dao. The higher degree of neutrality in this exploration of structures becomes apparent when we compare it to the strong benefits ascribed to having *qing* in section 16. *Qing* is the human component of the universe, and when the Dao is described in its absence its unitary form is being emphasized. In other words, it includes what is within our grasp and what is beyond us. As we transition to sections 8–9, limitations arise and the human component shifts into prominence.

One of the consistent attributes of the Dao is that because it can encompass what is vastly beyond our understanding, *qing* becomes the bedrock of our moral cultivation. We can see the unique treatment of the term in its being described in universally positive language throughout the "Xing zi mingchu." If we compare the role of *qing* to nature, a concept Mencius sees as our guide for self-cultivation, we immediately notice that section 1 takes pains to tell us "Being good at it and also [not good at it are nature.]" This means that if we are to rely on nature in our quest for morality, we will be completely rudderless. All we can consistently trust is *qing*. This seemingly unassuming concept turns out to be the mechanism through which we interface with the cosmos; it is the common ground that lies between nature and the Dao: "The Dao starts with *qing*, *qing* is born of nature." The previous chapters of this book discussed the function of *qing* as a source of ritual, and this ethical framework is a way that we can connect as humans to larger elements such as the Dao and nature.

GROUNDING OUR UNDERSTANDING OF THE DAO

Section 5 begins with nature; following this is a chain of verbs that are each understood to be its modifiers. However, because this is linked to sections 6, 7, and 8 the group as a whole must be seen as having a strong interest in the Dao as well. The first character of the section is important as it sets the topic for the subsequent sentences. For example, each verb from section 5 is repeated in section 6, but after each verb the character for nature is inserted. This means that in section 5, the character for nature was intended to be carried through the section as an implied topic. The object that the verb is acting upon in section 6 is then repeated in section 7, along with a further explanation of what the term means. We must remember that the conclusion of 7, and by extension the last item in each section, relates to the Dao. Section 6 contains seven instances of the character *xing* 性 "nature," but this should be seen as only one component of the section's conclusion, "what grows nature is the Dao." The process is not simply unidirectional, it is intertwined as we saw in the first section: "The Dao starts with *qing*, *qing* is born of nature."

The following table shows each of the three sections divided into their seven items; in the original manuscript each section is presented consecutively, not parallel as is shown below. Rearranging the sections in this table shows the way that each item is expanded upon in the next section. There is a similar type of parallel between sections in "The Five Aspects of Conduct" that I termed double sorites in my first book. "Xing zi mingchu" has three sections, and these are also sorites since they simply provide a chain of ideas that are not particularly meaningful if unhooked from the rest of the series. Therefore it would seem fitting to call sections 5–7 triple sorites. The key with sorites analysis is to look at the chain as a whole to see what conclusions can be drawn from the vagueness of the connections from one item to the next. Here, the connections do not simply proceed down a single chain of ideas, but are also knitted horizontally from one section to the next. This makes it a two-dimensional network of vague meaning instead of a one-dimensional chain of reasoning. Based on the order of the sections, we can see increasing complexity in the network of meaning in each successive section. Section 5 is the starting point of the triple sorites, so its basic meaning is still relatively linear. The line of reasoning begins with the term "nature." As we move forward to read section 6, we are forced to consider the separate vertical progressions of the two sections in conjunction with the combined horizontal connections among each of their seven items. We must consider that because of the painstaking repetition between these two sections and a high degree of consistency, this web of connections must have been intentional on the part of the original author.

In reading section 7, we must consider a complex web of meaning in each item since they are distinct members of a vertical list that must also be connected horizontally to section 6 and/or section 5. The first item in section 7 "All that we see is called matter" becomes more clearly connected to the topic of nature in item 6 of the section where the object of cultivation is said to be our nature. This ties back to the sixth item of section 6 since this item is a clarification of "what nourishes our nature is cultivation." The precursor to this sixth item is in section 5, which simply states "some are nourished." This creates 420 possible paired combinations and infinite loops of co-interconnection.

Each box in table 3.1 will be termed an item, and they will be referred to as numbered from top to bottom in each column. Rather than explore all the possible combinations in the above table, we will focus on three sets of connections that are representative of the ways the sections combine. The first set of arrows show that the verb "move" is a modifier of the noun "nature" in the first section, and it is further explained as the type of movement that is caused by materials in the second section. This seems to be a hopelessly broad statement since the world is filled with things. The text continues to reinforce the idea that universality is exactly what is meant by the term "materials" in the last section where it tells us again that everything we see is a material. The relationship between these three items is both horizontal

Table 3.1

Section 5	Section 6	Section 7
凡性或動之 With all nature, some move it	凡動性者，物也; All that moves nature is a material;	凡見者之謂物, All that we see is called a material
或逆之 some welcome it	逆性者，悅也; welcomes nature is happiness;	快已者之謂悅, what makes you content is called happiness
或交之 some regulate it	交性者，故也; regulates nature is a special purpose;	物之勢者之謂勢, that which is the power within materials is powerful
或厲之 some sharpen it	厲性者，義也; sharpens nature is righteousness;	有為也者之謂故。a person who achieves something is said to have a special purpose.
或出之 some emit it	出性者，勢也; emits nature is power;	義也者，群善之蕝也。Righteousness is the standard of all that are adept.
或養之 some nourish it	養性者，習也; nourishes nature is cultivation;	習也者，有以習其性也。Cultivation is using cultivation for your nature.
或長之 some grow it	長性者，道也。what grows nature is the Dao.	道也者，群物之道。The Dao is the Dao of all things.

in that there is further explanation of the terms in each successive section. This also happens vertically in section 5 where it discusses seven ways that nature reacts. "Move it" is but the first item; it is part of a series of successive links that ends with "nourish it" and "grow it." Section 5 also describes a process that begins with the movement of nature and ends with its growth. The meaning of growth must be understood at first in the isolation of the single section and then expanded through horizontal connections to the other two. If we observe the seventh item in the second section, we see that growth connects to the Dao, a term with implicit moral overtones.

Nature provides a direction to materials; these are the various verbs found in section 5. However, lacking materials, these actions remain unrealized potentials that exist above forms. In section 6 we have the addition of materials in the first item and this physicality carries down through the section. The construct of materials is all encompassing; it seems to include an emotional state in the term "happiness" and a state of being moral in "righteousness." It is interesting that section 7 describes materials as everything visible, which is emphasizing physicality as necessary. In other words, this clarification supports the assertion that we can know of the various items in section 6 because their animation is made possible through their having a physical existence.

This question of physicality then becomes puzzling when we wonder what separates the smooth interconnectivity of the discussion in sections 5–7 and the struggle to overcome negativity that exists in other parts of the text such as section 16. There is no decisive element that convincingly distinguishes the transcendent from the immanent. Granted, the term "*qing*" is missing from the triple sorites sections 5–7, but section 15 contains a long discussion of loathing falseness and makes no mention of *qing*. The terms "nature" and "Dao" serve as bookends to the discussion of interconnectivity, but they are not absent from section 16.

Instead, the answer seems to be more subtle and related to a finer distinction; the triples sorites describe a harmonious interconnectedness that exists between nature and the Dao. This explanation is problematic because it could be accused of circular reasoning—it lacks negativity because it is not there. Because the text operates based on truths and higher truths, the discussion of harmony is not divorced from the sections that relate to negativity. If this were the case there would need to be a concrete concept such as righteousness that marks the boundary between a flourishing life and loathing. However, righteousness is discussed in its purely positive context of the triple sorites; "some sharpen it" becomes "sharpens nature is righteousness" and finally we see that "righteousness is the standard of all that are adept." There is no mention of being loathed but not refuted as we find in section 16.

Taking these three sections as a unit, we see that the focus is on nature and the Dao, and these constructs engender constant motion. For example, the starting and ending items in sections 5 and 7 are movement and growth. This is not so surprising for the Dao, but describing nature as moved by materials is somewhat similar to the caricature-like criticism of Gaozi that we find in *Mencius* 6A.2. "Gaozi said 'Nature is like rushing water, unblock it on the east and it flows east; unblock it on the west and it flows west. Human nature does not distinguish between good and not good, like water does not distinguish between east and west.'" 告子曰. 性. 猶湍水也. 決諸東方則東流. 決諸西方則西流. 人性之無分於善不善也. 猶水之無分於東西也.³ We can never know what Gaozi actually believed by looking at his ideas through the distorted lens of a critic, but in *Mencius* he sees nature as being as fluid as water, with no preference for high or low, good or bad.

The obvious difference in "Xing zi mingchu" is that in these three sections that focus on the development of nature, there is nothing included that can be characterized as negative. In contrast, there are items that would belong in the positive category, such as nourishing and righteousness. The combining of nature with the Dao is also indicative of sections 5–7 belonging in the first half of the text where universal concerns are the focus and the tangible impact on daily life is minimal. There is none of the dancing and beating of our breasts we see in section 12.

Returning once again to a more fundamental level, one question that is particularly difficult to answer is why there is a shift in the order of some of the items from section 6 to 7. The start of the shift is seen in the discussion of the term "power," which was the fifth item in sections 4–5. In section 7 it moves earlier to become the third item. This move to an earlier position in the sorites of section 7 forces "purpose" and "adept" to then drop by one position in the order of items discussed. In fact, "purpose" and "adept" are not themselves moving; they are just being displaced by "power" moving ahead in the sorites. The sixth and seventh items in section 7 are unaffected by the movement because it is only the three items above them that are being shuffled.

It is inherently difficult to analyze the specifics of a sorites, and this shift of items is but a small detail in a long chain of reasoning. Despite this challenge, we can begin to observe a stylistic shift between the fourth and fifth items in section 7 that could help explain the author's reasoning. Each of the first four items is a clarification presented as "'X' is called 'Y.'" "Y" is the carried over term from section 6, and "X" is a phrase providing further explanation of the term "Y." The end of section 7 has three items that differ significantly from the first four. Items 5–7 of section 7 do not follow "'X' is called 'Y'"; it changes to "'Y' ones are 'X.'"

In section 6 we have "'W' nature is 'Y'" with "W" being carried over from section 5: "some 'W' it." When we compare the first four items in section 6 to section 7 we notice that "Y" consistently remains at the end of the item. Put simply, there is a horizontal connection among the first four items in section 7 that follows a completely rigid formula that dictates the word order. The order of "Y" as occurring at the end of the items in section 6 and the starting four items of section 7 is indicative of the care the author exerted in preserving consistency among the sections. It is interesting that we find a contrast to the strength of the horizontal consistency, with vertical inconsistency in the form of two items shifting from one section to the next. In the last three items of section 7, the horizontal order is also broken and this change must relate to why two items from 6 had to move to either the group of the first four or the last three.

These last three items of section 7 stand out for breaking both horizontal and vertical consistency. A closer look at them reveals they have other unique features. It is normal for the text to generalize; every section starts with the character 凡 *fan*, "all." However, the first and last of the three items contain the character *qun* 群, "all/group," which reconnects these items to the universal context that starts each section. Righteousness is connected to the collection of what we are good at, which can also be translated as "adept." It might seem that the group "adept" would include a variety of things in which we are skilled, but a surprisingly different understanding is given in section 1, and this is "being good at it or not good at it." This is not to say that adept always has to appear with its opposite; section 16 has one such example. Another possible expectation is that righteousness might appear with *qing*, as it does in sections 1 and 8. Again, this following of other patterns does not appear. Even the term "standards" is used only one time in the text, and this is in section 7 with righteousness.

The next member of the group of three final items in section 7 states "Cultivation is using cultivation for your nature." Not much can be made of this definition except that it specifies that the object of cultivation is "nature." Nature is everywhere in the world, so it represents a collection of things akin to the term "group" that is used with righteousness in the previous item. The last instance of all/group is in the context of the Dao, which is said to relate to all things or materials. This mention of materials establishes an important connection with nature since these terms are connected to each other in sections 1 and 2.

The above analysis has shown why the item related to righteousness has to appear closer to the end of section 7; it becomes a member of a set of three stylistically similar items to form a conclusion of the triple sorites. However, this does not yet answer the question of why the set does not remain consistent in sections 5 and 6. We can see that emitting comes before nourishing in these two sections, and we also know that emitting often appears before internalizing as was discussed in chapter 1 of this book. It is possible that nourishing falls under the category of internalizing; the text does not say this specifically, but it is a fairly plausible assumption. In contrast, the concept of sharpening is used in *Lushi Chunqiu* and *Xunzi* as a preparatory step done prior to sending troops into battle.[4] If this loose group of assumptions is correct, then it would mean that sections 5–6 are describing preparation, emitting then nourishing, three phases of cultivation that need to proceed in that specific order.

The item in section 7 related to power that does jump forward to the third position is fascinating for the ways it overlaps with pairings of connected terms in section 1. In particular, the question of emitting and nature is significant in both sections. "…Emits nature is power…that which is the power within materials is powerful" 出性者, 勢也…物之勢者之謂勢. Section 1 tells us that nature is emitted (emerges) from endowment, but this quote raises the possibility that the unspoken force that drives this reaction is power. Power does not appear frequently in the text. In addition to the above three instances of the character, it occurs only one more time in the following quote: "Likes and dislikes are nature. What you like and what you dislike, are materials. Being good at it and also [not good at it are nature.] What you are good at or not, is power." 好惡, 性也. 所好所惡, 物也. 善[不善性也,] 所善所不善, 勢也. Each of these two sentences contains repeated structures from the other and this produces a multiplication of inferences. What this means is that the term "materials" in the first carries over to become intertwined with "power" in the second because both terms are modifying nature in similar grammatical structures. Power becomes the catalyst for reifying what you like or dislike in nature. Materials then become the structure that allows for a display of power in what you are good at or not, in the second sentence.

The echo of material and power in the first section then continues to reverberate when it returns in section 7. Naturally, there are significant differences between the two sections. Section 1 includes positive and negative descriptors for materials, nature, and power, while section 7 is neutral. But it is the result of this reverberation that causes us to ask why neutrality appears in section 7. More questions are raised than can be answered. Exactly why power moves earlier in section 7 when materials are introduced remains for the moment somewhat mysterious. One point we can be certain of is that this third item holds quite a remarkable place in the triple sorites.

MUSIC AND FUN

The reward for transforming ourselves is more than an abstract promise of virtue; the "Xing zi mingchu" tells us that the results are palpable and fun. A transition from a discussion of harmonious interconnectedness toward a discussion of people having a good time is what occurs in section 8.

> In the entire Dao, the heart's technique is chief. The Dao has four techniques, only the human Dao can be spoken of as a Dao. As for the other three techniques, one does no more than speak of them. Odes, Documents, Rites, Music, their inception is in the needs of humankind.
>
> The Odes successfully make it;
>
> The Documents successfully speak it;
>
> The Rites and Music successfully gather it.

The sage compared the categories [of the classics] and by expounding, assembled them; observed the sequences [of the classics] and going with the flow, stabilized them; embodied the morality [of the classics] and by ordering, refined them; organized the *qing* [of the classics], express and internalized them. After this they can again be used for instructing. Teaching is that by which you give birth to virtue from the center. Ritual is created from *qing* when something excites it. Confront affairs according to the method and standardize them, the chronology of this sequence is the Dao of righteousness. When something is sequenced it becomes etiquette and is thus embellished. Devoting yourself to ornamenting your appearance is that by which patterns become etiquette. A noble person has beautified his or her *qing*, made venerable his or her righteousness, is good at etiquette, made the utmost of his or her appearance, enjoys the Dao, delights in teaching; thus he or she is made respectful by them. Honoring that by which □□□ he or she praises embellishment. Wealth is that by which you build trust and its verification, he or she regulates the righteous Dao. Laughter is the surface of ritual; music is the depth of ritual.

凡道, 心術為主。道四術, 唯人道為可道也。其三術者, 道之而已。詩、書、禮、樂, 其始出皆生於人。

詩, 有為為之也。

書, 有為言之也。

禮、樂, 有為舉之也。

聖人比其類而語會之, 觀其先後而逆順之, 體其義而節文之, 理其情而出入之, 然後復以教。教, 所以生德於中者也。禮作於情, 或興之也。當事因方而制之, 其先後之序則義道也。或序為之節則文也。致容貌, 所以文節也。君子美其情, [貴其義] 善其節, 好其容, 樂其道, 悅其教, 是以敬焉。拜, 所以□□□其徵文也。幣帛, 所以為信與征也, 其治義道也。笑禮之淺澤也。 樂, 禮之深澤也。

This rather long quote is the entire section 8 of the "Xing zi mingchu." The starting sentence invokes the hierarchy of the full versus the human Dao, which was discussed in the previous chapter. Following this, there is an obvious shift to focus on the immanent. The shift is exemplified by the listing of the Odes, Documents, Rites, and Music, which are said to emanate from people. By not narrowly assigning core terminology such as *qing* or righteousness directly to individual classical texts, section 8 treats these accomplishments in a distinct manner. It is possible that this is because these texts convey much more than a single concept, or they are seen as higher in importance than specific moral actions we might perform. Classic texts possess global abilities, and these are not narrowed to a singular specific trait such as righteousness. A sage appears next in the section and there is some vagueness regarding what is meant by comparing categories.

I take this and the next four sentences as referring back to the previously introduced classics. My interpretation is supported by their being four statements about what the sage does, and this is consistent in number with the four books. There is no obvious connection between the sage's actions and any individual book; instead it just seems that the four things a sage does relates to these books in a general manner.

Section 8 follows an orderly trajectory that begins with situating the classic texts and their creation in the cosmic context of the Dao. The final part of the section examines the propagation of moral learning. This involves teaching people about virtue, *qing*, ritual, and music. Within this discussion there is an inclusion of regulation, which I translate as "etiquette." When the text describes how the sages adapt the Dao through texts to transform others, it involves a process of conveying a pattern. The transfer of the pattern can be seen in ritual being created from *qing*. Ritual itself is a pattern of behavior and *qing* is a conduit for the Dao and emotions. The text then tells us there is a sequence that is "The Dao of righteousness" and this sequence leads to embellishment. The combination of those factors creates a regulation of our lives based on natural factors that we absorb with the aid of sages and the books they created.

The crucial element here is that the passage details the process of cultivating *qing*, and it begins with reading texts. These texts represent a historical basis of the process in that they were created by sages in the past but are used to teach people in the present. Their value is constantly revived since they produce the excitement that creates ritual from our *qing*, and this is an ongoing process. Once again, we need to reference the entire section to remember that classic texts are the underlying sources of embellishment that noble people use to beautify their appearance and their *qing*. Self-cultivation involves a combination of following the established guidance of past scholars and also relying on our refined *qing* to create new standards. There can be a number of ways that regulations impact our lives. In the "Xing zi mingchu" they start outside us, but the concept of *qing* in particular points to an utter absorption of these regulations into even our involuntary emotional reactions. Section 8 connects this to embellishment and regulation, which can be read as shorthand for its being in harmony with the Dao.

Further information on how this pattern affects our lives is presented at the end of the section. There is an intense eloquence in the situating of ritual between laughter and music. "Laughter is the surface of ritual; music is the depth of ritual." This term I am translating as "music" in the text could also be rendered as "joy" in English. The content here makes it completely appropriate to translate the term either way. In texts of this period ritual and music are often interlinked, so the translation of "music" is easy to support. On the other hand, laughter appears on the front half of the couplet so "joy" is also a good choice. The point of going through these details is of course to illustrate how both meanings are important to the text. In other words, it is fine to translate this as "happiness is the depth of ritual" as long as we understand happiness as having musical undertones. What this means for our understanding of the impact of the patterning on our lives is that it is a joyous event. Exactly how we are supposed to parse the divide between laughing, music, and joy is not as important as appreciating the fact that ritual resides comfortably in its midst.

HEART-NATURE-DAO

This part of the chapter will begin by discussing Dao using an idea from Roger Ames known as focus and field. The Guodian text "Tang Yu zhidao" discusses the Dao of emperors Yao and Shun. The brief moment of abdication can be considered their Dao, but this instant of focus as a slice of time cannot be divorced from the field, an assembled collection of events that constitute the lives of these great emperors. Following this there will be an analysis of the metaphysical features of the Dao that are present in section 1 of the "Xing zi mingchu." This section is challenging to analyze because it contains strongly universal constructs of heaven and the Dao alongside our feelings of happiness and sadness. The interplay of these concepts will be shown to follow the same basic approach of focus and field.

The challenges of section 1 are significant, and it will take several repeated passes over the section to highlight a series of essential structures. Nature as emotion will be introduced first to show the transient side of the term. Following this we will see when either nature or heart are implied in section 1 when examined from a variety of angles. First, the punctuation marks in section 1 will show the shift that could make either nature or the heart more likely candidates for the focus of self-cultivation. Next, three terms will be tested to see if they relate more closely to either nature or heart. These three terms are "reaction," "activity," and "establish." The conclusion of the Heart-Nature-Dao part of this chapter will be a contextualization of nature and heart by including other texts and the question of Dao.

The original question we started with is centered on the term "Dao" and what it means to the "Xing zi mingchu" in general and to the triple sorites specifically. The simple answer is that it incorporates the breadth of meanings articulated in sections 5–7 and encapsulated in section 8. In these sections Dao is something that starts with the movement of nature and then progresses through an interaction with matter and finally human moral cultivation. Section 7 concludes by seeing the Dao as a concept that relates to the accumulated materials of the world. The basic outline of the cosmology here is consistent with the first section that states "The Dao starts with *qing*; *qing* is born of nature." Although the term "*qing*" is absent from the triple sorites, there is a neat parallel with section 5 starting with the movement of nature and the conclusion of section 7 discussing the Dao.

There are two other Guodian texts that can provide some context for understanding what Dao could mean here. These are "The Five Aspects of Conduct" and "Tang Yu zhidao." Here we find two significantly different usages of Dao that can demonstrate possible meanings of the term as a single entity or something that spans multiple ethical cores. In other words, the implicit scope of Dao changes importantly in different contexts. In its smallest sense, we will see that Dao can refer to what a person does at a single moment. This singularity is combined with subsequent moments to construct a composite of the various actions that one undertakes in following the Dao. In other words, there are certain places in Guodian texts where the Dao is used in a very small sense, but this does not exclude the sum total of these actions also being combined into an expansive Dao that is larger in scale.

This reading of Guodian texts is indebted to the notion of focus and field that Roger Ames explores. Roger Ames disagrees with Chad Hansen's position of part versus whole since the individual is not disengaged from the society.[5] Instead, he adopts an aesthetic language that I like to imagine as similar to a telephoto lens that zooms in on a single flower or is more expansive such as the wide-angle view of the same scene where a panorama of flowers is seen. These are two ways to view a coherent entity, one that is focused and another that is expansive. The difference I find in Guodian is that both the focus and field perspectives are captured in the single term "Dao."

An example of the smallest usage of Dao is found in the first line of "Tang Yu zhidao." As the title of the text indicates, it is concerned with the Dao of the sage emperors Yao and Shun. The complete sentence that the title is taken from states: "Tang Yao and Yu Shun's Dao was to abdicate and not pass [through inheritance]." 唐虞之道, 禪而不傳.[6] A similar sentence ends what we today consider the first paragraph of the document: "Therefore Tang Yao and Yu Shun's (Dao was abdication)." 故唐虞之 (道, 禪)也.[7] As an actual event, abdication would have been confined to a specific ceremony performed over a relatively brief span of time. The problem is that if you take the meaning of the term "Dao" literally in these two sentences, its diminutive nature makes it difficult to believe that this moment of abdication is a comprehensive encapsulation of two great people, Yao and Shun.

In my first book, *Guodian: The Newly Discovered Seeds of Chinese Religious and Political Philosophy*, I argued that Yao and Shun were not merely concerned with abdication but instead were interested in finding balance in a world they saw as comprised of binary opposites. The following is a short reassessment of a lengthy argument made therein that will serve to clarify the two sides of the term "Dao." The two specific morals that Yao and Shun worked to bring into balance are humanity and righteousness. "Loving the family you forget the outstanding; you are humane but not righteous. Elevating the outstanding distances you from the family; you are righteous but not humane." 愛親忘賢, 仁而未義也. 尊賢遺親, 義而未仁也.[8] What is interesting about this quote is that it is divided into two sides, each of which is represented by a positive moral trait: humanity and righteousness. Elevating the outstanding represents the action of abdication, since at the end of Yao's reign we are told that he promoted the best person he could find as his replacement. When this action is undertaken it is an example of righteous behavior and is the opposite of acting humanely.

The world of "Tang Yu zhidao" is a political one, and the question of succession is paramount. This world can be divided into two halves: the humane and the righteous. The first half of the quotation is really the pivotal part, because it states that we would actually neglect the outstanding people of the world and show preference for family. This action is an example of humanity, not righteousness. If we were to look at this text in isolation, we would have to measure the weight of balancing family versus abdication against the start of the text where only abdication is the Dao. It is in this tension that the focus-field explanation is helpful; the momentary action and the sum total of what Yao and Shun accomplished are mutually inclusive. Several other recently excavated texts support this analysis of the balancing of opposites in Guodian.[9] "Xing zi mingchu" is part of this Guodian context. One clear example is the binary grouping of humanity and righteousness in section 16. The difference in "Xing zi mingchu" is that the terms are more deeply mired in friction than other texts such as "Tang Yu zhidao."

So far these examples have illustrated the division between humanity and righteousness in Guodian manuscripts. In the first paragraph of "Tang Yu zhidao," the Dao is described as abdication, which represents only the righteousness half of the equation. This raises an important issue: Could the Dao could be seen as contradicting humanity in this specific text? If we look at other quotations in "Tang Yu zhidao," we will see that in actuality, a harmonization of these opposites is the full characterization of the actions of Yao and Shun. So strictly speaking, their full Dao must not be limited to righteousness. One example of this is where the text states "The practice of Yao and Shun was to love family and elevate the outstanding." 堯舜之行, 愛親尊賢.[10] Although the quotation uses the term "practice" and not "Dao," the importance of both the family and the outstanding indicates that both sides are nurtured by these ancient sages. If we take the Guodian context seriously, then we must consider that "Tang Yu zhidao" is not merely advocating abdication but is instead open to the option of either abdication or selecting the next sovereign based on family connections. In both cases one of the two concepts, humanity or righteousness, will be marginalized. Both morals are important so the text is suggesting that instead of a moral impasse, balance is restored over time.

Further evidence that the sages, and by extension any notion of their Dao, was not limited to a single moment can be seen near the conclusion of the text where at twenty ancient sages are mature, at thirty they have a family, at fifty they govern all under heaven, and at seventy they have perfected governance. Although this does not contradict the Dao being used to refer to an isolated facet of Yao and Shun, it embeds such an interpretation into a larger narrative. A much more plausible explanation of Dao in this text is that it can be representative of a single moment but not if this moment can only be understood in exclusion to a collection of such thin slices of time. These slices must be combined in Guodian to assemble a complete picture of ethical cultivation.

This combination of slices model of Dao raises an important question of transcendence. Is the Dao a unified whole or is it merely a combination of moments? If it can be whole, then this is important for establishing that transcendence is present in a text. Hall and Ames argue that an examination of the whole always reveals it is made of slices, so the unitary element is negated and transcendence is absent.[11] The problem I see with this model is that it is not supported by the usage of the term in the Guodian texts. If we force Dao to become shorthand for its composite parts, it becomes ungainly. In the situation of Yao and Shun, where there is no implied metaphysical side to the Dao, it would seem an ideal example to support the Hall and Ames model where single-ordered entities are absent. The problem is that "Tang Yu zhidao" is discussing two very coherent entities, Yao and Shun. All the minute details that went into the lives of Yao and Shun suddenly vanish as their Dao is discussed. Ultimately, they are known for abdicating and that is their Dao. Despite our realizing that the sum total of their lives does include many other important elements, the term is at that moment representing Yao and Shun in their sum. These two people are seen as coherently whole in the same way all people have a strong sense of self, that is all people with the rare exception of some very enlightened Buddhists. Dao can be used as a unified whole and it can be focused in a momentary action, and both of these meanings are present at the start of "Tang Yu zhidao."

Humanity and righteousness exist in tension that must be harmonized over a span of time. The question of succession is confined to a short moment, but balancing it against the negative impact this has on the moral balance of the society is something that takes time to resolve. We must assume that in the case of abdication, subsequent efforts would have to be made to strengthen the role of humanity in the society. On the contrary, if hereditary transmission were selected, righteousness would have to be promoted at a separate time. It is the importance that specific moments have on these subsequent efforts to maintain balance that allowed the author to boldly state that the entire Dao of the sages was encapsulated in the single act of abdication. The full understanding of what that moment entails is then expanded upon in the rest of the text.

In "Xing zi mingchu" there is an identical tension between moments that dissipates when combined into an enduring span of time. This tension is in the Dao of humans, but the universal Dao absorbs the friction. What is different is that the smallest slice of Dao in "Xing zi mingchu" is human and understood in a generalized manner; it is never used as something that relates to an individual person the way Yao and Shun have their Dao. Looking at the question of how we understand the Dao in this context, we can see that the term is more universally oriented in "Xing zi mingchu." "Tang Yu zhidao" is closer to the *Analects* in seeing the Dao as the way specific people cultivate. "Xing zi mingchu" is situated midway between the *Analects* and *Laozi* in that the Dao is metaphysical but still has a strong human connection. The concept of Dao shares important common ground in that there is a love of discussing divisions of the Dao. This can be the difference between abdication as a moment versus the span of an emperor's reign. Another is the split between the human and the universal. Either way, the context of "Tang Yu zhidao" is a valuable tool for understanding "Xing zi mingchu."

Section 1 of the "Xing zi mingchu" contains a collection of items that exist only momentarily, such as specific emotional states. There are also items that exist along a span of time, such as in the second sentence of the section which starts with materials and ends with being established. The third level is a metaphysical overview of our universe. Section 7 ended with the statement "The Dao is the Dao of all things," so understanding these three levels in section 1 contributes to our comprehensive understanding of Dao in the text.

All people, despite their nature, have hearts with no stable will ■. Awaiting materials, then there is a reaction; awaiting happiness, there is activity ■; awaiting cultivation, it is established ■. The *qi* of being happy, angry, sad, and grieved are nature ■. If they are seen externally, materials obtains them ■.

Nature emerges from endowment, endowment descends from heaven ■.

The Dao starts with *qing*, *qing* is born of nature ■.

When you start you are close to *qing* ■, when you end you are close to righteousness ■.

Those who know *qing* can express it; those who know righteousness are able to internalize it.

Likes and dislikes are nature.

What you like and what you dislike, are materials.

Being good at it and also [not good at it are nature.]

What you are good at or not, is power.

凡人雖有性, 心無定志■, 待物而後作, 待悅而後行■, 待習而後定■。喜怒哀悲之氣, 性也■。及其見於外, 則物取之也。

性自命出, 命自天降■。道始於情, 情生於性■。

始者近情■, 終者近義■。

知[情者能] 出之, 知義 者能入之。

好惡, 性也。

所好所惡, 物也。

善[不善性也,]

所善所不善, 勢也。

In this section there are two concepts that have the potential to impact our lives. The first is nature, which at the start of the section seems to have little relevance to our lives. In the middle part this changes and it is shown to have great significance as it is connected to endowment and heaven. Nature emerges from endowment in a manner similar to a matryoshka doll; it comes out of endowment, which in turn descended from heaven. The doll model does not establish dominant or subordinate positions but instead is intended as an epistemological statement about how we understand our world. Ultimately, this discussion of our universe is tied directly to the human realm through metasensory emotional elements. The second concept is the heart, which seems to have a more important role than nature at the start of the quote, but since it is not mentioned again we quickly lose sight of its role in the quote. How nature and heart might or might not relate to the rest of section 1 is a difficult question.

Nature is an important term in the text, but it is not limited to the smallness of our bodies or the vastness of the universe. It is in the juxtaposition of the personal and the universal that this can be best understood. In the middle of the first section, we see that the discussion of our cosmos begins and ends with nature: It is the alpha and the omega. This is strikingly different from the first instance of nature in the text where it is unable to provide stability to the heart. The difference between heart and nature is based on the inclusion of the term "although" at the start of the section 1. This takes the character *sui* (雖 although) as meaning that despite the presence of nature, it provides no stabilizing function. When we look at the second sentence, based on the English parsing, the "it" refers to an unexpressed subject in the Chinese text. Stability can only be found through practice, but we are unclear if this refers to the stability of nature, the heart, or both.

If nature is unlike the heart, then the impact of nature on our lives could be a surprisingly ethereal force in this section. Such a possibility remains, but something is observing the impact of the awaiting in the second sentence of the quote and it should be nature as it relates to the human. In its transcendent state, nature is unable to bring stability. If this is the case, then both nature and heart need to be activated by materials in our world. The text states that stability can be acquired through self-cultivation, and since it is not specific, if taken in isolation, it could refer to either the heart or nature.[12]

Nature is all encompassing, and because of this it is connected to a wide range of emotions early in section 1. This strengthens the possibility that as the text continues it is still discussing nature and not both heart and nature. Nature in the second strip of the text is changeable, but this could support either reading nature as unconnected to the heart or in need of cultivating in order to provide stability. "The *qi* of being happy, angry, sad, and grieved are nature." 喜怒哀悲之氣, 性也. The quotation here could be an expansion of the phrase "awaiting happiness, there is activity" in the first strip of the text. This is conceivable since although the characters for happiness are different in each of the two instances, they are synonyms. The problem is that it is difficult to see how the other two items that nature is said to await from the first strip, materials and cultivation, might connect to the discussion of nature in an emotional context on the second strip. Despite this problem, the first strip has a phrase stating "awaiting happiness there is activity" 待悅而後行. This could be expanded to include reactions to awaiting the other emotions of anger, sadness, and grief. It cannot be known if the results of awaiting these other emotions would also be classified as active, but it is plausible.

The term "materials" from the first strip of the text is further clarified on strip 4 "What you like and what you dislike, are materials." 所好所惡, 物也. All that we can conclude from this without reference to its more lengthy discussion in paragraphs 4–7 and 16 is that the text understands "things" as all encompassing. There are two reasons for seeing them as widespread. The first is its connection to both positive and negative attributes, since providing such a complete range implies great breadth. A second reason is its connection to nature, which is itself universal. Attempting to understand the first paragraph of the text within its own context is quite impossible if we do not make full use of the clues we are given to the meaning from the bamboo strips.

The main difference between the Shanghai and Guodian versions of "Xing zi mingchu" is that the Shanghai strips have black squares (■) on them indicating idea breaks. These marks are clues that were inserted to help us follow a meaning otherwise easily obscured. I have included these marks in both the English translation and Chinese text in this chapter because they are particularly important to the content. Some Guodian texts such as "The Five Aspects of Conduct" have these markers as paragraph divisions, but the greater frequency of the marks in "Xing zi mingchu" means that they are closer to the modern sentence. The challenge we face in tracing the orderly flow of ideas we find in the text is partially one of finding the force and direction of ideas that have to overcome the inertia born of divorcing idea from teacher for millennia. Following these markers and paying close attention to the order and repetition of ideas found in the bamboo text are key tools we can use for uncovering otherwise obscure ideas.

On the first strip of the text, we have "awaiting" with matter creating a reaction. This is followed by "awaiting" happiness causing activity. At this point we find the second marker of the text and it is separating these first two from the third "awaiting," which is with self-cultivation. This third item makes sense as separate from the first two since it results in "settling," a contrasting term to the first two that are active. Following this third item, the character for "settled," we find the third mark on the text separating it again from the next series of terms. We have two active terms at the start that relate to matter as an emotional reaction, happiness. After the distinctly different mention of self-cultivation bringing a settling, we have a return to a description of nature and emotion. This emotion is the raw uncultivated substance that we have within us, and as the next phrase tells us, it can be manifest externally. There is a separation from the internal description and the external manifestation that is underscored by the fourth marker on the bamboo strip. What is noteworthy is that there is no such marker dividing external manifestation from the most interesting and difficult to understand eight characters of the text "Nature emerges from endowment, endowment descends from heaven." This is nature on a universal transcendent level. With the breaking of the corporal barrier, what is outside our body becomes what others see. It is at this moment that the text raises a connection between nature, endowment, and heaven.

As we continue to try and understand what could be driving the movement of nature as it emerges, it is important to consider the role of material as was described in section 6: "All that: moves nature is a material." Material is not mentioned in the first sentence of section 1, but it seems unlikely that the reason nature cannot stabilize the heart is because it lacks material. The only way this could be possible is if the text is imagining humans existing in a disembodied state of flux prior to obtaining a body. Once we have a body we can become stable and self-cultivate. This would work nicely with the middle of the section where the metaphysical relationship between nature, heaven, the Dao, and *qing* are explained. However, there are no other clear instances in the "Xing zi mingchu" of the preexistence of humans in some sort of stasis, so the idea should be abandoned.

Discarding the possibility of ghosts in the text underscores the importance of answering the question of what the subject of "awaiting" is in the first sentence of section 1. The sentence seems to be pointing to nature as reacting to things encountered with activity, but it could just as easily be our heart or possibly something else. What remains a mystery is the relationship between reaction (作),[13] activity (行), and establish (定). Neither nature nor heart seems particularly established or stable in the text. Section 11 relates sorrow and joy to our nature in a similar way that section 1 has the *qi* of our emotions as nature. Section 10 has the heart being harmonized by music, which could be similar to being established, but in 12 anguish and delight are parts of the heart.

Since stable and establish have not produced a definitive link to the heart or nature, the third item to consider is "activity." One way to contextualize the term "activity" is to examine its role in another Guodian text, "The Five Aspects of Conduct." In my previous study of the text, I translated the title "The Five Aspects of Conduct." Here, *xing* is the term "conduct" in the title, but how we act is divided into morally charged activity and regular activity. The assessment of what you do depends on your ability to form five different types of moral conduct in your body: humanity, righteousness, the rites, wisdom, and sagacity. The first of these types of morality, humanity, is consistently related to happiness.[14] Paragraph 19 of "The Five Aspects of Conduct" states what is meant by happiness when the text states that it is the type derived from interacting with other people (以其中心與人交, 悅也). This is similar to what appears in reverse order in the second and third items of section 6 of "Xing zi mingchu": "welcomes nature is happiness; regulates nature is a special purpose." 逆性者, 悅也; 交性者, 故也. One challenge to building further on this line of analysis is that the term "nature" is conspicuously absent from "The Five Aspects of Conduct."

Despite the problem of lacking the term "nature," there is a similar interest in balancing opposites in both texts. "The Five Aspects of Conduct" is interested in connecting five different types of moral conduct that are organized into groups of binary opposites. At the start of the text we find five parallel sentences that are identical except that each one substitutes a different character for moral conduct. "When humanity forms within [your heart] it is called virtuous conduct. If [humanity] is not formed within it is called a mere act." 五行: 仁形於內謂之德之行, 不形於內, 謂之行.[15] The next sentences conform to a tightly parallel structure and only differ in that they begin with righteousness, the rites, wisdom, and sagacity. In "Xing zi mingchu" we have emotional responses emerging and then being eclipsed by an opposite feeling. It might seem strange to compare happiness and sadness to humanity and righteousness, but these feelings are more than simple emotions. Being connecting to our feelings allows us to become one with the Dao.

Immediately following the first five sentences of "The Five Aspects of Conduct" that represent morality action in its purely segmented stage, it turns to the combination of these distinct instances into two different types of Dao. "There are five aspects of virtuous conduct, that, when united, are called virtue itself. When only four of these actions are united it is called being adept [at virtue]. Adeptness is the Dao of humans while virtue is the Dao of heaven." 德之行五和, 謂之德, 四行和, 謂之善. 善, 人道也. 德, 天道也.[16] Elsewhere in the text, we see that "Sages know the Dao of heaven" 聖人知天道也.[17] In isolation, we cannot be sure if the first quote understands people as able to attain a combination of all five types of moral action, but in combination with the next quote we see that this is something sages can accomplish. These two quotations tell us three things about the relationship between the development of morality and being connected to a higher power. A hierarchy exists between a lower level of attainment comprised of four actions that regular people are able to achieve and a higher level of attainment that is connected to heaven. Next, the highest ideal of the text is to figure out how to combine these different ways of acting morally into a harmonious Dao. The final point we need to understand about Dao is that it is comprised of separate segments that we need to combine to achieve the highest ideals of the text.

This question of how we combine segments is important for understanding how "activity" is joined with other constructs in the "Xing zi mingchu."

As we have discussed, the first strip of the text has nature in contrast to the heart because of the character *sui* (雖 although). Since the second half of strip 1 relates to nature, we see that there is the potential to be both active *and* stable. It is important to remain conscious of the order in which the relationship between reacting and stability appears in the text to properly understand the meaning. The three results on strip 1 are react, active, and stable, which are the product of happiness and cultivation. React and materials are a starting point, completely neutral in that it appears any phenomenon in the world would be capable of initiating the process. The second stage is one that begins to produce positive change in that happiness is mentioned. Admittedly, by themselves, the characterization of these two stages is tentative at best. It is only when considering the third item of self-cultivation producing stability that the pattern of two items becomes identifiable. Section 6 follows the same pattern as strip 1. The starting point of the phrase is again an interaction with materials producing motion. After this we see that happiness occurs, and after this we have cultivation nourishing nature "All that…nourishes nature is cultivation" 凡…養性者, 習也.

The final segment that we need to combine in the first sentence of section 1 of "Xing zi mingchu" is *xi* 習 (practice, or cultivation). This term appears only five times in the text and it is a positive attribute. Strip 1 contains the first appearance of the term and this is the instance we are trying to understand. Section 6, item 6 has "nourishes nature is cultivation." 養性者, 習也 There is a similar phrase of course in section 7, item 6 that links cultivation to nature: "cultivation is using cultivation for your nature." 習也者, 有以習其性也. The one clear pattern that emerges is that nature is something that is supposed to be cultivated in the text. It is therefore logical to conclude that this is a process that begins with interaction, then happiness, and finally stability. At this moment we must remember that in many instances such as section 4, nature is omnipresent: "Within the four seas, our nature is the same" 四海之內, 其性一也. This sameness does not mean it is static; the section explains that nature is the hardness and softness we experience. What we are supposed to transform is not soft into hard or some other miracle of a minor sort. Instead, our goal is to transform everything in our immanent world into a true reflection of the transcendent Dao. When we do this we perform a very important activity: We nourish nature.

"Xing zi mingchu" does not understand nature as something that is innately good like in the *Mencius*; we have to work for its development. Xunzi also sees nature as something that is generally the same among all people, but at times he does state that it is transformable. Since there are only a few instances of Xunzi stating that nature is transformable but many instances where cultivation relates to man-made phenomena such as ritual and music, transforming one's nature should be understood as a superhuman feat that could only be accomplished by a sage. I have yet to find an example of Xunzi describing our nature as having the power to stabilize the heart. He would be more comfortable with sources outside of our nature as performing positive functions for our moral practice.[18]

There is an important similarity in the views in *Mencius* and *Xunzi* on nature in that both texts see the nature of all people as being able to serve as a source of goodness, either innately so or after being transformed. This is strikingly different in "Xing zi mingchu" since *qing* is the construct that guides our life. Our nature does other things. One thing it does is it relates to our mood, which means that on any given day my nature itself will be different. It is also possible to transform our nature, and this might produce a stable heart. However, the process is one of manifest diversity even though there is consistency on a transcendent level. This acceptance of the bipolar mood swings as part of the immanent side of the process seems to be a trend where a higher degree of individuality is recognized in Guodian texts than in the received tradition.

The degree of individuality becomes apparent when contextualizing "Xing zi mingchu" with "The Five Aspects of Conduct." Lacking the construct of nature, we instead find emphasis in "The Five Aspects of Conduct" on the body and its activities. Here, the corporal quality is accentuated in changes to the skin and voice that are observable in those who develop morality. The skin of ones who excel in self-cultivation becomes like jade (玉色) and their voice like a bronze bell (金聲). Hearing and seeing people like this who have transformed themselves is a necessary part of self-cultivation and also connects one individual to another.[19] What we see is that once again a person manifests significant physical changes as he or she connects to the transcendent.

In the "Xing zi mingchu" transcendent connections are based on our knowledge being built on the Dao as we saw at the start of section 8. "In the entire Dao, the heart's technique is chief. The Dao has four techniques, only the human Dao can be spoken of as a Dao." Chief (*zhu* 主) means it is in a superior position, and it exerts control over our ability to connect to the Dao. This underscores the importance of cognitive agency in the smallest slices of time. The term "*zhu*" could just as easily be translated as "ruler" to highlight this administrative aspect. In light of this, Dao starting in the immanently human concept of *qing* begins to make more sense. If all that the Dao encompasses is related, in some way or another, to the technique of the heart we are seeing a term that connects the highly specific subset of cognitive interactions to the world at large. We may not be able to directly know about the world beyond the human realm, but we are still connected to it through our *qing*. The power of *qing* to bridge from the human to the cosmic is therefore a mechanism that allows us to transcend our limitations. Dao here has a sense of being of limited scope because of its connection to a micro-human context, but it is also used adjacent to heaven so it also points to a more universal concept such as the Dao of Laozi, the fountainhead of all things in the universe. Both sides of the Dao are discussed in the text. The limited aspect can be seen in the focus on the human element in section 8 of the "Xing zi mingchu," but the universal side is brought out in section 7. In sum, both sides are emphasized by the author of the text.

DANCING WITH THE DAO

In "The Five Aspects of Conduct," hearing and seeing a person who has already attained a high level of self-cultivation is indispensable. In the "Xing zi mingchu" the category of what is important to hear and see changes to music. What is interesting is that in many instances of the term for sound 聲 (sheng) the original character in the text was sagacity 聖 (sheng). This reinforces the importance of music to moral cultivation in the text that is found in sections 9–10 where being a sage and hearing music is discussed.

Section 9

Of all sounds, when they emanate from one's *qing*, are trusted; furthermore, after it enters and moves a person's heart it is profound.

If you hear the sound of laughter, you smile broadly and are happy.

If you hear a ballad, you are carefree and vigorous.

If you hear the sound of the 7 and 27 string zither, you are moved and lament.

If you observe the "Lai" and "Wu" performed you are upright and constructive.

If you see the "Shao" or "Xia" music and dance you are diligent and restrained.

If you sing your thoughts and your heart is moved, you sigh deeply; one's residing with the rhythms of life is enduring; one's returning to what you are good at, and going back to where you start, is cautious; emanating and internalizing is following the flow; the start is in one's virtue. The music of Zheng and Wei is not the sort that can be followed.

凡聲，其出於情也信，然後其入撥人之心也夠。

聞笑聲，則鮮如也斯喜。

聞歌謠,則陶如也斯奮。

聽琴瑟之聲,則悸如也斯歎。

觀《賚》、《武》,則齊如也斯作。

觀《韶》、《夏》,則勉如也斯斂。

詠思而動心,喟如也,其居節也久,其反善復始也慎,其出入也順,始其德也。鄭衛之樂,則非其聲而從之也。

Section 10

Of all ancient sounds, they harmonize the heart, licentious music harmonizes intentions, all music instructs people. Lai and Wu music obtain [the empire for King Wu]; Shao and Xia [of emperors Shun and Yu] are the *qing* of music.

凡古樂龍心,溢樂龍指皆教其人者也。《賚》、《武》樂取《韶》、《夏》樂情。

A description of sound quality begins section 9 and we are told that the way to assess this is to understand its origin.[20] This means that we can know if a sound is coming from a person's *qing* or not just by listening to it. In the first chapter of this book *qing* was described as an emotional connection we establish with the universe, so this provides some clarity as to how we connect to each other. It is clear that this connection includes a strong auditory component. We should be cautious not to dismiss this as simply appreciating pleasant sounds. A transcendent element is present in section 16: "If you have not yet spoken and people [already] believe you, you are a person with a beautiful *qing*." There is sound that we physically hear and also another type that we perceive in a more complete way. The role of the ear in the whole process of assessment is not emphasized, and the understanding of sound in this text is quite unlike the physical waves of our modern scientific explanation. One way that we can understand this difference is the connection between a sound and our heart being moved.

As the text shifts from sounds in general to specific categories there is an important repetition of the connection between joy and music. Parallel grammar underscores the connection between hearing the sound of laughter and the sound of a ballad in these second and third sentences of the section. Because these two sentences come directly after a statement regarding the value of sounds coming from our *qing* and affecting our heart, we can see that this section is describing a process of genuine self-expression. The direct line that exists between the naturalness of a laugh reflecting our true emotional state is analogous to what we should experience when hearing a song. There are of course situations when a laugh is sarcastic and a song is flat, but these are the sort of sounds that do not touch the heart. It is important to see this connection between laughter and song as amplifying the phrase that ended section 8, "Laughter is the surface of ritual; music is the depth of ritual."[21]

Morality is seen as a joyous state of being in "Xing zi mingchu," and the first chapter of this book relied on section 12 to argue that ecstatic dancing to exhibit happiness is part of acting with *qing*. There is an important connection between this description of extreme happiness and the way that we respond to laughter and music in section 9. The order of the terminology used in both sections is repeated in the same order. Section 9 has "If you hear the sound of laughter, you smile broadly and are happy. If you hear a ballad, you are carefree and vigorous." 聞笑聲, 則鮮如也斯喜. 聞歌謠, 則陶如也斯奮. In section 12 we find "Happy and carefree, carefree and vigorous, vigorous and singing, singing and shaking, shaking and dancing. Dancing, happiness's end result." 喜斯陶, 陶斯奮, 奮斯詠, 詠斯猶, 猶斯舞. 舞, 喜之終也. The repetition of "happy," "carefree," and "vigorous" in section 12 is building upon the musical and ritual context the text established earlier.

The importance of this group of terms is not limited to "Xing zi mingchu"; it is also found in the "Tangong" chapter of the *Book of Rites*. Much of the chapter is concerned with the proper display of mourning, and in the section where this is found it is particularly interested in extreme displays of emotion.

> Youzi and Ziyou were standing alone and they saw a childlike mourner. Youzi said to Ziyou, "I for one have never understood hopping around at funerals. I have wished this practice were long gone. *Qing* is in this and it is correct."
>
> Ziyou replied, "In ritual, there are things that calm our *qing*, and there are things that excite us.[22] When there is genuine *qing* but obstinacy, this is the way of the foreign Rong and Di tribes. The way of ritual is not this way, when people are happy they are carefree, when they are carefree they sing, when they sing they shake, when they shake they dance, when they dance they become furious. Fury leads to being melancholy, being melancholy leads to lamentation, lamentation leads to beating your breast, beating your breast leads to hopping around. These standards and regulations are called the rituals."
>
> 慕者有子謂子游曰予壹不知夫喪之踊也予欲去之久矣情在於斯其是也夫
>
> 子游曰禮有微情者有以故興物者有直情而徑行者戎狄之道也禮道則不然人喜則斯陶陶斯咏[23] 詠斯猶猶斯舞舞斯慍斯戚戚斯歎歎斯辟辟斯踊矣品節斯斯之謂禮[24]

One term that is important here is the one I am translating as "furious." Understanding its nuances will lead to unlocking the connection between the passage and the "Xing zi mingchu."

The Chinese character I am translating is *yun* 慍, which generally means "angry." This is reflected in the explanatory note where it is said to mean *nu* 怒,[25] which is an extreme emotion, usually negative. The character appears at the apogee of an arc of emotions shifting at that moment from happy to sad. Because the text is precisely between these two emotions, *yun* represents a pivotal turning point, neither exactly positive nor negative. Legge translates it as "he gets into a state of wild excitement."[26] I see the moment as indicative of a person entering an ecstatic state as this turning point is reached. You can scream with fury but also dance furiously, making the translation particularly apt. However, there is something missing in the depiction of a wave of emotions that has climaxed and begun to revert. An underlying message of the text seems to be that the cresting of emotions is creating momentary ecstasy as the dancers become lamenters who then are beating their breasts.[27]

In isolation I would not want to go too far in extrapolating on a secondary meaning of a character used in an explanatory note, but it is supported by other more compelling evidence. In the first half of the quotation, the singing leads to shaking in a joyous manner. This moment in which people are unable to contain their enthusiasm points to a surge in emotion that overpowers normal limitations on its expression. What the term "ecstasy" conveys that is missing otherwise is a religious element that describes our travel beyond our normal understanding. This religious element is inescapable in the funerary context of the *Book of Rites*. There is no direct mention of a funerary context in the "Xing zi mingchu"; instead we find a different religious message of establishing a connection with higher powers such as the Dao and heaven. It would be difficult to deny the compatibility of a funerary context to both texts despite their differences. One reason they relate to each other is that the *Book of Rites* is specifically mentioned in section 8 of the "Xing zi mingchu." The discussion of music that concludes section 8 is continued in section 9, establishing a clear link.[28]

As we move deeper into section 9 we see more specific examples of what is meant by music. The text lists two types of zither as well as historical music from the states of Lai, Wu, Shao, and Xia. There seems to be a progression from laughter as the most obvious sound that connects with our heart to the human voice in song. Following this the text moves on to instruments and then historical music. The types of sounds become progressively removed from laughter, but the text is telling us that they should be just as able to reach within us to move our hearts. In describing how to judge sounds, the text concludes that music of a desirable sort can have a positive impact on our lives. What makes the characterization of music positive is that when we hear it we respond emotionally with happiness and excitement. Next the text describes moral progress such as being upright and diligent. The section comes full circle at the end and it shifts to a warning about what we should and should not follow in music.

The warning contrasts the positive music of the former kings such as Lai, Wu, Shao, and Xia against the negative music of the two states of Zheng and Wei. These last two states are famous for their overbearing and decadent music, and this is reflected in the text where it says that their music "is not the sort that can be followed." The problems with music from Zheng and Wei are discussed in various sources, most famously in the received texts the *Zuozhuan* and *Analects* of Confucius.[29] Based on these received sources, there seems to be a consistency in the divide between the music of the former kings that are preferred in section 9, such as the Lai, Wu, Shao, and Xia music, versus the more modern music of Zheng and Wei. What we cannot be sure of is what secondary associations are implied in this divide.

Section 10 seems to support the importance of a divide between helpful and hurtful music. It contrasts ancient sounds with licentious[30] music and again praises the music from Lai, Wu, Shao, and Xia. The negative side is where the section becomes messy. The problem is that while we could debate if the term "harmonize" is the correct translation for what is happening to our intentions after hearing what is licentious, the following statement of "all music enlightens people" is unambiguous. The term "enlighten" is literally "to instruct or teach" (*jiao* 教), and in this period the term is a positive one. This seems to drive a wedge between the previous section where the music of Zheng and Wei is said to be the sort you should not follow.

If we think more generally about the standards that the text follows, we will see that particularly with *qing*, the text does not see the world as existing in absolutes. *Qing* is a central part of the discussion of sounds that starts section 9, so it makes sense that a harmonization derived from opposites is what is being described here. There is continuity between the tension analyzed in the first chapter of this book between *qing* and committing an error. Another tension exists between humanity and righteousness on the one side versus the negativity of loathing and refutation on the other. Now in section 10, positive and negative moral constructs are both able to enlighten us. These positive and negative types of music can be instructive in the same way that acting morally but being hated helps us grow. This means that the text is making a subtle point about the difference between following something and learning from it. You can learn from anything, but not everything can be followed.

CHAPTER 4

Absolute versus Relative Morality

This book has explored moral behavior in early China almost exclusively from the perspective of the recently excavated text "Xing zi mingchu." Q*ing* has been shown to establish a connection between the lower truths of a society where conflicts abound and the higher truth of the Dao where absolute harmony is possible. This raises an important question: Is this dualist worldview exclusive to Guodian or does it resonate with other texts from the same period? Context will bring clarity.

Recent scholarship has demonstrated an important connection between section 1 of the "Xing zi mingchu" and the list of emotions found in Xunzi's chapter, the "Rectification of Names" 正名. Yan Binggang argues that the similarities with Xunzi are far more compelling than other theories that have sought to connect the "Xing zi mingchu" with either Mencius or Zisi. The major divide he sees is that Mencius understands *qing* and nature differently. Yan feels these two concepts are fundamental to the philosophy of the "Xing zi mingchu" and that they are more importantly similar to Xunzi than any other source. The "Rectification of Names" is one chapter that he uses to illustrate this similarity convincingly.[1] Due to the importance of this similarity, quoting the chapter at some length is needed.

> The later kings' establishment of names: names of punishments followed the Shang Dynasty, names of nobility followed the Zhou Dynasty, and refined cultural names followed ritual practice. Common names were given to the myriad things, thus following the established customs of China, and made certain that such names could be used in distant regions whose customs are different, so that a common means of interaction could be established thereby.

> These are the common names that apply to people. That which is as it is from the time of birth is called nature. That which is harmonious from birth, which is capable

of perceiving through the senses of responding to stimulus spontaneously and without effort, is also called nature. The likes and dislikes, happy and angry, sad and joy of nature is called *qing*. When *qing* is aroused and the mind makes a choice from among them, this is called thought. When the mind conceives a thought and the body puts it into action, this is called conscious activity. When the thoughts have accumulated sufficiently, the body is well trained, and then the action is carried to completion, this is also called conscious activity. When one acts from considerations of profit, it is called business. When one acts from considerations of duty, it is called [moral] conduct. The faculty which allows people to have understanding is called knowledge. Understanding which has practical applicability is also called knowledge. The understanding which makes people capable of something is called ability. Capability which has practical application is also called ability. Injuries to the nature are called sickness; unexpected occurrences which one meets with are called fate. These are the common names that apply to people, the names that have been fixed by the kings of later times.²

後王之成名。刑名從商。爵名從周。文名從禮。散名之加於萬物者。則從諸夏之成俗曲期。遠方異俗之鄉。則因之而為通。散名之在人者。生之所以然者。謂之性。性之和所生。精合感應。不事而自然。謂之性。性之好惡喜怒哀樂謂之情。情然而心為之擇。謂之慮。心慮而能為之動。謂之偽。慮積焉能習焉而後成。謂之偽。正利而為。謂之事。正義而為。謂之行。所以知之在人者。謂之知。知有所合。謂之智。智所以能之在人者。謂之能。能有所合。謂之能。性傷謂之病。節遇謂之命。名之在人者也。是後王之成名也。³

Correcting the assignment of names is a valuable tool for fixing something larger—human society. This tool crosses spatial and political boundaries, to solve what the author sees as a systemic problem. The text can be divided into three parts. The start of the quote describes the history of naming, with reference to the dynasties that were the first to correct certain types of names. In the original Chinese text, there are no paragraph markers. However, the start of the second paragraph as divided in Watson's translation contains a shift toward the metaphysical. Here, the term he translates as "apply to" (*zai* 在) is taken by Knoblock more literally as "The various names for what is within man."⁴ The awkwardness of his gendered mass noun aside, there is an important literalness that his translation signals as the text shifts toward a discussion of what is inside us all. This discussion moves beyond what is tangible to explore systems that initially appear to be a detour from the discussion of naming; the focus is now on nature and *qing*. It is here that *qing* is given a succinct definition: "The likes and dislikes, happy and angry, sad and joy of nature is called *qing*." Chapter 1 of the "Xing zi mingchu" also says that nature contains emotion and three out of the four it lists are the same as Xunzi. "The *qi* of being happy, angry, sad, and grieved are nature" 喜怒哀悲之氣, 性也.

Following the discussion of *qing*, we find the final part of the quotation, which describes the names of general actions and moves on to the names of moral actions. The quote concludes with a description of how we name problems. In the first and last sections, we find more similarities in that the quote begins with a history of how names came about and concludes with specific examples of these names. The middle section is extraordinary, and its conclusion is the point where the text connects *qing* with naming. "When *qing* is aroused and the mind makes a choice from among them, this is called thought. When the mind conceives a thought and the body puts it into action, this is called conscious activity." This term that we see at the end of the quote, "conscious activity" (*wei* 偽), can also be translated as "artifice," and is particularly important for Xunzi.

Wei can refer to what is false, as in not authentic. The meaning in its negative context comes from its indicating that something was fabricated by a person instead of being the genuine article. Xunzi takes this negative term and essentially inverts its meaning. It still connotes what is made by humans, but it comes to refer to the great things we make such as rituals and music. The negative side disappears, so instead of being something we have falsified, it comes to mean something we have created. "The nature of humans is evil, goodness is conscious activity." 人之性惡. 其善者偽也.[5] In the above section from the chapter the "Rectification of Names," *wei* originates in thoughts that in turn are the result of *qing* being aroused. Put simply, goodness arises from *qing* and so far, Yan Binggang's analysis seems unproblematic.[6]

While this list of emotions in "Xing zi mingchu" and Xunzi at first appears similar, a more comprehensive analysis of Xunzi shows that there are deeper structural differences. This is not to say that I disagree with Yan's findings; he is correct that Xunzi is closer to the "Xing zi mingchu" than Mencius, but the point is that when the analysis extends beyond the "Rectification of Names" chapter, these differences become daunting.[7] Ouyang Zhenren argues that in Xunzi, the meaning of three characters are importantly linked: nature, *qing*, and desire (性, 情, and 欲). Among these three, however, he sees *qing* as having a different meaning in Xunzi and "Xing zi mingchu." The main difference he sees is that Xunzi is critical of *qing*, but it is praised in "Xing zi mingchu."[8] Xunzi's criticism centers around a need to control *qing*, and this is particularly apparent in the "Human Nature Is Evil" chapter. In the first chapter of this book, I detailed the positive role that *qing* plays, and "Xing zi mingchu" never describes *qing* as something in need of regulation. Quite the contrary, the text celebrates instances of wild emotional swings. In contrast, Xunzi generally sees *qing* as a freewheeling attitude that is harmful.

> Today, people who are transformed by the methods of their teachers who accumulate refinement and learning and follow the Dao, ritual and righteousness, they are noble people. Those who set free their nature and *qing*, who would let loose tyranny, and those who violate ritual and righteousness, they are vile people. From this perspective, it is plain that the nature of people is evil and our goodness is from conscious activity.
>
> 今人之化師法。積文學。道禮義者為君子。縱性情。安恣睢。而違禮義者為小人。用此觀之。然則人之性惡明矣。其善者偽也。⁹

Many pre-Qin texts also advocate controlling our emotions. One example where emotions are understood as in need of regulation is the *Zhongyong*, and this was explored in chapter 1 of this book. Masayuki Sato sees the times in which Xunzi lived as providing important context for understanding why *qing* needed to be controlled. In particular, he cites the texts *Guanzi* and *Lüshi chunqiu* as sharing a similar interest in controlling the *qing* of a ruler. The concern is that if a ruler is overindulgent, resources will be insufficient to satisfy need and the result will be widespread misery.¹⁰ In the first chapter of this book, my analysis of *qing* saw section 16 as containing numerous markers of religious leadership. Such leaders are shown to operate outside normal avenues to solve social problems, so it would seem logical that they could also be seen as immune to the common failings of leaders. In Xunzi, nature, *qing*, and emotion are not capable of guiding the world; instead we have to rely on what we create, and that is ritual. Granted these rituals are based on what Xunzi feels we need as humans to live a flourishing life, so they are not created in the sense of being unnatural. Placing what we create as the focus of our project of moral cultivation is unlike "Xing zi mingchu" where we embrace what we all have in our possession, *qing*, in order to connect with what surrounds and imbues all things, the Dao.

While *qing* in the "Xing zi mingchu" may not resonate with the majority of Xunzi's writings, it is similar to a number of other texts. He Shanmeng 何善蒙 found important similarities between the *Daode jing*, the *Analects*, and the "Xing zi mingchu" in a recent article, and he did so because of his unique perspective. His interest is in the aesthetic history of *qing*. In his analysis of this topic, he moves freely between Confucianism, Buddhism, and Daoism schools of thought beginning in the Warring States and concluding in the Wei-Jin period (220–420 CE).¹¹ This concept of *qing* has also been shown by Halvor Eifring to be big enough to support diachronic comparisons from early China through the Ming and Qing dynasties.¹² It is important to note that in both of these studies the "Xing zi mingchu" has served to anchor the discussion in the pre-Han period. The point of this is to show that the concept of *qing* in the "Xing zi mingchu" has been established as a concept that can connect what is conventionally deemed disconnected. In what remains of this chapter, *qing* will elucidate an important link between Laozi and Confucius. It is hoped that this will provide groundwork for further studies of Confucianism to look at roots more broad than Confucius and Mencius.

Having established a link between *qing* and naming in Xunzi's "Rectification of Names" chapter, further analysis was hampered by conflicts existing in other chapters. This idea of rectifying names is also found in the *Analects*, and here we will find that it functions similarly to *qing* in the "Xing zi mingchu." The role of naming in the *Daode jing* is also importantly similar to the *Analects*. I realize including the *Daode jing* in this is surprising, but it will be explained in due time. An overview will provide a good starting point.

Names function similarly in three main ways. First, when Confucius is asked how to govern and he replies that names have to be rectified, he is describing a solution that can touch every single person. Every person with even minimal mental capacity uses language, so fixing this tool will allow this fundamental ability to function properly. A minimalist account of the issue in the *Daode jing* centers on the first line of the text where Laozi warns us of the limitations of names. In this statement, he is in his own way rectifying names. Names are confused with the ultimate truth of the Dao and this leads to massive confusion. Elsewhere in section 14 of the received and Mawangdui versions of the *Daode jing*, names play a role in the initial stage of self-cultivation. This role will be explored in detail in the final chapter of this book. The universality of *qing* is emphasized in the "Xing zi mingchu" where we see that we are told in section 16 "Of all people's *qing*, it can be delighted."¹³

Second, once rectification allows names to revert to performing at their original capacity, they have the ability to hasten important positive results. The main result that is produced is an improved connection between people once names function properly. This can be understood as the benefit of having a communication tool that operates effectively. In the *Analects*, there is a practical side that is similar to chapter 14 of the received *Daode jing* where names help us learn about the unknown. The benefit of establishing these connections via names in both of these texts also has a moral side, which is an important attribute of *qing* in "Xing zi mingchu."

Understanding this relationship will allow us to appreciate the way that "naming" works in a similar fashion in both the *Daode jing* and the *Analects*. All three of these texts have important areas in which they overlap. Since this book started with *qing* and has explained its function in detail, this chapter will begin at the opposite end of the triple relationship by exploring the *Analects*. After this the final chapter of the book, The Rectification of Names, will work backward through this puzzle by showing the connection that "naming" has to the *Daode jing*. The book will end with a conclusion that ties the texts together from the perspective of the "Xing zi mingchu."

The immediate value of understanding the connection between these three texts is that it will help clarify the seeming contradiction between the correctness of those who uphold morality and the messiness of those who loathe it. How and when chaos is accounted for in a religious system is useful in measuring the distance between its ideals and its practice. It can also help us to understand how much value is being placed on the individual versus the collective. The *Analects*, *Daode jing*, and "Xing zi mingchu" all see the actions of an individual as paramount in establishing a harmonious society.

Confucius sees the rectification of names as an action that is correct in an absolute sense; the actions of this person are seen as able to spread morality across the empire without exception. Laozi sees names as an important tool in a person's understanding the Dao, which exists as an absolute. However, the process of reaching this understanding involves first wrestling with the relativity of the differences we perceive in our surroundings. The "Xing zi mingchu" is the most interesting in that it details the futility of striving for uniform acceptance of moral behavior. There exists an absolute morality in the Dao and we can achieve it through understanding our *qing*, but that will not stop others from still hating us.

RELATIVISM

The way relativity and universality is being used in this chapter departs in important ways from the way it appears in previous scholarship, so an explanation is in order. Zhuangzi's famous attack on reason as a viable mechanism for fully understanding the Dao spawned a significant amount of scholarship that investigated his claim from the perspective of Western philosophy. Hansen, for one, argues that there are multiple Daos in *Zhuangzi*, which undermines the possibility of either there being or our comprehending an absolute Dao. In response to this type of characterization, relativism was largely dismissed by Slingerland as only relating to its radical formulation where humans are unable to comprehend grand universals such as a unified Dao.[14]

"Xing zi mingchu" is different in that there are passages where the Dao is multiple and others where it is singular. When analyzed from the context of other Guodian texts, the previous chapter argued that momentary slices of insight can be assembled to comprise a composite notion of Dao. This means that there is not a contradiction between multiple and singular. A pivotal element that we have at our disposal is the ability to use a clear connector between the relative human Dao and the absolute Dao in the concept of *qing*. Because of this, the anthropological perspective on relativism being both diverse but not opposed to universal human rights seems an important analogous construct.

Moral relativism and the partner concept cultural relativism arose from the common question of how we should study another person or culture without improperly imposing a universal standard. One issue this raised is how we might then be able to construct a single notion of human rights that does not violate the rights of different cultures to continue to follow their unique traditions.[15] This relates to the question from the "Xing zi mingchu" of how we understand those who resist morality. These people are not necessarily from different cultural backgrounds, but they are seen to have highly developed individuality.

Individuals may hate humanity and righteousness, but the higher Dao-level moral does not describe such friction. Understanding the resistance to the Universal Declaration of Human Rights helps to see the way that moral relativism can connect the higher order standards of an ethical system to the diversity of a population. Anthropologists famously opposed the creation of a universal declaration of human rights in the 1940s for this exact reason. The result has been an interest in defending the practice against the charge that moral relativism eliminates all universal standards and thus destroys ethics by undermining all claims of injustice. Extreme cases such as cannibalism and the killing of the sick or aged are often explored to try and arrive at a balance between relativity and universality.[16]

In contrast, the tension between morality and its opponents in "Xing zi mingchu" starts to seem more benign. The text does not detail the practices of its opponents, but we have plenty of examples of those who Graham aptly described as disputers.[17] None seem to rise to the level of contrast explored in modern questions of moral relativism, and I cannot help but wondering if too much attention might be paid to the fringes of socially acceptable practices in some of these modern studies. In the "Xing zi mingchu," universal claims are understood as moral actions that exist above other more common ways of acting. Universal is meant to signify the higher and broader significance of certain morals. The value of performing a universal action is not seen as limited. This issue of limitation can be seen as either a finite set of situations in which an action could be viable or a tendency to encounter entrenched opposition.

Relativity is not meant to be an exact opposite of universality; instead it is meant to connote something that requires reference to other constituent parts to completely define. In other words, it is not an absolute that exists in isolation. The two concepts work together in the texts. In the *Analects*, relativity is present in the way each person must interpret their own circumstances to figure out how to act. This is akin to the cultural relativity challenge in that each of our backgrounds requires unique solutions to the same problem. Defenders of cultural relativity argue that it does not threaten claims of universal moral standards, and this is true in the *Analects*. Confucius believes that despite the uniqueness of each person, all humans share a common set of moral requirements.

The tension between relativity and universality is best illustrated in the section of the *Analects* where an identical question when asked by multiple people elicits vastly different responses. Arguably the most famous is found in book 2:5–2:8 where Confucius is asked about acting filial by four people who use identical phrasing in their questions. Each answer is unique.[18] The first two passages will do nicely to illustrate the trend, and following this they will be compared with *Analects* 12:19. This later passage is useful for illustrating a moment when Confucius voices sharp disagreement with an interlocutor, so interpersonal difference is again present.

> 2:5 Meng Yizi asked about acting filial. Confucius replied: "Never deviate." Fan Chi was driving the master's carriage when the master said to him, "Meng Sun [i.e., Meng Yizi] asked me about acting filial, I responded saying, 'Never deviate.'" Fan Chi said: "What does that mean?" Confucius replied, "When alive serve them with the rites, when they die, bury them according to the rites, and set sacrifices according to the rites."
>
> 孟懿子問孝。子曰:「無違。」樊遲御, 子告之曰:「孟孫問孝於我, 我對曰: 無違。」樊遲曰:「何謂也?」子曰:「生事之以禮, 死葬之以禮、祭之以禮。」[19]
>
> 2:6 Meng Wubo asked about acting filial. Confucius replied: "Your parents are the only ones who worry about your illness."
>
> 孟武伯問孝。子曰:「父母唯其疾之憂。」[20]

Meng Yizi is the first to pose the question about acting in a filial manner and in response Confucius tells him to never disobey. The answer is further clarified to explain that one must observe ritual when people are alive and after they die. Meng Wubo is the son of Meng Yizi and is the next person to ask the identical question about acting filial. He is told to avoid letting his parents worry about his health. From this we can see that contrary to modern popular belief, Confucius is not telling children to obey their parents, as I have heard numerous parents proclaim when they bring their children to see the large character for "filial" in the Confucian temple in Tainan, Taiwan. The actual lesson we need to learn from this is highly context specific. Based on what we are told in this passage alone, it seems that if the son is old enough to be consulting with Confucius, then Meng Yizi's own father must also be fairly old. This implies that following ritual during a funeral and afterward offering sacrifices to the deceased is the specific context in which a person should simply obey. The advice is being given to a person about to embark on this process or possibly already in engaged in mourning.

Reading the advice of 2:5 as valuable for a person preparing to begin mourning is supported by the appearance of a partial repetition of this passage in *Mencius* 3A2. Here, Mencius is advising the crown prince after the death of Duke Ding of Teng. The prince's tutor meets with Mencius who quotes Confucius's words regarding the importance of following ritual during a funeral and after death. In other words, it is not taken as general advice about obeying at all but instead is specific to a person who wants to know how to bury someone properly. In valuing this context and individuality, the *Analects* demands that the most exacting standards of filial orthopraxy be decided upon based on our own relative circumstances. What this implies is that at any given moment, one has the potential to be absolutely correct, but a different person in the same situation could not mimic this behavior and also be correct. We each have a responsibility to act differently.

It is worth mentioning that this positional relativity caused May 4–era thinkers to misunderstand the system as hopelessly hierarchical. Open access to completely correct behavior is understood as available to all people, and this is an important component of refuting this long antiquated misperception.[21] The above examples from Confucius illustrate this as they are absolutist in the correctness that a single person could enjoy at a given moment. Simultaneously, when viewed as a collection of questions and answers, we see that the way to react is relative to who we are and what we are doing. Absolute correctness is not imagined as manifest in the same way across a spectrum of individuals; it can only be found through each of us figuring out what to do. At an individual level we can access absolutes, but as a group there is a high degree of relativity.

In the "Xing zi mingchu," we have already explored how individuals cannot act in a way that will be universally acceptable at an immanent level. Orthopraxy will always be seen negatively by a certain percentage of people. This is not so much a contrast from the *Analects*; Confucius did not imagine a world without critics or threats. As a roving consultant he understood that the path toward morality was not easy.[22] Despite this, he provides advice as to how to act in an absolutely correct manner in a highly specific circumstance. This inclination can be seen in passages 12:11 and 12:17 where he provides an extremely terse prescription for how the world can be governed with absolute morality. A clearer illustration can be found in the more contentious passage 12:19, where he describes the power of morality as wind over grass.

> Ji Kangzi asks Confucius about governing: "What do you think of killing the people who do not have the Dao and bring close those who have the Dao?" Confucius replied, "You are governing, what use is there in killing? If you desire goodness, the people will be good. The noble person's virtue is like the wind, the lesser person's virtue is like grass. When the wind blows over the grass it must bend."
>
> 季康子問政於孔子曰:「如殺無道以就有道, 何如?」孔子對曰:「子為政, 焉用殺? 子欲善而民善矣。君子之德, 風; 小人之德, 草。草上之風, 必偃。」[23]

There are two individuals having a conversation in 12:19, Confucius and Ji Kangzi. When Confucius says that the character of a noble person (*junzi*) causes the will of the people to bend, we can find two meanings. The first is that a potential exists for a ruler to be a noble person, and in such a case the position of power can be used to spread morality among the people. As an idealized situation, this first interpretation has to be taken with a degree of suspicion. There is also a second meaning, which comes from Ji Kangzi being corrected by Confucius. It is here that my analysis is breaking with tradition. If pushed to select which person is the noble one in their conversation, I feel that the clear choice is Confucius. This makes Ji Kangzi the grass that Confucius is hoping to sway with his answer about how to run the country. The difference between these two interpretations is that one is based on a theoretical situation of good leadership and the other understands that Ji Kangzi is at this moment exhibiting shockingly ignoble leadership by proposing that wholesale slaughter can solve his moral problems.

It is interesting that this Ji Kangzi passage is also quoted in *Mencius* 3A2. The scenario contains interesting parallels. A crown prince is reluctant to follow proper mourning practices, and the wind over grass quotation convinces him of the importance of his actions. He comes to believe that what he does will have a strong influence on others. What he fails to see is that in actuality, while his position is seemingly above others, he is in fact being influenced by Mencius. This puts Mencius in the role of powerful wind over grass, based on morality that someone in a politically higher position might enjoy based on military might. The crown prince is not the real source of the wind at all, but Mencius is hoping to use him as an amplifier to quickly propagate his moral lesson.

The difference between the actual events of the Warring States, where rulers were rarely noble in character and suggestions that in a perfect world they would be, is a clear divide between my analysis and that of Yuri Pines. In his recent book *In Search of Eternal Empire*, he goes to great lengths to explain that the power of the ruler remained unchallenged in early China. This takes a very literal reading of the encounters between advisors such as Confucius and Mencius by insisting on the ideal of perfect rulers being paramount. When meeting a ruler, Confucius and Mencius spent the bulk of their time correcting their behavior. If the ideal of perfect rulers were really the dominant paradigm, then there would not be the need for such chastening encounters. In other words, we should not impose upon these exchanges a limitation that denies the extent to which power was being negotiated.[24]

The key is that there is a single standard across society, and Confucius is seen as in full possession of its intricacies. When Confucius advises his students and his rulers, he understands the specifics of his interlocutor's situation prior to telling them what to do. This means that the system is not moral pluralism; there are not a number of standards involved. Instead, the plethora of diverse factors in a person's background that must be understood form the relativity in the system. The presence of relativity does not block Confucius from understanding what is correct; he never hesitates. If he were unable to offer precise solutions to the myriad problems he encounters, then it would be nihilism, an entirely different way of seeing the world.[25]

In fact, the *Analects* is filled with statements about how to act with absolute morality, such as the start of book 12 where one person acting morally for one day could spread this to the entire empire. At this moment, Confucius does not add a proviso regarding an exceptional circumstance that could possibly impede this spread of morality. A similar type of optimism, derived from having open access to the highest moral truths, is seen much earlier in 2:1. Here, governing with virtue makes us akin to the North Star, and there are numerous other passages where Confucius sees our ability to act in a correct manner as existing as an absolute truth. "Confucius said: 'Governing with virtue, is comparable to the North Star. It resides in its place and the other stars encircle it.'" 子曰:「為政以德, 譬如北辰居其所, 而眾星共之。」 [26] Human diversity was not seen as creating moral conflict; on the contrary, acting morally was seen as having an influence that was no less than stellar.

While the friction of orthopraxy in the "Xing zi mingchu" seems irreconcilable with the persuasive power of morality in the *Analects,* that is but one side of the story. The "Xing zi mingchu" also envisions a harmonious interconnectedness with the Dao that is free of friction. It is at this universal level of truth that we find a corollary with Confucius's North Star. Despite this area where we can connect the two texts together, another more basic difference remains. Understanding the Dao in the "Xing zi mingchu" is inseparable from the prevalent ecstatic displays of happiness and sadness. What this points to is that Confucius is glossing over some of the sharp edges that the "Xing zi mingchu" revels in exploring. It would seem that this process of presenting an idealized side of Confucius has stripped both the low end of the spectrum in terms of the depth of disputation but also the high end where people leap with joy.

There is one interesting passage where Confucius bemoans a lack of deep passion in his times. He feels that most people do not have a deep enough love for humanity. This is explained in passage 4:6, but what is left out is a musing about the low end of the spectrum where people could also hate someone for acting with humanity or righteousness.

> Confucius said: "I have never seen one who really likes humanity, and one who truly dislikes inhumanity. There is nothing more esteemed than one who likes humanity. Those who hate inhumanity, they act for humanity and discouraging inhumanity is what they contribute to themselves. Can it be possible to have the ability for one day to use all your strength for humanity? I have never seen someone whose strength was insufficient. If they exist, I have never met them."
>
> 子曰:「我未見好仁者惡不仁者。好仁者, 無以尚之; 惡不仁者, 其為仁矣, 不使不仁者加乎其身。有能一日用其力於仁矣乎? 我未見力不足者。蓋有之矣, 我未之見也。」 [27]

Moral behavior was not something that elicited negativity, and his advice was not often qualified by a stipulation that it should be done differently if certain circumstances changed. This is not to say that different people should not act in different ways; quite to the contrary he did not have a single recipe such as a Ten Commandments for all to follow.

The disagreeable response of people who hate the implementation of humanity or righteousness in "Xing zi mingchu" is not a diametric opposite to the worldview of the *Analects*. Since Confucius sees us each as highly unique individuals it is not impossible to imagine friction arising from two working on the same issue in opposite ways. The difference is that if such friction is imagined by Confucius, it can only be found buried deep in the subtext of his interactions. In 6:26 Zilu is unhappy with Confucius for visiting Nanzi, a woman of ill repute. Passage 13:3 contains a more direct challenge when Zilu questions a statement on morality by Confucius. Similar to all the discussions in the text, this one does not contain much back-and-forth debate, and Confucius quickly overrides the objection. The passage concludes with Confucius having the last word and he presumably convinces Zilu of the value of his position, but this is nicely representative of the diminished nature of friction we can find in the *Analects*.

It should be recognized that when building an ethical system from questions by diverse individuals such as we find in the *Analects*, it will inevitably dictate different solutions to construction challenges than when working with a treatise model such as the "Xing zi mingchu" or the *Daode jing*. The naturally abundant entropy that Confucius's compositional style injects into the *Analects* must be counterbalanced by the cohesion of individually attainable absolutes. Each person who talks to Confucius has a separate background, so the response is tailored to suit this. As such, it is easy to appear scattered and lack the singular message of a treatise. Bryan Van Norden has sought to overcome this eclecticism by demonstrating the compatibility of Confucianism to virtue ethics.[28] His work provides a framework for connecting the assorted points made over a series of dialogues. However, the metaphysical construct of the Dao in "Xing zi mingchu" and the *Daode jing* is so robust that these two texts can more easily survive the test of denying access to absolutes within society. Since both of these texts were found in the Guodian tomb, it is also interesting to find such a nice contrast with the *Analects*, a text that was not found there.

We should hesitate to interpret this from an overly simplistic view of the *Analects*, one that merely provides an opposite perspective on government and society from the *Daode jing*. Doing so imposes a false sense of balkanization on early China and fails to appreciate the importance of dialogue during this epoch. Instead, the next chapter will show that names are an important part of knowledge acquisition and self-cultivation in both of these texts. Names are a construct that represent a mechanism for humans to achieve absolute correctness in a social context in the *Analects*. This can be seen in its obverse, a failure to rectify names causing a spread of chaos. In the *Daode jing*, names are the way that we extend our knowledge into the unknown and begin to grasp the Dao. In much of the *Daode jing*, knowledge is gained from observing nature so the political relevance of the text and even the role humans play in establishing names are easily obscured.

The *Daode jing* sees the intense variety of our observable world as all coming from the Dao. Because of this a higher-level understanding reveals a Dao that forms a unity that interconnects the world's diversity. Names function for Laozi as a tool for gaining understanding of this unity. There are people who believe the world is completely relative, but that is because they cannot grasp the higher-level absolute continuity behind phenomena. As we gain understanding we move from being deluded by relativity to understanding the absoluteness of morality.

Similar to the *Analects*, "Xing zi mingchu" shares a belief in the potential of a single concept, this time *qing*, to engender harmony across a society. The major difference is that this harmony is transcendent instead of immanent. Confucius believed that the society he lived in could be pacified, but in Chu harmony became something that you would experience only by seeing through the dichotomy of anger and happiness. It seems that sitting in the state of Chu on the eve of its annihilation resulted in a pessimistic view about the ability to promote morality without encountering the opposing forces of discord. In that time, harmony could only be understood as existing on a higher level of the Dao. This creates a strong contrast with the *Analects* where absolute correctness exists here in society. There is a higher degree of overlap in the way names are used in the *Daode jing* in that they function as a tool for accessing a harmony that transcends the human experience. The corollary term for the "Xing zi mingchu" is a tool we rely on to attain harmony, *qing*, the emotional conduit that connects us to the Dao.

CHAPTER 5

The Rectification of Names

How does the "Xing zi mingchu" address people who respond to righteousness with loathing? Are they left out of the higher-level discourse in the way that sinners in the Western tradition might be denied access to salvation? Or could it be that diverging beliefs are embraced as part of the process of appreciating the Dao? The fact that some people are left out even at one stage could be a sign of a fatal flaw in the system. On the contrary, it could just be the way that religious systems of the time tended to construct their beliefs. A final and more optimistic perspective can be found by returning the "Xing zi mingchu" to the context of the times in two important received texts, the *Analects* and the *Daode jing*. This chapter will explore this final perspective and show how the ideal of the "Xing zi mingchu" was to include everyone, but the author was also realistic enough to know that this would not be easy.

It is easy to categorize the "Xing zi mingchu" as a Confucian text. The text values many of this group's core moral tenets such as humanity, righteousness, and the rites. Sages are seen as having preserved these morals in the core classical texts of the Confucian tradition, the Odes, Documents, Rites, and Music. In short, the answer is yes, the *Analects* of Confucius does overlap in important ways with the "Xing zi mingchu."

As was demonstrated in the previous chapter, correct names emanate from *qing* in Xunzi's "Rectification of Names." However, other chapters of his text see morality as something we need to construct in order to live harmoniously. This constructive version is absent from "Xing zi mingchu." Instead, the analysis below will explore the means of obtaining absolute truth in three texts. An important similarity exists between absolute social morals that are immanent in Confucius with the transcendent concept of

Dao in the "Xing zi mingchu." Absolute morality is also transcendent in the *Daode jing*. Naming is the means of obtaining this absolute in the *Analects* and *Daode jing*, while in the "Xing zi mingchu" it is through *qing*.

In the *Analects* of Confucius, "Rectify names" stands out as abundantly clear and simple to execute. As such it is similar to the lack of friction we find with the Dao in the "Xing zi mingchu" where connecting with this transcendent concept allows us to overcome the challenges we face at a social level. Since the *Analects* shaped religious institutions and governments across East Asia for two millennia, it also would seem to provide a convenient dividing line with another foundational religious manual, the *Daode jing*.[1] The received version of the *Daode jing* begins by telling us that nameable names are not eternal, a seemingly insurmountable obstacle for any attempt at their rectification. Instead of a clean divide between the *Analects* and the *Daode jing*, these two texts will be shown to contain important similarities in the way they see the value of naming. This is not to imply that they are identical. The point is that the differences do not represent an irreconcilable division when analyzed in the light of the "Xing zi mingchu."

A study of a single individual concept such as the rectification of names can provide a much more accurate historical understanding of early China when compared to trying to work at the more problematic school level.[2] An individual is able to spread morality across the empire by rectifying names in the *Analects*. This does not override the position of other passages where the characteristic of the individual would still encompass a high degree of diversity relative to his or her background. In short, we do not become homogenous. Laozi sees names as bridging another divide, that which exists between the unity of the Dao and the disunity we must understand in the process of reaching this understanding. While "Xing zi mingchu" does not contain the character for name (*ming* 名) even once, *qing* serves a similar bridging function between the chaos of society and the harmony of the Dao.

One of the dangers of relying on schools for measuring the tripartite relationship between two ostensibly Confucian texts the *Analects* and "Xing zi minghchu" versus *Laozi* is it is a methodology predicated on the assumption that each of these texts are religiously and philosophically consistent. In fact each text has areas of overlap with the others but these do not fall along neat lines. Even as we are finding ever earlier copies of transmitted texts, accretional theories, both new and old, have pointed to a distinct lack of coherence. The problem is that when a text is divided into strata, it can simply impose a new expectation of coherence on subsections. In the *Analects* the differences of absolute and relative can be seen in the actions of one person versus a group of people so the tension here is created from the grain of detail, not accretion.

There is a final reason for being particularly interested in the concept of naming when developing context for the recently excavated manuscript "Xing zi mingchu." The character *ming* 命 is translated as "endowment" in my translation in that it is something that we receive from heaven in the first section of the text "endowment descends from heaven" 命自天降. However, the term can have another entirely different meaning in early Chinese sources. The character for endowment *ming* 命 can also mean "name" since it is a cognate with *ming* 名 (name). Both terms can be used to mean the act of naming in early China.[3] Despite these two characters being cognates, it is just impossible to develop a substantial analysis of endowment in the "Xing zi mingchu." Instead, I feel that the structural similarities between *qing* and naming are far more compelling.

ANALECTS

The *Analects* has two famous passages that explain the importance of names in spreading morality, 12:11 and 13:3. Here we find the rectification of names in the context of Confucius arguing that the most important objective for a ruler is to ensure that names are appropriately assigned. The implication is that names are intimately related to what might be loosely termed the highest goals of the text. This term "goal" is less than a complete characterization as the text is not interested in fixed concepts, but rather refers to the appropriate or well-functioning social interrelations that Confucius describes through discrete events laden with instructive power for his assumed reader. Although function is essential, it is the *process* that is of greater importance than an endpoint as a single goal that could be achieved and then concluded. Nonetheless, names play an important role in harmonizing these social interworkings. This gives the sense that a name is similar to a handle for adjusting the action of individuals—names indirectly shape people.

> 13:3: Zilu said, "The ruler of Wei is waiting for you to help his government. What will you do first?" Confucius said, "Certainly I will rectify names." Zilu said, "Is that so? You are wide of the mark. Why should there be rectification?" Confucius said, "You! How uncivilized! With regard to what a noble person does not know, he should maintain an attitude of humility. If names are not rectified, language will not accord. If language does not accord, deeds will not be completed. If deeds are not completed, then ceremonies and music will not flourish. If ceremonies and music

do not flourish, then punishment will not be on target. If punishments are not on target, then the people will not know where to put their hands and feet. Therefore, the noble person's naming will certainly be something that can be discussed, and these discussions can certainly be put into action. With a noble person and his or her language, there is nothing that can be careless, period."

子路曰:「衛君待子而為政, 子將奚先?」子曰:「必也正名乎!」子路曰:「有是哉, 子之迂也! 奚其正?」子曰:「野哉, 由也! 君子於其所不知, 蓋闕如也。名不正, 則言不順; 言不順, 則事不成; 事不成, 則禮樂不興; 禮樂不興, 則刑罰不中; 刑罰不中, 則民無所措手足。故君子名之必可言也, 言之必可行也。君子於其言, 無所苟而已矣。」⁴

There are two aspects to this passage that are important to explore: the large structure and the specific details of the descent into chaos that results from a lack of rectification. The large structure is that we have a sorites where the unraveling of society is set against a backdrop of Confucius and Zilu addressing each other quite directly, in what appears to be heated disagreement. One has to consider this context in analyzing the speech that concludes the passage. We have an example of two people failing to communicate; Zilu flatly states that Confucius is wrong and the Master responds by calling his student uncivilized. This brings to mind a situation where the heat of argument has retarded the ability of participants to appreciate what the other side is presenting. The solution to this type of impasse is a clarification of terminology. From this part of the passage alone, we cannot infer that we have encountered a broadly applicable principle of government, but we will be able to see this kind of general implication of naming more clearly by analyzing it in conjunction with other passages such as 12:11. It is interesting though that naming per se as a topic for discussion is not that prevalent in the *Analects*; it only appears in a total of six passages.[5]

The sorites that comprises the second half of 13:3 has two features. The first is the connection between neighboring terms, which are closer. The second is the implication of the sorites as a whole, which is more loosely constructed but of greater importance to conclusions we might draw from our analysis. The relationship between neighboring terms can be seen in comparing names and words. Names are a subset of words, so we see the sorites progressing in the direction of expansion. This trajectory is repeated in the third term, "accomplishing things." Speech and speech acts are only one subsegment of the actions a person performs. Following this, we have what might seem to be a narrowing in rites and music, which is followed by punishments. Rites and music could be seen as a smaller category since even a dedicated musician is only performing a few hours per day. This is a misleading line of analysis since rites and music are supposed to be transformative. They should inform all that we do, even if we are not always conscious of the impact. We might continue this same line of expansion with punishments, but this starts to look incompatible since Confucius is opposed to punishments as a primary source of social transformation. In other words, the argument that we begin from the small sphere of naming to a universal analysis of punishments begins to break down.

We can overcome this obstacle of understanding the trajectory of the sorites by seeing the first three terms as related to one individual, which is then dramatically expanded to the state level with mention of the rites and music. If we consider the context of the sorites, we can see that the individual behind the first three terms is Confucius working in the state of Wei. By considering context, we can turn the passage around and see that Confucius would rectify names, then expand to his words and deeds in his interactions with others in court. This would alter the meaning of rites and music of the state, and the application of (or possibly a lack of need for) punishments. The end result would be that the common people of the state would know what to do at all times or literally know where to place their hands and feet. It must be pointed out that the passage then shifts from a discussion of the people to how the noble person contributes or participates in the process. This shift can still be seen as compatible with the expansive impact of naming in that naming reaches its terminus with the people and then feeds back to being reconnected with the aristocracy.

Before proceeding, let us pause to consider how the above findings compare with the "Xing zi mingchu." First, names serve a pivotal role in 13:3; they move these two individuals from friction to agreement. Second, the action of rectification has an impact on the society far larger than anything explainable by common logic. Both of these characteristics are comparable with *qing* in "Xing zi mingchu." In section 16 we began by using our *qing*. When *qing* developed into a connection with the Dao in the second half, friction disappeared. The impact on society, even in the first part of the section, was extraordinary. We did not need to speak, teach, or punish, yet the society enjoyed great benefit. Various tasks of government are mysteriously accomplished by our self-cultivation's maturation.

The terms that bookend the sorites in 13:3 are useful for understanding how Confucius understood his role as an outside consultant in government. We see that it begins in response to a question of governance and expands to include all people knowing how to act. This shows that the passage is a discussion of duties and responsibilities rather than simply names in isolation. Passage 12:11 again explicitly discusses government, and as such it is a strong candidate for further explaining 13:3. The connection between the passages is underscored by the similar unraveling that results from a person not living up to his or her name; both instances end with a total paralysis. In 13:3, the unraveling ends with the inability to know how to move, and in 12:11 it ends with having grain but being unable to eat.

> 12:11: Duke Jing of Qi asked Confucius about government. Confucius replied, "Ruler, ruler; minister, minister; father, father; son, son." The duke said, "Excellent! If the ruler is not a ruler, the minister not a minister, the father not a father, and the son not a son, although there is grain, can I obtain and eat it?"
>
> 齊景公問政於孔子，孔子對曰:「君君、臣臣、父父、子子。」公曰:「善哉! 信如君不君、臣不臣、父不父、子不子, 雖有粟, 吾得而食諸?」 [6]

Here we see the same trajectory from the action of the central government in the ruler and minister emanating out into a larger sphere of fathers and sons. This is a corollary pattern to the above analysis of 13:3 where Confucius, rectifying names in Wei, engenders ever expanding reverberations until the actions of the common people are transformed. The scope of these two passages is also similar in that we see names tied to the actions of people, not entities that are inanimate or abstract. The discussion is not expansive enough to be considered universal, but it does encompass what we could classify as the range of the human experience. This is particularly evident in 12:11, which includes a range of individuals from ruler to son that are meant to represent all human relations.

The ability to draw a comparison between 13:3 and 12:11 is further supported by the parallel styles of the two passages. Both present their ideas in sorites. Passage 13:3 is interesting in that it utilizes the same sorites progressing from ruler to son in both positive and negative forms. The result is that the implied connections between terms are of greater importance than the explicit mechanisms that secure the linkages. In actuality, there are no explicit connections between the terms in either passage. Meaning can only be seen by comparing the arrangement of the terms, resulting in order and position being the only guides. Both passages begin with the actions of the ruler and proceed to the reverberations that are felt by the people. Although this trajectory has been detailed for passage 13:3 above, 12:11 needs further clarification. In 12:11, the son is not the son of a ruler since the sorites has already expanded from the first term, "ruler," to the second, "minister." Fathers and sons then should relate to the society at large.

It might seem that names are a feature that only relate to the context of a ruler extending influence outward to transform the people. Although this is the undeniable trend of these two passages, the *Analects* does emphasize the context of each situation.⁷ Therefore, a slightly more context-sensitive reading would see names as an important religious concern of central governments but not necessarily a tool they are exclusively privy to employ. One strong reason for this is that Confucius himself served largely as an outside advisor to governments. A fully context-sensitive reading would see that names are important to the governments of Duke Jing of Qi and the ruler of Wei. However, this is too narrow an interpretation since even if such a reading were all that could be concluded at the moment of these conversations, their inclusion in the text of the *Analects* immediately creates a broader significance.

If we take 12:11 as the model for reading 13:3, then this certainly cannot be seen as beginning with Confucius and ending with the ruler since 12:11 starts and ends with the noble person. Again, this takes the parallel too far since 13:3 begins with a question of what Confucius himself would do and the answer is "rectify names." In fact, the opposite could be much more plausible. In 12:11, we hear Confucius state that a ruler should be a ruler. This statement *is* the rectification of names starting with the ruler and extending to the people. Following this, the ruler repeats Confucius's statement, which is comparable to the occurrence of the noble person at the end of the passage. Passage 13:3 is the same in that it begins with a statement by Confucius, is followed by a sorites that progresses to the people, and then moves back to a noble person discussing names in their rectified state.

The broadest role of names can be seen in 17:9 where Confucius is describing the value of reading the *Book of Odes*. He concludes the passage by saying, "it arouses you, it improves your ability to observe, to get along with others, and to express resentment. Near, it helps you serve your father; far it helps you serve your ruler; and you can know more of the names of birds, animals, and plants." 可以興, 可以觀, 可以羣, 可以怨. 邇之事父, 遠之事君; 多識於鳥獸草木之名.」⁸ The value of names here is similar to 13:3 and 12:1 in that they are simply part of the process of clarifying and ordering our world. However, each part of passage 17:9 is only loosely connected, so beyond observing that there is a relationship based on the context of the passage, it is difficult to draw inferences that are more specific.

H. G. Creel doubted that 13:3 should be seen as part of the original *Analects*, and his primary reason was the inclusion of punishments. Instead, he believes the passage was added later, with the process continuing possibly as long as into the Han dynasty. The issue he has with the passage comes from the praising of punishments. He argues that punishment belongs to legalist thinking and is not something Confucius would embrace. In 13:3, after names are not rectified, a whole host of problems will arise and he feels that all of them should relate to issues that Confucius cares about deeply.⁹ The loss of rites and music is a good example of this sort of concept; they are discussed and praised by Confucius on a regular basis.¹⁰

In contrast to the rites and music, passage 2:3 tells us specifically that punishments by themselves are not a good mechanism for promoting morality.

> The master said, "Lead them with politics, regulate them with punishment, and the people will be evasive but have no sense of disgrace. Lead them with virtue, regulate them with rituals, and they will have a sense of disgrace and moreover will be reformed."
>
> 子曰：「道之以政, 齊之以刑, 民免而無恥。道之以德, 齊之以禮, 有恥且格。」¹¹

There are several counterpoints that refute the exclusion of 13:3, particularly in light of 2:3. The first is that Confucius is not uniformly opposed to punishments; in 4:11 he says that a noble person should "cherish punishment" 懷刑. The second is that the category of legalism that Creel employs has been shown to be anachronous and misleading when applied to Warring States texts.¹² Important parallels have been established between 13:3 and the less problematic 12:11 in earlier parts of this chapter. Finally, even if 13:3 is a later addition, Creel's Han date for the terminus ad quem for the interpolation is generous. More recent scholarship has estimated it was inserted in the middle of the third century while 12:11 has been dated to the last third of the fourth century.¹³ This span of time nicely bridges the closure of the Guodian tomb. Being skeptical of such an exact attempt to date passages to precise years, I feel that we can be confident that they were included in the *Analects* somewhere around 300 BCE. Since the "Xing zi mingchu" is also found outside of the Guodian tomb, its existence after the tomb closure is certain. This makes a comparison between the two sources historically valuable.

DAODE JING

The interest in examining the issue of naming is its ability to improve our understanding of "Xing zi mingchu." At the start of this chapter, the concern was that the text might be disturbingly comfortable with leaving people out of its moral system. In the above analysis of the *Analects*, the ability of naming to transform society has raised a question: Could *qing* have a similar ability to function as a social panacea? Any ability to draw such a conclusion will require a first step of uncovering a social concern in the importance of naming in the otherwise transcendentally oriented *Daode jing*. Then we will have to demonstrate that the "Xing zi mingchu" needs to be read in this larger context, and by doing this *qing* becomes part of a program that could at least mollify social problems.

Before we can reach this conclusion we have to deal with a final perceived division between our sources. Likely the strongest argument for a split between the *Analects* and the *Daode jing* relies on contrasting the first stanza of the *Daode jing* in isolation, "The name that can be named is not the eternal name," with *Analects* 13:3, "Confucius said, 'Certainly I will rectify names.'" However, we must ask ourselves what circumstances could produce these statements. Unless we count ourselves amongst the true believers, we are unlikely to accept that the authors' pure enlightenment was the source of the idea. An objective assessment would have to conclude that discontent over the use of names would have likely inspired the authors to advocate a complete abandonment of the project of naming. With this or some similar circumstance as inspiration, concerns for shaping a more perfect society must come from fixing the naming problem.

Working from this position of doubting opposition, it is possible to explain the issue of naming in the *Daode jing* and the *Analects* as being similar by observing that both texts are concerned by the misappropriation of names. It is even plausible that a prevalence of improperly assigned names inspired both authors of these texts to propose slightly different solutions to the same problem. If this were the case then the *Analects* would be following a restorative approach where names are returned to their former correctness along the lines of Xunzi. The opposite route to the same conclusion would be the abandonment of names in the *Daode jing* in order to downplay their importance. This reduction of names overall would allow us to properly understand phenomena without being clouded by these bad names. Even when comparing these two quotes in isolation, we can see that both philosophies share a concern for names and their proper use in society. This approach can bring the two texts philosophically closer, but it is only a starting point for understanding their similarities. In fact, speculating as to the stimulus that sparked these discussions of naming in the *Analects* and *Daode jing* is the weakest analytical avenue we will explore, but it provides a segue to the consideration of further commonalities that belie schoolcentric analysis.

Naming is used in two ways in the *Daode jing*. There are passages where naming is unconnected with understanding the Dao, but there is also one that uses names in a discussion of our ability to broadly develop comprehension. These two positions intersect since they represent a progression during the process of self-cultivation: Names assist us in gaining our initial understanding of the Dao but are different from the Dao itself. If we read stanza 1 as indicating a lack of connection between naming and the Dao, this becomes a warning not to conflate the assistance provided by naming in the initial stage with the ultimate understanding that we can achieve at a higher stage. We will begin with the first stanza of the text, as it would at first blush seem to provide the greatest challenge to congruence with the *Analects*.

There are two ways that we can interpret the first stanza's second sentence in the received *Daode jing*. These two ways hinge on the reading of two groups of four characters: *wu* (無 absent or lack) and *ming* (名 name), and *you* (有 present or have) and *ming* (名 name). The first way to read these two groups is to see them as containing four separate words that can be read as "absent is the name" and "present is the name."

> The Way as "way" bespeaks no common lasting Way, The name as "name" no common lasting name. Absent is the name for the sky and land's first life, Present for the mother of all ten thousand things. Desire ever-absent: Behold the seed germs of all things; Desire ever-present: Behold their every finite course.[14]
>
> 道,可道,非常道。名,可名,非常名。無名,天地之始; 有名,萬物之母。故常無欲,以觀其妙; 常有欲,以觀其徼。[15]

This reading sees the universe divided into what can be named "absent" and "present." Names remain important in the first *and* second halves of the second sentence in the quotation. The result is that all things in the universe, including the sky and land's first life, relate to names.

The second way to read the characters is as two groups of only two separate words, "the nameless" and "the named." This second reading is supported by seeing parallelism in the subsequent line's negation of desire. However, if the negation is really the object of desire, then the line reads "Desire the ever absent."

> The ways that can be walked are not the eternal Way; the names that can be named are not the eternal name. The nameless is the origin of the myriad creatures; the named is the mother of the myriad creatures. Therefore, Always be without desire in order to observe its wondrous subtleties; Always have desire so that you may observe its manifestations.[16]
>
> 道,可道,非常道。名,可名,非常名。無名,天地之始; 有名,萬物之母。故常無欲,以觀其妙; 常有欲,以觀其徼。[17]

In this reading, the nameless and named exist in hierarchy since the second half of the first sentence indicates that named names are not eternal. Although unnamed names in the first sentence are different from the nameless in the second, there is a basic level of similarity in the hierarchy of naming that can be seen in each sentence. The significant difference from the first reading of this passage is that names cease to relate to the origin of all things.

The project of naming in sentence one of the text is contrasted with what is termed "the eternal name." This is a difficult statement to understand, as it is hard to know what an eternal name is. We cannot be certain that even if we follow the second reading either or neither of the nameless or the named might in fact refer to nameable names or eternal names. What we have are simply four categories of names: the nameable, the eternal name, the named, and the nameless. This becomes more complicated by the fact that in the first reading we have names absent and present, which are also not obviously eternal. Drilling down to the most fundamental question, we must admit that we do not know if eternal is good or bad.

A sage is admired for not having a constant mind in stanza 49, indicating "eternal" is a negative attribute. However, in stanzas 32 and 37,[18] being eternal is an attribute of the Dao, and that means it should be admirable. Having two stanzas repeat the same character as a descriptor of the Dao is strong evidence that the Dao is eternal. Working more generally, we can see that enduring is a positive characteristic in the text. The valley spirit is said not to die,[19] an enduring attribute in stanza 6. Later in stanza 12, the wearing out of our senses is a warning that incorrect behavior will inhibit our ability to endure.[20] If higher or more advanced understanding involves a comprehension of the eternal way, then eternal names are those that pertain to the Dao. Eternal names are then not the same as the names we would encounter at the beginning stage of our quest for understanding.

Appreciating a potential lack of opposition to naming in the *Daode jing* is but the preliminary objective of this analysis. Ultimately, it will be argued that naming is also important for understanding the phenomenal world in the text. The *Daode jing* discusses a more abstract perspective pertaining to the unobservable and unnameable, attributes of the universe that are accessible through a study of phenomenon. The first hint that this is a beginning stage and not looked down upon is in stanza 1. We must remember that it states that the name that *can* be named is not the eternal name. This is different from the text stating that you should not name names since they are not eternal. Such a phrase would be unequivocal evidence of names simply being an impediment to understanding. Instead, what we find is that the *Daode jing* tells us that the use of names is perfectly acceptable, but we are also cautioned that these names are separate from unchangeable names. Since the above discussion of eternal points to passages that connect the description of "eternal" with the Dao, we can theorize that names not being eternal means there is a higher order of understanding that is beyond regular names. The other implication of this theory is that eternal names should actually be compatible with understanding the Dao.

In stanza 14 of the *Daode jing*, names are important to understanding the phenomenal world. As such, this process stands out in the text as an example of names functioning in a very special manner: They assist in the comprehension of the natural order of the world, which is synonymous with the Dao. These names are not common names, and as such are the best candidates in the text for being examples of eternal names.

> 14: When you look but do not see, you name it dark; when you listen but do not hear, you name it faint; when you probe but do not find, you name it minute. Each of these three cannot be further examined; therefore, we combine them into one. Above it is not clear, below it is not dark. Unending, it is nameless and returns us to the void. This is called the shapeless shape, the formless form, it is called hazy. Facing it you do not see its head, following it you do not see its rear. Holding the ancient Dao, is used to manage our existence today, being able to know the ancient origins, this is called the Dao's pattern.
>
> 視之不見名[21]曰夷，聽之不聞名曰希，搏[22]之不得名曰微。此三者不可致詰，故混而為一。其上不皦，其下不昧，繩繩不可名，復歸於無物。是謂無狀之狀，無物之象，是謂惚恍。迎之不見其首，隨之不見其後。[23] 執古之道，以御今之有，能知古始，是謂道紀。[24]

In the process of probing the unknown, we construct names to represent what is just beyond our senses of sight, hearing, and touch. The stanza continues by stating that these three are common since they are all part of a single unity, which in turn is related to the Dao of ancient times. This Dao is transcendent; it crosses space and time. Names are immanent since they are something we create that allows us to improve upon our sensory perceptions. Our understanding progresses from pushing beyond the limitations of perception to an awareness of what exists beyond phenomena. In other words, this process of naming allows us to transition from simply perceiving something as faint to understanding what cannot be seen.

This process is further explained as the stanza continues "Each of these three cannot be further examined; therefore we combine them into one. Above it is not clear, below it is not dark." What we see here is the recognition that the phenomenal world can be difficult to comprehend. These three are representative of the various inputs we receive from our senses. When this sensory information is assembled together, we are able to comprehend the unity that lies beyond what we ascertain from our senses. What lies below would tend to be dark, and what is above is not clear so the world is opposite our expectations. It is important to recognize the two elements that are central to transforming vague sensory inputs into this higher order understanding. The first factor is naming. By affixing a name to a blurred sensation, we begin to make sense of what we have failed to understand. Prior to naming, all we have are failures by our sensory organs to grasp what we are encountering. After we have affixed a name, we are able to work toward forming a synthesis. The three sources of information are brought together and we are able to understand unity.

Unity in the *Daode jing* is not merely a combination of information. Something important occurs when we bring together sensory data that is able to be synthesized after it has been named. This unity is synonymous with the Dao. We should be careful to observe at this point that there is a difference between early and advanced stages of understanding the Dao. Early stages involve our sensory organs and the process of naming, and later stages involve comprehending unity. Nonetheless, naming in stanza 14 leads to the transcendent and could be the eternal names referred to in stanza 1.

Although names lead to an understanding of the eternal Dao, there are no details provided as to how the early stages relate to the later stages, aside from being part of the same process of knowledge acquisition. In other words, we might begin to understand the Dao by employing our senses, but by these senses alone, we are unable to grasp the Dao in its entirety. In summary, we can see that the Dao exists beyond names, but names are a means by which we understand our world. This helps us understand stanza 1 where it states that some names are eternal and others are not. Names are distinct from the unity of the transcendent universe since they are not of themselves eternal, but they can lead us to this understanding as in stanza 14.

The importance of naming to our understanding of the universe is confirmed in stanza 21, where it states "From present time to ancient day These names have not been forgotten; Through them we can scrutinize The myriad millions' genesis."[25] 自古及今，其名不去，以閱衆甫。[26] Using names to observe the myriad things in the above quotation is similar to stanza 1, where we have the name present (or the named) connected with the mother of the myriad things. The difference in stanza 21 is that we also have a statement that these names are eternal, or at least they have been enduring since ancient times. If we consider enduring in the context of stanza 14, we see that the reason why these names are eternal is they are being unified. Names are not connected with the eternal when they are simply named individually, as we saw in stanza 1. Instead, if we combine them we can understand the Dao through names and that makes them enduring names.

In contrast to stanzas 1, 14, and 21, there are several stanzas where the process of naming might appear to be unconnected to understanding the Dao. Likely, the strongest of these are stanzas 32 and 37,[27] which state "The Dao is eternally nameless." One could argue that since it is nameless, the process of naming contradicts understanding the Dao. Far from being an isolated stanza, we find a similar perspective in stanza 25: "I do not know its name, but I dub it the Dao. If forced to name it, I call it great." 吾不[28]知其名，字之曰道，強為之名曰大.[29] Here, there is no name for the Dao and the only name that one might affix to it is done through force, which implies it is unnatural. Finally, stanza 41 states "The Dao is dark and unnamed" 道隱無名.[30] This stanza is particularly interesting since it begins by discussing the uselessness of hearing the Dao. If the Dao is heard, the best it says you can do is laugh at it. These passages consistently raise the possibility that the *Daode jing* is opposed to the process of naming.

There are several ways to interpret the relationship between stanzas that might oppose naming and others that seem to advocate naming. The first way to interpret the relationship is to conclude that stanzas 14 and 21, where naming is viewed as important, are irreconcilable with stanzas 32, 37, and 41, where the Dao is nameless. Being irreconcilable could support the argument that these two groups of stanzas come from different strata of the text or might have been authored by different people.

A second and more exact way to interpret the relationship between seemingly conflicting groups of stanzas is to adhere to a close reading of the text. Stanzas 32, 37, and 41 are really only stating that the Dao is nameless. This close reading allows the two stanza groups to be harmonized by seeing them as describing two distinct parts of the process of understanding the Dao. The first group of stanzas, 14 and 21, describe the function of naming in the initial stage of the process. Names assist in the comprehension of what exists beyond our senses of sight, hearing, and touch. By bringing together the incomprehensible data collected from these three sensory sources, we can understand the unity of the universe, which leads to knowing about the Dao. The first group of stanzas never state that the Dao itself can be named or is nameable. This means that in a close reading they do not actually contradict stanzas 32, 37, and 41. The second group of stanzas is simply emphasizing the second stage of understanding the Dao, and this does not include naming. The Dao is beyond names, just as certain things are beyond our senses.

The complex entity that the Dao represents is in fact distinct from any name. This means that the name "Dao" is not an eternal name, or even a very good regular name. However, this does not change the fact that the text recognizes the existence of eternal names. This is why stanza 41 states "The forward Way seems backward. The level Way seems bumpy."[31] 進道若退，夷道若纇。[32] Names for things and the truth that a name can lead you to are thus distinct, so if someone tells you the Dao, then all you can do is laugh at them.

> 41: When the superior person hears the Dao, he or she is diligent and puts it into practice. When the average person hears the Dao, it seems he or she has it, and it seems he or she loses it. When the inferior person hears the Dao, he or she laughs greatly. If he or she did not laugh, it would not be sufficient to be taken as the Dao.
>
> 上士聞道，勤而行之。中士聞道，若存若亡。下士聞道，大笑。[33]不弗笑，不足以為道。[34]

The process of understanding the Dao can never be so simple that it can be described in language that does justice to its entire scope. We can bring this idea of words being unable to fully explain the Dao back to the first reading of the first stanza of the *Daode jing* that we discussed earlier in this chapter: "The names that can be named are not the eternal names."

If we put aside the issue of learning momentarily and reanalyze the second group of stanzas ontologically, we can reach an importantly different conclusion as to the relationship between names and the Dao. First, it is no surprise and no indication of special status that names are in fact related to the Dao since the Dao is supposed to be the source of all things. Stanza 42 states "The Dao gives birth to the one, the one gives birth to the two, the two gives birth to the three, the three gives birth to the myriad things." 道生一，一生二，二生三，三生萬物。[34] One should then be able to trace the thread of any phenomenon back to the Dao despite the connection being potentially highly convoluted. According to this line of reasoning, names are not privileged in their cosmic connection to the Dao. They are only special in their ability to connect people to the Dao. This is how the Dao is both nameless and knowable through names.

All things, including humans and their creations, such as names, relate to the Dao. However, a connection is not the same as equivalence. In stanza 1, there is a clear hierarchy amongst things. We see that the experiential Dao, or what is capable of being spoken of or walked upon, is not the same as the entire eternal entity of the Dao. This is also reflected in the process of assigning names or the citing of a name being distinct from the eternal unchanging entity being termed. If we take the maternal metaphor of stanza 42 seriously, we can see that emanating from a single source does not mean that it is all the same. Five children from the same mother can be very different, despite having vague similarities such as hair color, height, or other sundry features.[35] This means that being of one family is a call for unity more than a claim of homogeneity. Appreciating the unity behind the diversity of the world is therefore the importance of understanding the names of things.

There are two ways to understand the distinctions between stanzas 42 and 1. The sense of rupture stems from the first stanza, stating that certain things are not the same as others: A nameable name is not the same as an eternal name.[36] This is difficult to understand in light of stanza 42 where all things are said to emanate from the Dao. The first way to overcome this obstacle is to see that all things having a common origin is not the same as all things being identical. The problem with this observation is that identical or not, there is supposed to be a fundamental commonality among things. If things are of common origin, why are names different from eternal names? Focusing on a distinction between types of names seems to contradict stanza 42. The solution is to see that although things in the world are all interconnected, an understanding of this can only be obtained by understanding the countless varieties of things in our world. Names play a vital role as a guide for proceeding from the seemingly endless differences in phenomena to an understanding of their connectedness. The result we attain at the culmination of the process is that although things are identical at a higher level, their differentiation at a name level continues to be an indispensable stage in our learning.

The second way we can understand this contradiction is to see the first stanza as serving as a warning against differentiating. There is an eternal Dao and an eternal name, but people fail to appreciate this when they are obsessed with the experiential Dao and the nameable name. We are blocked from getting to the truth of things by our focus on what is at hand, or directly accessible. This sense of warning is underscored by passages that describe the Dao as nameless. The problem with this second way of understanding the contradiction is that stanza 1 does specifically say that the experienced Dao is not the same as the eternal Dao. What this means is that the world is more than a purely homogeneous mush without edges that separate one thing from another—differentiation is necessary. However, the purpose of this differentiation is that it serves as a means for enabling us to understand the ultimate unity of things.

CONTRAST

We must remember that theoretical perspectives must not be built on overly generalized assumptions about the theme of a text but instead they have to be constructed from careful empirical observations. In this chapter theoretical assumptions were based on a specific issue, naming. The relevant passages on the subject in both the *Daode jing* and the *Analects* see names as important for their ability to bring order to our world. In the *Analects*, order is brought to a variety of interpersonal relationships through the rectification of names. The impact of this ordering is seen as expansive, emanating from a virtuous government outward to encompass every action of the common people. Since the *Analects* does not discuss the world outside of human society, we can see names as providing structure and order to the universe, as defined in the pages of the text.

In the *Daode jing*, the scope of the text is larger and its consideration of the universe encompasses all things in all times. Here names function as our means of comprehending the unity behind the diverse phenomena of our world. Names are not equatable with either the phenomena of the world or its unity, but names allow us to understand both of these things. Interestingly, *qing* functions the same way. *Qing* is not the same as the phenomena we experience; emotional content, ritual, and music are different from *qing*. While *qing* and names are different from the Dao, they can create a link for us to both the world around us and the transcendent unity that lies beyond.

Order is attainable by developing our ability to comprehend our world, but the *Daode jing* and "Xing zi mingchu" see us as separated from the source of order in society, which is not the case in the *Analects*. From this perspective, the *Daode jing* can be seen as analytically much smaller since the ordering is not described as something that one constructs on the outside in society after the internal process of comprehension is complete. The text sees order as preexisting in the world in the form of the Dao, so the only project that remains for us to complete is the enacting of the same order internally. One vehicle for achieving this order is the correct use of names when examining the external world.

The importance of finding the function of names in the *Daode jing* is that it uncovers the human element in a text that initially seems concerned with nature and little more. The natural unpolluted world is the substance of the Dao that we are supposed to understand through the comprehension of names. However, absent the human conduit of these names, the vehicle by which we could connect to the Dao remains obscure. A reader would sense a nagging lacuna when trying to understanding the *Daode jing* without a clear sense of how one could begin to access the methods described in the text. By mistakenly reading the first stanza as only a warning against employing language in the quest for understanding, further progress is impossible. *Qing* in the "Xing zi mingchu" plays the same role of acting as a human connection to the transcendent Dao.

Although it is the human element that is brought forward in the discussion of naming in the *Daode jing*, seeing this issue as a parallel with the *Analects* gives us a new window into Confucius's views of the world beyond language. There is a value that names have beyond what can be analyzed from a purely utilitarian perspective. Names function as more than a convenient way of referring to the human relations we encounter. These names represent a web of connections that prevent our descent into chaos. We see this power in the description of the unraveling in 13:3. By observing the trajectory of influence from a constructive direction, we can see that all you need to do in government is rectify names. Everything else seems to simply fall into place. In actuality, there is much more involved, but names are really the keystone that enables other factors such as the rites to function properly.

A more abstract way of describing the impact of analyzing names in the *Analects* and the *Daode jing* is to divide the two texts into micro or macro processes of self-cultivation. What is referred to by these categories is the importance each text ascribes to the transformation of society (macro) versus a single individual (micro). In the *Analects*, names immediately radiate out into society and help to bring order to all in the empire. The *Daode jing* would seem to be more micro focused since one person correctly comprehending names in the understanding of the Dao is not explicitly connected to even one other person following the same process.

Again, a tandem analysis helps to get beyond this simple juxtaposition. The *Daode jing* sees the Dao as already perfected and thus not in need of our intervention. The process of naming is described in the text from an individual or micro perspective: It brings clarity to what is beyond our senses. However, names are social constructs. They are conventions that one person establishes and are then passed around for others to follow. Even the understanding that these names are distinct from the phenomenon they describe is a community-defining convention. The readers of the text obtain an outline for understanding that enables them to move forward toward comprehending the Dao and its unity. This is an implied social community that is constructed through the practice of properly applying names, and members would believe they understand the unity of all things. In this way, the text ultimately is uninterested in differentiating the micro or macro.

In the *Analects*, there is also a micro side to the rectification of names. Although 13:3 describes a social transformation that results from naming, the society in question is explicitly comprised of distinct individuals. These are the people who would not "know where to place their hands and feet" if names were not rectified. Individuals are transformed, and this transformation is physically manifest in the representative body parts of hands and feet. The corporal locus of the impact of naming brings out a distinctly micro side to the text.

The potentially negative impact of not rectifying names is another interesting point of comparison between the *Analects* and *Daode jing*. The decline that results from not rectifying names is clear in the *Analects*. There is an unraveling that permeates the macro society, meaning names have the potential for causing significant damage. Both passages 13:3 and 12:11 follow an interesting pattern in that they begin with a statement in the positive. In 13:3, Confucius begins by stating that he will rectify names, and in the first half of 12:11, "letting the ruler be a ruler" implies names are in their rectified state. Following the description of names being properly defined, these passages switch to what can happen when things go awry. In the "Xing zi mingchu" and *Daode jing*, order is already complete; our only task is to reach it. Because of this, the role of unraveling is sidelined in these texts.

The reason for describing the unfortunate consequences of improper names seems to be related to its rhetorical power in 13:3. Here, Confucius's student Zilu is unconvinced of the value of naming. When confronted by this, Confucius switches to a description of how wrongly assigned names can damage a country. Subsequent to this statement by Confucius, we do not have further questions or rebuttal from Zilu. This shows the persuasive power of a description of social unraveling. The same conflict and misunderstanding is not evident in 12:11 since after hearing the laconic statement of rulers as rulers, ministers as ministers, etc. Duke Jing simply agrees. However, we see the same shift toward the negative consequences of not enacting the policy. The combination of Confucius's great economy of words and the duke's understanding them to contain weighty implications for the health of the state causes the shift to the rhetorically powerful negative repercussions of not rectifying names for the assumed benefit of others who may have been present.

Confucius is describing a system where the internal understanding of names shapes an individual's actions in the society. Although negative examples are used for their ability to persuade, it is intended to encourage people to work toward the proper transformation of the society. This means that individuals are granted unfettered agency that has great power to bring about positive change. One might question the level of agency when both 12:11 and 13:3 could be seen as starting with the actions of the ruler that then filter down to the ministers and only then the people.

The first problem with seeing these statements as promoting a top-down hierarchy is that in 13:3 the agent of change is Confucius, who is certainly no sovereign. In addition, the connection of naming to the noble person is actually followed by mention of the common people. The second problem is that in 12:11 the negative description completes the circle of relations. It begins with the ruler, progresses to the son of a commoner, but finishes back with the duke having food he is unable to eat.

The potential negative impact of assigning names improperly in the *Daode jing* is quite different. First, there is no macro unraveling of society that we find from names being misunderstood. The text begins with a strong warning against misunderstanding names. This implies a division between naming as a convenience and names as part of learning about the perfected unity of the universe. However, a failure to understand names properly does not affect the Dao or the cultivation of others. Another reason why there is no chain of negative events described is that the objective of self-cultivation is to understand the unity that is already extant outside of us. Our actions can neither benefit nor hinder the Dao. Negative examples in the *Daode jing* are issues that affect our personal quest for understanding. This means that although the text begins with a statement that is seemingly much more negative toward the project of naming, the text actually sees names as having much less of a potential downside for the universe. The reason for this is that the *Daode jing* is interested in government and how this relates to the lives of the people, but it is unlike the *Analects* since it does not discuss a specific connection between governing and naming.

If we apply the lens of naming to the question of how much agency we have in the *Daode jing*, we see a very different situation from the *Analects*. In the *Daode jing* and "Xing zi mingchu," the goal is to understand the Dao, a unity that is outside of us. Agency is then very differently constructed since the best we can hope for is an internalization of this external perfection. In the *Analects*, we are creating perfection in our surroundings by rectifying names since this is bringing order. Any sense of ordering in the *Daode jing* and "Xing zi mingchu" is produced within our internal understanding of the universe in which we live. This universe exists at arm's length; we are unable to impact it in any negative way.

CONCLUSION

An analysis of the concept of naming in both the *Analects* and *Daode jing* has shown that the categories of micro and macro are not disconnected;

each builds upon the other in important ways. While these two texts can be seen to emphasize micro or macro categories, this is but the foreground of a multidimensional argument. As we traced the interconnections between micro and macro, the conduit underpinning the analysis was "Xing zi mingchu." In these final pages I will return to this underlying structure and show how the challenge in section 16 of finding room for those who deny the value of morality is better understood in the context of the rectification of names.

The process of cultivating *qing* in the "Xing zi mingchu" is similar to naming in the *Daode jing* in that both processes highlight the personal or micro side. Sound is modified by *qing*, and this is relevant to the production of music in section 9. There is a similarity in the role that *qing* plays in how we express ourselves with music and the way that names give voice to the pushing back of mists that inhibit our senses in the *Daode jing*. Everyone has emotions in the same way names are ubiquitous. It is only when we refine these tools that they can enable us to reach beyond ourselves to connect to the Dao.

Extending perception is how we begin to establish this connection in the *Daode jing*, and it is akin to the role of sensory organs that lies at the core of the "Xing zi mingchu." By this I mean that joy and sadness are triggered by what we see and hear. In both texts our senses are part of the process of becoming one with the Dao. Tang Yijie, for one, has questioned whether the Dao we seek in the "Xing zi mingchu" is the same as the *Daode jing*. He argues that the "Xing zi mingchu" has more of a social Dao like Confucius, while lacking the metaphysical elements of Laozi. In particular he points to the importance of *qing* as a conduit for understanding the Dao as an indicator of the text's social emphasis.[37] I disagree with his assessment, and a significant factor is the similarity between *qing* and Laozi's use of names in self-cultivation. Names are themselves a social construct and Laozi is happy to make use of them in his text.

The social function of names in Laozi helps clarify a major concern for how dissent is accounted for in the "Xing zi mingchu." While the "Xing zi mingchu" is clear that there will be those who reject the moral project of the text, locating the source of goodness in *qing* forces the cultivation to be understood as containing a universal component. Further support for universality is found in statements that contextualize nature, the heart, and materials as inclusive of more than what is merely human in sections 2–4. This is unlike *Mencius*, where nature is a human trait and an important part of how we are distinct from animals. These animals are unlike us; he sees them as a lower form of life. An interest in seeing humans in a context that is larger than immanent society is a characteristic more commonly associated with the *Daode jing*. Here we see the Dao as transcending the human realm to emphasize the natural world. It is a shame that section 3 of the "Xing zi mingchu" is so badly damaged because its inclusion of cows and geese in its discussion of all hearts possessing wills points to an important move toward the inclusion of all nature. The best we can approximate its meaning is by comparing it to the next section which uses trees and rope to underscore the unity of nature. Somehow the two sections must be working in a similar direction, and this is one where the human and the natural universe are unified.

It is easy to misconstrue an interest in the natural world as diminishing the importance of human society. This would be a mistake because the "Xing zi mingchu" places a high value on bringing the external harmony of the Dao into our personal view of the world through *qing*. The specific details of how we enact this change are left somewhat amorphous. Section 16 tells us that when we hear the Dao we reflect it above, below, and personally. I am interpreting these statements as connected to the opening lines of the section, which say that all people's *qing* can be delighted. The opening continues to tell us that acting with *qing* is an important element of how our behavior will be judged. Details of how our *qing*, empowered by the Dao, will produce results is left to the vague promise that we will spread this in all directions.

This is where the context of the rectification of names in the *Analects* proves particularly valuable. The *Analects* is a text that is keenly focused on immanence. Moral value is measured with reference to human society and metaphysical claims are relegated to the periphery. This would seem a solid candidate for pragmatic explanations of how we produce results in society. However, the correcting of social ills that we see driven by rectified names defies mere pragmatic explanation. Names are changed and the result is almost magical. Everyone is included in these positive changes, but no real details are provided of how the process works. Instead, we have a leap of faith that is necessary for accepting the way a simple prescription for change could produce such epic results. What this means is that a lack of specificity in the working of *qing* in "Xing zi mingchu" can be similarly understood as a sign of an element of faith in the text: By setting our emotions free, we become one with the Dao.

The "Xing zi mingchu" conveys a level of sincerity in how completely it embraces the lives of the people it hopes to improve. There is no flattening of the complexity involved in the human condition to only allow idealized elements a role in self-cultivation. Instead, life includes the messy emotional outflows that many in the Warring States would rather bury. Valuing extreme expressions of joy and sorrow, there is a belief that passion can lead us to a greater understanding of the world.

Conflicting concepts are present in the "Xing zi mingchu," but we are tasked with finding a way to embrace the harmony of the Dao that transcends these opposites. This is what we gain by developing our *qing*. The solution to these conflicting perspectives is not to divide the text into separate sections. On the contrary, the text is part of a Guodian context where unification is urgently important. Believing that Dao, a transcendent source of morality, could help alleviate disunity was a compelling idea during China's Warring States Period. The historical relevance should be abundantly clear, and so should the importance of maintaining the "Xing zi mingchu" as a single unified document.

Appendix

Translation of the "Xing zi mingchu" 性自命出 or "Xing qing lun" 性情論

There are two major versions of this text that are almost identical, Guodian and Shanghai. The Guodian transcription is the primary one used here, but all major Shanghai variants are provided in the footnotes. Numbers in open circles indicate ends of Guodian strips ①; closed numbers are for Shanghai strips ❶. The Shanghai edition has square blocks ■ that separate semantic segments of the text; these are not present in the Guodian edition. Because of this I only provided them in the Chinese text and did not transfer them to the English translation. The placement of the strip marks in the English text is approximate because the word order is changed. Following these marks is useful for seeing the change in order between the Guodian and Shanghai editions.

This transcription relies heavily on the four transcriptions and thorough notes found in Ding Yuanzhi 丁原植, *Chujian Rujia "Xing qing shuo" yan jiu* 楚簡儒家《性情說研究》 (Taibei: Wanjuanlou, May 2002). The notes are authored by Ding and will be referred to as (DZLBX) "Ziliao bianxi yu jieyi" 《資料辨析與解義》 regardless if they are part of the actual 辨析 *bianxi* "analysis" subsection or 申論 *shenlun* "discussion." Based on the order in which they appear in the book, the first two transcriptions are by Li Ling and are the (DGDJDJ) "Guodian jian 'Jiaoduji' jiaodingben shiwen" 郭店簡《校讀記》校訂本釋文 and (DSHJDJ) "Shanghai jian 'jiaoduji' jiaodingben shiwen" 上海簡《校讀記》校訂本釋文. The first *D* in these abbreviation distinguishes these two chapters as republications in Ding's book. In fact, they are corrections of transcriptions that were published two months earlier as (SHCJSP) Li Ling李零, *Shanghai Chujian sanpian jiaoduji* 上海楚簡三篇交讀記 (Taibei: Wanjuanlou, March 2002). The third and fourth transcriptions Ding provides are the original Guodian Wenwu transcription (DGDWW) *Guodian chumu zhujian* 郭店楚幕竹簡 (Beijing: Wenwu, 1998) and Ding's republication of the Shanghai Guji text (DSHGJ) Ma Chengyuan 馬承源, ed., *Shanghaibowuguan cang Zhanguo Chu zhushu (yi)* 上海博物館藏戰國楚竹書（一）(Shanghai: Guji, 2001). There are a couple of instances where notes from the 2001 Guji texts are cited that Ding does not include, at which point it will be referred to without the *D* (SHGJ).

Several characters are provided as modern equivalents in the JDJ that are supported in the annotations of the ZLBX. For example, DGDJDJ has 心無定志 and DGDWW has心亡奠志, but in the DZLBX, 32 and 34 it states that *wang*亡 should be read as *wu*無 and that *dian* 奠 is a phonetic loan for *ding* 定. My transcription is thus心亡（無）奠（定）志. Brackets [] are used to indicate characters interpolated from broken strips in the Guodian edition that are inserted from the Shanghai text. If both versions are damaged, theories as to what the text may say can be found in the footnotes.

Other editions that will be referenced are (SHDB) Ji Xusheng季旭昇, *Shanghaibowuguan cang Zhanguo Chu zhushu yi duben* 上海博物館藏戰國楚竹書（一）讀本》 (Taibei: Wanjuanlou, 2004); (LZ) Liu Zhao 劉釗, *Guodian chujian jiaoshi* 郭店楚簡校釋 (Fujian: Remin, 2003); and (CW) Chen Wei 陳偉 et al., *Chudi chutu Zhanguo jian ce (Shisan zhong)* 楚地出土戰國簡冊（十三種）(Beijing: Jingji kexue, 2009).

Section 1[1]

凡人唯（雖）又（有）眚（性），[2]　　　心亡（無）奠（定[3]）志■，待[4]勿（物）而句（後）复（作），[5] 待兑（悅）而句（後）行■，待習而句（後）① 奠（定）。　■ 意　（喜）惹（怒）帔（哀）[6]悲之熒（氣），眚（性）也■。及丌[7]　（其）見[8]於外，則勿（物）取之❶也。眚（性）自命出，命　②自天降■。衒（道）司（始）於青（情），青（情）生於眚（性）■。司（始）者近青（情）　■，終者近義■。智（知）[青（情）者能]③　　出之，智（知）宜（義）　者能入[9]之。

好❷亞（惡），眚（性）也。

所好所[10]亞（惡），勿（物）也。

善[不眚（善）性也，] ④

所善所不善，執（勢[11]）也。

All people, despite their nature, have hearts with no stable will. Awaiting materials, then there is a reaction; awaiting happiness, there is activity; awaiting cultivation, ① it is established. The *qi* of being happy, angry, sad, and grieved are nature. If they are seen externally, materials obtains them❶. Nature emerges[12] from endowment, endowment ② descends from heaven. The Dao starts with *qing*, *qing* is born of nature. When you start you are close to *qing*, when you end you are close to righteousness. Those who know *qing* can③ express it; those who know righteousness are able to internalize it.

Likes ❷ and dislikes are nature.

What you like and what you dislike, are materials.

Being good at it and also [not good at it are nature.] ④

What you are good at or not, is power.

Section 2

凡眚（性）為宝（主），勿（物）取之也■。金石之又（有）聖（聲）[也,¹³ 弗鉤（擊¹⁴）⑤不鳴❸□□。]¹⁵ 唯（雖）又（有）眚（性）心，弗取不出。

All those who make nature their master it is materials that obtains them. Bronze and stone [instruments] having sound, [without striking ⑤ they do not ring ❸ ...]. [For people,] although there is nature, if the heart does not obtain it will not emanate.¹⁶

Section 3

凡心又（有）志也，亡（無）与（與）不□□□□¹⁷⑥　蜀（獨）行，猷（猶）口之不可蜀（獨）言也。牛生而倀（長），雁¹⁸生而戟（伸），丌（其）眚（性）□□□¹⁹⑦而學或叟（使）²⁰之也。

All hearts have wills, without offering there is not ... ⑥ acting alone, is like the mouth not being able to speak alone. Cows are born and grow, wild geese are born and extend, its nature ... ⑦ and studying or enabling.

Section 4

凡勿（物）亡(無)不異²¹也者。

　剛之桓(樹)也，剛取之也。

　柔之 ⑧約，柔取之也。

四洦（海）²²之内，丌（其）眚（性）弌（一）也，其甬（用）心各異■，耇（教）叟（使）肰（然）也。

With all materials, everything is different.

Of a hard tree, you get hardness.

Of soft ⑧ rope, you get softness.

Within the four seas, our nature is the same,²³ but we use our heart differently; teaching makes it so.

Section 5

凡眚（性）⑨或勭（動）之■，或迬（逆）之■，或交²⁴之，或萬（厲）²⁵之，或出²⁶之，或羕（養）❹之，或長之■。

Appendix [115]

With all nature ⑨ some move it, some welcome it, some regulate it, some sharpen it, some emit it, some nourish ❹it, and some grow it.²⁷

Section 6

凡軋（動）眚（性）❿者，勿（物）也■；迬（逆）眚（性）者，兌（悅）也；交眚（性）者，古（故）也；萬（厲）眚（性）者，宜（義）也；出眚（性）者，埶（勢）也；❺羕（養）眚（性）①①者，習也■；長眚（性）者，術（道）也■。

All that: moves nature ❿ is a material; welcomes nature is happiness; regulates nature is a special purpose; sharpening nature is righteousness; emits nature is power; ❺ nourishes nature ①① is cultivation; grows nature is the Dao.

Section 7

凡見者之胃（謂）勿（物）■，快於己（已）²⁸者之胃（謂）兌（悅）■，勿（物）①②之埶（勢）²⁹者之胃（謂）埶（勢）■，又（有）為也❻者之胃（謂）古（故）■。義也者，群善之蕝也。習也 ①③者，又（有）以習亓（其）眚（性）也■。術(道)也者,³⁰ 群勿（物）之術(道)。

All that we see is called a material, what makes you content is called happiness; that which is the power within materials ①② is powerful; a person who achieves something ❻ is said to have a special purpose. Righteousness is the standard of all that are adept. Cultivation is ①③ using cultivation for your nature. The Dao is the Dao of all things.³¹

Section 8

凡術（道），心述（術）❼為宔（主）■。術（道）四述（術），唯 ①④人術（道）為可術（道）也。其參（三）述（術）者，術（道）³²之而已■。時（詩）、箸（書）、豊（禮）、樂，其司（始）出皆生①⑤於❽人。

　　時（詩），又（有）為為之也■。

　　箸（書），又（有）為言之也。

　　豊（禮）、樂，又（有）為舉（舉）之也■。

聖人比其 ①⑥頪（類）而侖（論）³³會之，雚（觀）其之（先）逡（後）而❾迬（逆）訓（順）³⁴之，體其宜（義）而即（節）³⁵廈（文）之，里（理）①⑦其青（情）而出內（入）之，肰（然）句（後）復以㪘（教）。㪘（教），所以生悳（德）於中者也。豊（禮）❿ 复（作）於青（情），①⑧或興³⁶之也■。堂（當）事因方而折（制）之■，其先後之序³⁷則宜（義）道也■。或³⁸序為①⑨之即（節）則廈（文）也。❶❶至（致）頌（容）窅（貌）,³⁹所以廈（文）即（節）也。君子媺（美）其青（情），[貴其宜（義）]②⓪善其節，好其頌（容），樂其術（道），兌（悅）其㪘（教），是以敬安（焉）■。⁴⁰拜，❶❷ 所以□□□②①⁴¹ 其徵⁴²廈（文）也⁴³也。幣帛，所以為信與諽（征）⁴⁴也，其訶（治）⁴⁵宜（義）道也。芺（笑），豊（禮）⁴⁶之淺澤也。②②樂，豊（禮）之❶❸深澤也。

In the entire Dao, the heart's technique ❼ is chief. The Dao has four techniques, only ①④ the human Dao can be spoken of as a Dao.⁴⁷ As for the other three techniques, one does no more than speak of them. Odes, Documents, Rites, Music, their inception is in the [needs] ①⑤ of ❽ humankind.

The Odes successfully make it;

The Documents successfully speak it;

The Rites and Music successfully gather it.

The sage compared ①⑥ the categories [of the classics] and by expounding, assembled them; observed the sequences [of the classics] ❾ and going with the flow, stabilized them; embodied the morality [of the classics] and by ordering, refined them; ①⑦ organized the *qing* [of the classics], express and internalized them. After this they can again be used⁴⁸ for instructing.⁴⁹ Teaching is that by which you give birth to virtue from the center. Ritual ❿ is created from *qing* ①⑧when something excites it. Confront affairs according to the method and standardize them, the chronology of this sequence is the Dao of righteousness. When something is sequenced it becomes ①⑨ etiquette⁵⁰ and is thus embellished. ❶❶ Devoting yourself to ornamenting your appearance is that by which patterns become etiquette. A noble person has beautified his or her *qing*, made venerable his or her righteousness, ②⓪ is good at etiquette, made the utmost of his or her appearance, enjoys the Dao,⁵¹ delights in teaching; thus he or she is made respectful by them. Honoring❶❷ that by which □□□ ②① he or she praises embellishment. Wealth is that by which you build trust and its verification, he or she regulates the righteous Dao. Laughter is the surface of ritual; ②② music is the ❶❸ depth of ritual.⁵²

Section 9

凡聖（聲），其出於情也。⁵³信，肤（然）句（後）其内（入）拔（撥）⁵⁴人之心也敏（敫）■。⁵⁵②③

誾（聞）芙（笑）聖（聲），則鱻（鮮）女（如）也斯⁵⁶悥（喜）。

昏（聞）訶（歌）誂（謠），❶❹則陶⁵⁷女（如）也斯奮。

聖（聽）琴瑟之聖（聲），②④則謑（悸）女（如）也斯歎（歎）。⁵⁸

雚（觀）堥（《賚》）、《武》，則齊⁵⁹女（如）也斯复（作）。

雚（觀）卲（《韶》）、頧（《夏》），則免（勉）女（如）也❶❺②⑤斯僉（斂）。⁶⁰ 羕(詠)思而勤（動）心，　藋（喟）⁶¹女（如）也,其居即（節）⁶²也舊（久），其反善復訶（始）也②⑥　斳（慎）■，其出内（入）也訓（順），司(始)其悳（德）也。奠（鄭）聟（衛）之❶❻樂，則非其聖（聲）而從之也■。②⑦

Of all sounds, when they emanate from one's *qing*, are trusted;⁶³ furthermore, after it enters and moves a person's heart it is profound. ②③

Appendix [117]

If you hear the sound of laughter, you smile broadly[64] and are happy.

If you hear a ballad, ❶❹ you are carefree and vigorous.

If you hear the sound of the 7 and 27 string zither, ②④ you are moved[65] and lament.

If you observe the "Lai" and "Wu" performed you are upright and constructive.

If you see the "Shao" or "Xia" music and dance you are diligent ❶❺②⑤ and restrained.

If you sing your thoughts and your heart is moved, you sigh deeply; one's residing with the rhythms of life is enduring; one's returning to what you are good at, and going back to where you start, ②⑥ is cautious;[66] emanating and internalizing is following the flow; the start is in one's virtue. The music of Zheng and Wei ❶❻ is not the sort that can be followed. ②⑦

Section 10

凡古樂龍心，益(溢)⁶⁷樂龍指皆𣎳(教)其人者也。　　坴(《賚》)、《武》樂取■侶(《韶》)⁶⁸、頄(《夏》)樂情■。②⑧

Of all ancient sounds, they harmonize[69] the heart, licentious music harmonizes intentions[70] all music instructs people. Lai and Wu music obtain [the empire for King Wu]; Shao and Xia [of emperors Shun and Yu] are the *qing* of music. ②⑧

Section 11

凡❶❼至樂必悲，哭亦悲，皆至其情也■。依(哀)、樂，其眚(性)相近也■，是古(故)其心②⑨不遠■。哭之勲(動)心也，澃(浸)⁷¹淺(殺)■，⁷² 其❶❽刺(烈)⁷³纞(戀)纞(戀)⁷⁴女(如)也，戚肰(然)以終。樂之勲(動)心也,③⑩濬(浚)⁷⁵深鹹(鬱)舀(陶)，其刺(烈)則流女(如)也以悲，條(悠)肰(然)以思。

Of all ❶❼ utmost joy, there is the starting point of grief, crying is indeed grief; these two together are the utmost of your *qing*. Sadness, and joy they are close to our nature, for this reason they are not far from our heart ②⑨. Crying's movement of the heart, in tears and isolated, you are ❶❽ intensely unable to bear parting, melancholy [76] with the end. Joy's movement of the heart reaches ③⑩ deep and becomes giddy;[77] if you are intense then you are tearful[78] and in grief; leisurely in contemplation.

Section 12

凡惥(憂)思而句(後)悲，③①　　凡❶❾樂思而句(後)忻,凡思之甬(用)心為甚。戁(歎)，⁷⁹ 思之方也。其聖(聲)乁(變)則[心從之矣。]⁸⁰ ③② 其心乁(變)則其聖(聲)亦肰(然)。❷⓪ 誇(吟)⁸¹遊⁸²依(哀)也，㠱(噪)，遊樂也。湫(啾)⁸³遊聖(聲)，嗸(謳)⁸⁴遊心也■。⁸⁵③③ 憙(喜)斯慆(陶)，慆(陶)斯奮，奮斯羕(詠)，羕(詠)斯猷(猶)，猷(猶)斯辶(舞)。辶(舞)，憙(喜)之終也。㤙(慍)斯惥(憂)，

悥（憂）斯慼（戚），⁸⁶ 慼（戚）③④ 斯歎，歎斯辟（辟），⁸⁷ 奔（辟）斯通（踊）。通（踊），
㤅（慍）之終也。③⑤

Of all anguished thoughts, afterwards there is grief; all musical/joyous thoughts afterwards there is delight.⁸⁸ ③① All ❶❾ thoughts use the mind deeply. Lamentation provides a method for [expressing] your thoughts. Sound changes thus [the heart follows.] ③② When the heart changes the sound also changes this way. ❷⓿ Chanting, reveals your sadness; "*zao*" chirping reveals your joy; "*jiu*" chirping reveals resonance,⁸⁹ singing folk songs reveals the heart. ③③ Happy and carefree, carefree and vigorous, vigorous and singing, singing and shaking, shaking and dancing. Dancing, happiness's end result. Angry and anguished, anguished and grieving, grieving and melancholy, melancholy ③④ and beating your breast, beating your breast and hopping around.⁹⁰ Hopping, anger's end result. ③⑤

Section 13

凡⁹¹學⁹²者隶（求）其❸❶心為難，從其所為,㐭（近）得之㠯（矣），不女（如）以樂
之速也。③⑥　唯（雖）能其事，不能其心，不貴。求其心又（有）為(偽)⁹³也，弗得之
㠯（矣）。人之不能以為也，③⑦可智（知）也■。[不]⁹⁴迲（過）十㪯（舉），其心必
才（在）安(焉)，　𢒫（察）其見者，青（情）安（焉）⁹⁵遱（失）才（哉）？❸❷
察，⁹⁶宜（義）之方也■。③⑧宜（義），敬之方也■。敬，勿（物）之節也。篤，㤅（仁）之
方也。㤅（仁），眚（性）之方也,眚（性）或生之。忠,信③⑨ 之方也。信,青（情）之
方❸❸也。青（情）出於眚（性）■。

㤅（愛）頪（類）七,唯眚（性）㤅（愛）為近㤅（仁）■。智頪（類）五,唯④⓿
宜（義）衍（道）為忻（近）忠。亞（惡）頪（類）参（三），唯亞（惡）不㤅（仁）為
忻（近）宜（義）。所❸④為衍（道）者四,唯人衍（道）為④①可衍（道）也■。

Of all who cultivate, seeking ❸❶ one's heart is difficult. You obtain it by following what you are close to, but this is not as effective as doing what you enjoy.⁹⁷ ③⑥ Although this is acceptable for work, it is not suitable for your heart and should not be treated as venerable. If you seek your heart with any falsity, you will not obtain it; we know ③⑦ people are unable [to do it] with falsity. Do not go beyond the ten types of actions,⁹⁸ the heart must be present in it; investigate what you see, how could the *qing* be lost? ❸❷ Investigation is the method of righteousness. ③⑧ Righteousness is the method of respect. Respect is the regulator of materials. Earnest is the method of humanity. Humanity is the method of nature; nature gives birth. Loyalty⁹⁹ is the method of faith③⑨. Faith is the method of *qing* ❸❸. *Qing* emanates from nature.

There are seven ways to love one's kind, only the nature's love is close to humanity. There are five ways to knowing one's kind, only ④⓿ the righteous Dao is close to loyalty. There are three ways to hate one's kind, only hating what is not humane is close to righteousness. There ❸❹ are four Daos, only the human Dao ④① can be known.

Section 14

凡甬（用）心之臊（躁）者，思為甚。

甬（用）智之疾者，患為甚。

甬（用）青（情）之④②至❸❺者，依（哀）樂為甚■。

甬（用）身之覓（弁）¹⁰⁰者，兌（悅）為甚■。

甬（用）力之肁（盡）者，利為甚。

目之好④③色，耳之樂聖（聲），鹹（鬱）舀（陶）之燹（氣）也，❸❻人不難為之死。又（有）其為人之迴（節）迴（節）女（如）也，④④ 不又（有）夫柬柬¹⁰¹之心則采。又（有）其為人之柬柬女（如）也，不又（有）夫亙（恒）怡（殆）¹⁰²之志則縵（漫）■。¹⁰³❸❽人之孜（巧）④⑤言利訂（詞）¹⁰⁴者，不又（有）夫詘詘之心則流■。人之兑（悅）肰（然）可與和安者，不又（有）夫懽（奮）④⑥ 炸（作）之青（情）則悉（侮）■。

又（有）其為人之快¹⁰⁵女（如）也，弗牧不可■。

又（有）其為人之蓂（淵）¹⁰⁶女（如）也，④⑦弗校（輔）不足■。

Of all those who use the heart impatiently, it becomes particularly apparent when contemplating.

Those who use wisdom in a hurry, it becomes particularly apparent in adversity.

Those who use *qing* ④② to the utmost, ❸❺ it becomes particularly important in times of sadness and joy.

Those who use their body with urgency, it becomes particularly apparent in times of joy.

Those who use their strength to the utmost, it becomes particularly apparent when they seek advantage.

Eyes like ④③ sex, ears delight in sound, if it is with giddy[107] *qi*, it is not difficult for ❸❻ people to die. Some people are upright,[108] ④④ but if they do not have honesty in their hearts, they will be falsely adorned.[109] If they have honesty, but their conscience is not careful and concerned, then they will be disrespectful. A person ❸❽ with clever ④⑤ words and endearing statements who lacks honesty will be rootless. A person who can be happy and can be at peace with others, but does not have a *qing* of vigorous ④⑥ action then will be insulted.

There are people who are intelligent, but if they do not nurture it then it fails.

There are people who are cautious, ④⑦ but if they are not coached it is not enough.

Section 15

凡人憍(偽)為可亞(惡)也。憍(偽)斯吝¹¹⁰荳(矣)，吝斯慮荳(矣)■，慮斯莫與之
④⑧結■荳(矣)。訢(慎)，息(仁)之方也，肰(然)而其怠(過)不亞(惡)。速，
悔(謀)之方也，又(有)怠(過)則咎■。人不訢(慎)❸❾斯又(有)怠(過)，
信荳(矣)。❹①④⑨

Of all people who act falsely, they are loathsome. Acting falsely they will have regrets, having regrets they will start scheming, schemers¹¹¹ do not have people who ④⑧ associate with them. Being cautious is the method of humanity, but if they are excessively cautious they are still not loathed. Eagerness (speed?) is the method of planning, but if it is excessive there is blame. People who are not cautious ❸❾ are excessive, this is something true. ❹①④⑨

Section 16

凡人青(情)為可兌(悅)也。句(苟)以其青(情)，唯(雖)怠(過)不亞(惡)；
❷⓪ 不以其青(情)，唯(雖)難不貴。⑤⓪句(苟)又(有)其青(情)，唯(雖)未
之為，斯人信之荳(矣)■。

未言而信，又(有)娩(美)青(情)者也。

未羑(教)⑤①而民互(恆)，眚(性)善者也。

未賞而民懂(勸)，含福¹¹²者也。❷❷

未型(刑)而民惺(畏)，又(有)⑤②心惺(畏)者也。

戔(賤)而民貴之，又(有)惪(德)者也。

貧而民聚安(焉)，又(有)衍(道)者也■。⑤③

蜀(獨)処(處)¹¹³而樂，又(有)內其(體)¹¹⁴❷❸者也。

亞(惡)之而不可非者，達於義者也。

非之⑤④而不可亞(惡)者，管(篤)於息(仁)者也■。

行之不怠(過)，智(知)道者❷④ 也。

昏(聞)道反上，上交者也。⑤⑤

昏(聞)衍(道)反下，下交者也。

昏(聞)道反昌(己)，攸(修)身者也■。

上交近事君，

下交得¹¹⁵⑤⑥近從正(政)■，

攸(修)身近至息(仁)。

同方而交，以道者也。不同方而❷⑤[交以古(故)者也。]¹¹⁶⑤⑦

同兌(悅)而交，以惪(德)者也。不同兌(悅)而交，以獻者也。

門內之絧(治)，谷(欲)其⑤⑧艄(逸)¹¹⁷也。❷⑥ 門外之絧(治)，谷(欲)其折(制)也。

Of all people's *qing* it can be delighted. If you use your *qing*, although you are excessive you are not loathed; if you do not use ❷❶ your *qing*, although you do what is difficult you will not be treated as venerable. ⑤⓪ If you have your *qing*, although you do not act, other people will believe you.[118]

> If you have not yet spoken and people [already] believe you, you are a person with a beautiful *qing*.
>
> If you have not yet taught [them] ⑤① and people are [already] enduring, you are a person whose nature is good (adept).
>
> If you have not yet [bestowed] reward and people are [already] hard working, you are a person with concealed moral abundance. ❷❷
>
> If you have not yet [meted out] punishments and the people are [already] respectful, you are a person with ⑤② respect in your heart.
>
> One who is destitute but treated by the people as venerable, is due to a person having virtue.
>
> One who is poor, but the people flock to you, is due to a person having the Dao. ⑤③
>
> One who lives alone but happy, is due to a person having inner substance. ❷❸

When people loathe you but you cannot be refuted you are one who has reached righteousness.

When people refute you ⑤④ but you cannot be loathed you are one who is earnest in humanity.

Acting but not being excessive is a person with wisdom of the Dao.

> Hearing the Dao and reflecting[119] it to those above is someone who interacts with those above. ⑤⑤
>
> Hearing the Dao and reflecting it to those below is someone who interacts with those below.
>
> Hearing the Dao and reflecting it personally is someone who cultivates his or her body.[120]

> Interacting with those above is close to serving a noble,
>
> interacting with those below achieves ⑤⑥ closeness with engaging in politics,
>
> cultivating your body is close to achieving humanity.
>
> Interacting with people of the same station ❷⑥ is a person who uses the Dao.
>
> Interacting with people of a different station [is to use the special purpose 故]. ⑤⑦ Interacting with people with the same happiness is a person who uses virtue.
>
> Interacting with people with different happiness is a person who uses planning 猷.

The regulation of what is inside[121] is ⑤⑧ at ease. ❷❻ The regulation of what is outside needs control.

Section 17

凡兌（說）[122]人勿憪（吝）[123]❷❾[124]也，身必從之，言及則⑤⑨明辵（舉）之而毋憍(偽)。

When you speak with others you should not have regrets ❷❾. You must follow what you say; your words can be clearly followed ⑤⑨ and not be deemed false.

Section 18

凡交毋刔（刺），[125]必貞（使）又（有）末■。

Of all the interactions none should be intense, they must have a reasonable outcome.

Section 19

凡於道[126]毋悁（畏），毋蜀（獨）言■。蜀（獨）⑥⓪処（處），則習❸⓪父兄之所樂。句（苟）毋（無）大害，少枉內（入）[127]之可也，已則勿復言也。⑥①

Of all the Dao there should be no disrespect, do not speak when alone. When living ⑥⓪ alone, practice what brought joy to your ❸⓪ father and brother. If no great disaster ensues when a small mistake is tolerated, it is acceptable. After things are finished there is no need to discuss it again. ⑥①

Section 20

凡悥（憂）患之事谷（欲）玨（任），樂事谷（欲）後■。[128]

身谷（欲）青（靜）而毋歆(羨)，[129]

慮谷（欲）困（淵）而毋憍（偽），[130]⑥②

行谷（欲）恿（勇）而必至，

笛（貌）谷（欲）壯(莊)而毋杲（伐），[131]

谷[132]（欲）柔齊[133]而泊，

悥（喜）谷（欲）智而無末，⑥③

樂谷（欲）睪（懌）而又有[134]志，

悥（憂）谷（欲）僉（儉）[135]而毋惛（昏），

悲（怒）谷（欲）涅[136]而毋夆（希），[137]

進谷（欲）孫（遜）而毋攷（巧）■，⑥④

退谷（欲）易（肅）而毋巠（輕），❷❼

谷（欲）皆廌(敏)[138]而毋憍（偽）■。

君子執志必又(有)夫坓(廣)坓(廣)之心■，出言必又(有)⑥⑤夫柬柬[139]❷❽之信，
　賓客之豊(禮)必又(有)夫齊齊之頌(容)■，
　祭祀之豊(禮)必又(有)夫齊齊之敬■，⑥⑥
居喪必又(有)夫㝈(戀)㝈(戀)之忨(哀)。❷❾[140]君子身以為宝(主)心。口口
口口口口口口⑥⑦[141]

In all anguish and adverse times, you should want to receive an official post; in musical events you should want to come after others.

> Your body wants stillness but not excess.
>
> When considering things you should want caution but no falseness. ⑥②
>
> When you act you should want bravery but there must be attainment.
>
> In your appearance you should want to be solemn but not arrogant.
>
> You should want to be soft,[142] pure, and tranquil.
>
> When you are happy you should want wisdom but not superfluous things. ⑥③
>
> With music you should want joy and have the correct will.
>
> When in anguish you should want to show restraint and not be overly dark.
>
> When you are angry you should want what is thick, not what is thin.
>
> When making progress you should want to be modest and not act clever. ⑥④
>
> When you decline, you should want to be respectful but not frivolous. ❷❼
>
> Desire all of these intelligently and no falseness.

A noble person grasps his or her will and must have a broad mind. Words that you express[143] must be ⑥⑤ upright and ❷❽ honest.

> The ritual for guests must have solemn tolerance.
>
> The rituals for worship must have solemn respect. ⑥⑥

When in mourning you must have sadness from being unable to bear parting. ❷❾

A noble person's body treats this as the chief of his or her heart. □□□□□□
□⑥⑦

NOTES

PREFACE
1. Kenneth W. Holloway, "Can an Understanding of Guodian Manuscripts Help Bridge Divisions in Chinese Buddhism?" in *Proceedings of the Second World Buddhist Forum* 第二屆世界佛教論壇語文集 (Beijing: Preparatory Office of the World Buddhist Forum 世界佛教論壇籌備辦公室, 2009), 361–72.
2. This presentation resulted in the following publication: Kenneth W. Holloway, "An Inquiry into the 'Xing zi mingchu' from the Perspective of the 'Five Aspects of Conduct,'" 從《五行篇》的角度探討《性自命出》 *Taiwan Journal of East Asian Studies* 臺灣東亞文明研究學刊 6, 1 (June 2009): 203–210.

INTRODUCTION
1. The problem is that the term "nature" (*xing* 性) is often translated "human nature." This does not work here because nature is more than human in the text. Next, the term "endowment" (*ming* 命) can mean "heaven's mandate" in several texts in early China. In the context of the quote, we are even told that this endowment descends from heaven. I resist this because endowment is not well developed in the text; it only occurs two times in one single sentence connecting nature to heaven. It is tantalizing to speculate how this tells us about our connection to heaven, but heaven is even less important to the text than "mandate." Heaven appears only one time in the entire text. Instead of focusing the attention of the reader on endowment or mandate, I have decided to leave the title transliterated as "Xing zi mingchu." The other option would be to adopt the less prevalent title "Discourse on Nature and *Qing*," which is a far superior title for the text. Unfortunately, this title was proposed after numerous publications decided it should be called "Xing zi mingchu." So, faced with the choice of translating a bad title or using a more obscure one, I felt that transliteration was the only solution.
2. Tang Yijie 湯一介, "'Dao shi yu qing' de zhexue quanshi—Wulun chuangjian Zhongguo jieshixue wenti" "道始於情"的哲學詮釋—五論創建中國解失學問題" *Xueshu yuekan* 7 (2001): 40–44. "Emotion in Pre-Qin Ruist Moral Theory: An Explanation of '*Dao* Begins in *Qing*,'" Brian Bruya and Hai-ming Wen, tr., *Philosophy East and West* 53, 2 (2003): 271–81.
3. Liao Mingchun 廖名春, "Guodian Chujian Rujia zhuzuo kao" 郭店楚簡儒家著作考, *Kongzi yanjiu* 孔子研究 (1998): 69–83.
4. Ding Sixin 丁四新, "Lun Kongzi yu Guodian Rujian de tianming, tiandao guan"論孔子與郭店儒簡的天命、天道觀*Xiangtan shifan xueyuanbao* 湘潭師範學報 21, 5 (2000): 25–29.
5. See chapter 2 for further discussion.

6. Huang Huaixin 黃懷信, *Lunyu huijiao jishi* 論語彙校集釋 (Shanghai: Shanghai Guji, 2008), 25.
7. Finding this connection between the socially conceived ethical system of "Xing zi mingchu" and other religious systems is particularly exciting in light of the numerous twentieth-century monastics who advocate humanistic Buddhism. Some see this modern trend as reconnecting Buddhism with its early Chinese roots of Confucianism. Two groups that see Confucianism as part of humanistic Buddhism, are the Taiwanese Buddhist groups Foguangshan and Ciji. Stuart Chandler, *Establishing a Pure Land on Earth* (Honolulu: University of Hawai'i Press, 2004), 237; Elise Anne DeVido, *Taiwan's Buddhist Nuns* (Albany: State University of New York Press, 2010), 31, 50, 53.
8. Li Tianhong 李天虹, *Guodian zhujian "Xing zi ming chu" yanjiu* 郭店竹簡《性自命出》研究, *Xinchu jianbo yanjiu congshu* 新出簡帛研究叢書 (Wuhan: Hubei jiaoyu, 2002), 8.
9. Lian selects a few of phrases from the "Xing zi mingchu" and then decontextualizes them through an overreliance on transmitted sources. Comparisons to other excavated texts exist but are minimal. Any hope of reading the quotes in a Guodian context is thus lost. Lian Shaoming連劭名, "Lun Guodian Chujian 'Xing zi mingchu' zhong de 'Dao,'" 論郭店楚簡《性自命出》中的《道》 *Zhongguo zhexue shi*中國哲學史 4 (2000): 36–40.
10. The first article here discusses the connection with Zisi. The second article cited here relates to the division of the text. Liao proposes that strips 1–35 should be one chapter, 36–49 should be the middle chapter, and 50–67 should be the final. Strip 50 is section 16 in my appendix. In my analysis, I am careful to demonstrate connections between what comes before and after strips 35 and 50. In my first book I spent a significant amount of time criticizing the assignment of texts to Zisi in early China. There is no need to rehash these ideas here. Liao Mingchun, "Guodian Chujian Rujia zhuzuo kao"; Liao Mingchun "Guodian jian 'Xing zi mingchu' de bian lian yu fenhe wenti" 郭店簡《性自命出》的編連與分合問題, *Zhongguo zhexue shi*中國哲學史 4 (2000): 14–21; Kenneth W. Holloway, *Guodian: The Newly Discovered Seeds of Chinese Religious and Political Philosophy* (New York: Oxford University Press, 2009).
11. Holloway, *Guodian*.
12. On page 13 of *Thinking Through Confucius*, they offer the following definition of strict transcendence: "A principle, A, is transcendent with respect to that, B, which it serves as principle if the meaning or import of B cannot be fully analyzed and explained without recourse to A, but the reverse is not true." I believe that their definition holds true for the *Analects* where heaven is always discussed in a human context. However, there are passages of the *Daode jing* where the Dao is explained without reference to people, so by this same simple test the Dao is transcendent. The question is: Can we fully analyze these passages without reference to people? I believe it can be done. For this reason, I agree with Van Norden that the Dao is at least causally transcendent. David L. Hall and Roger T. Ames, *Thinking Through Confucius* (Albany: State University of New York Press, 1987), 12–17; 204–208. Bryan W. Van Norden, "Method in the Madness of the Laozi," in *Religious and Philosophical Aspects of Laozi*, Mark Csikszentmihalyi and Philip J. Ivanhoe, eds. (Albany: State University of New York Press, 1999).
13. Wm. Theodore de Bary, *The Trouble with Confucianism* (Cambridge, MA: Harvard University Press, 1991), 9–12, 49, 57–59.
14. My thinking about embodiment has benefited from the work of my colleague at Florida Atlantic University, Dr. Richard Shusterman.

15. There are many alternate readings for these characters and important notes to my translations. Please refer to the appendix for these details.
16. "Govern/regulate" (*zhi* 治) is used this way in many instances in early China including *Analects* 8.20 "Shun had only five ministers but was able to govern all under heaven." 舜有臣五人而天下治. Huang Huaixin黃懷信, *Lunyu huijiao jishi* 論語彙校集釋 (Shanghai: Guji, 2008), 724.

CHAPTER 1: *QING*, FROM CONFLICT TO ECSTASY

1. Please note that the terms "like" (*hao* 好) and "dislike" (*e* 惡) are understood to represent a range of assessment from being mildly fond of something to having a deep affinity for it. In the obverse, there is a range from being displeased with something to absolutely abhorring it.
2. Michael Pye has shown that the juxtaposition of higher and lower truths is something we find in the much later Mādhyamika approach to Buddhism. The development of upāya within Buddhism itself is still unclear at this point in history. I believe that this similarity in method is not the result of Buddhist influence on Guodian. Instead, this similarity is important from the perspective of how native religious concepts in China represent a fertile foundation for the later development of Buddhist ideas. The idea of looking at pre-Qin texts to understand later developments in Buddhism was explored by Chun-fang Yu in her analysis of the way that Guanyin was transformed in China. In much later periods, Christine Mollier has shown that there was significant cross-pollination that occurred between Buddhism and the native religion of Daoism. By the mid-Tang period, Buddhism and Daoism borrowed entire scriptures from each other with only cursory changes in titles and characters. However, the cross-pollination began from the moment Buddhism arrived in China. Through an exploration of the religious dimensions of pre-Qin excavated manuscripts, it is hoped that we can better understand a lost chapter in the development of religion in the Han and following periods of Chinese history. Michael Pye, *Skilful Means: A Concept in Mahayana Buddhism,* 2d ed. (London: Taylor & Francis Routledge, 2003), 109–10; Chun-fang Yu, *Kuan-yin, The Chinese Transformation of Avalokitesvara* (New York: Columbia University Press, 2001), 153–58; 408–13; Christine Mollier, *Buddhism and Taoism Face to Face* (Honolulu: University of Hawai'i Press, 2008).
3. Rebecca Nedostup, *Superstitious Regimes, Religion and the Politics of Chinese Modernity* (Cambridge, MA: Harvard University Asia Center, 2009); Mayfair Mei-Hui Yang, ed., *Chinese Religiosities, Afflictions of Modernity and State Formation* (Berkeley: University of California Press, 2008).
4. For his discussion of the ability of the Zhou religious and cultural practices to cross political boundaries, see chapter 6 of von Falkenhausen's book. Lothar von Falkenhausen, *Chinese Society in the Age of Confucius (1000–250 BC): The Archaeological Evidence* (Los Angeles: Cotsen Institute of Archaeology, 2006), 13.
5. Holloway, *Guodian*, chapter 3.
6. Holloway, *Guodian*, chapter 5.
7. More precisely, this is an interpolation based on the context of the quotation that begins on strip 15: "Odes, Documents, Rites, Music, their inception is in the [needs] ①⑤ of ❽ humankind." Following this are several sentences that specifically expand upon the attributes of these texts, and from there is an implicit connection that I highlight in my translation through interpolations in brackets. The other option for interpolation is that it could be describing the Dao, and in a sense, it is doing just that.

8. Another possibility is that as in the *Odes*, it refers to someone whose husband has passed away, but the happiness part would seem odd if this were the case. See *Book of Odes* 毛詩, "Guofeng" 國風, "Tang Feng" 唐風, "Ge sheng" 葛生.
9. There are enough passages like this to constitute a theme in the *Analects*. I will only list a few representatives, such as 4:11, 4:12, and 4:16, where morality and profit are described as being separate paths. Passage 4:5 tells us not to seek wealth if it is immoral.
10. One exception is section 16 where humanity and righteousness appear in mirrored sentences.
11. The character translated as "enter," *ru* (入), originally appears in the text as 內 *nei*, "inside." In other words, transcribers argue that the character should in fact be read as "enter." One possible exception to entering and emitting always appearing in tandem is section 19 where the characters appear in the transcription. The reason this exception is not being considered is that the explanation of the character is different here. In this instance, 內 *nei*, "inside," is being taken as 納 *na*, "accept." So "enter" is not the understood meaning in section 19. A similar usage of *na* as "accept" is seen in *Mencius* 3B.7 where a violation of propriety means a person is not kept locked out of a room and is not "admitted." This "admitting" is the same character I translate as "accepting" in section 19.
12. William V. Harris, *Restraining Rage: The Ideology of Anger Control in Classical Antiquity* (Cambridge, MA: Harvard University Press, 2001), 285–316.
13. Barbara H. Rosenwein, "Worrying about Emotions in History," *The American Historical Review* 107, 3 (June 2002): 821–45; Linda A. Pollock, "Anger and the Negotiation of Relationships in Early Modern England," *The Historical Journal* 47, 3 (September 2004): 567–90.
14. Ruan Yuan 阮元 (1764–1849), *Li ji zhengyi* 禮記正義, in *Shisanjing Zhushu* 十三經注書 (1815; repr., Taipei: Yiwen, 1960), "Zhong Yong" 中庸, 879.
15. Kwong-loi Shun provides a comprehensive survey of pre-Qin material on *qing* and nature with a particular focus on *Mencius*. This survey provides an excellent update to the work of A. C. Graham, who proposed that *qing* should be translated as "essence." The issue had been explored earlier in the January 1991 issue of *Philosophy East and West*, which was dedicated to the question of "Emotions East and West." An outgrowth of that issue was a volume edited by Marks and Ames on *Emotions in Asian Thought*. Kwong-loi Shun, "Mencius on Jen-hsing," *Philosophy East and West* 47, 1, *Human "Nature" in Chinese Philosophy: A Panel of the 1995 Annual Meeting of the Association for Asian Studies* (January 1997): 1–20; A. C. Graham, "The Background of the Mencian Theory of Human Nature," *Tsing Hua Journal of Chinese Studies* 6 (1967): 215–71. Reprinted in A. C. Graham, *Studies in Chinese Philosophy and Philosophical Literature* (Albany: State University of New York Press, 1990), 7–66; Joel Marks and Roger Ames, eds., *Emotions in Asian Thought: A Dialogue in Comparative Philosophy* (Albany: State University of New York Press, 1995).
16. John Berthrong, *Expanding Process: Exploring Philosophical and Theological Transformations in China and the West* (Albany: State University of New York Press, 2008), 95; Wing-tsit Chan, *Chu Hsi and Neo-Confucianism* (Honolulu: University of Hawai'i Press, 1986), 278–80.
17. There are of course differences between Neo-Confucianism and "Xing zi mingchu" that none of these authors deny, but areas of overlap raise tantalizing questions about how lost texts can inform historical events even a millennium hence. A further complicating factor is the gap that exists between the English category I am

using, Neo-Confucian, and the more precise terms of Lixue 理學 and Daoxue 道學 used in these Chinese articles. Stephen Angle discusses this problem and finds it valuable as an analytical structure. An exchange on the subject between de Bary and Tillman nicely presents both sides of the debate. Peng Guoxiang 彭國翔, "Continuity between Classical Confucianism and Neo-Confucianism: As Seen through Archeological Finds of Confucian Texts" 從出土文獻看宋明理學與先秦儒學的連貫性—郭店與上博儒家文獻的啟示, *Social Sciences in China*, April 2007; Li Yujie李玉潔, "Guodian Chujian rujia zhexue sixiang yu Songdai Lixue" 郭店楚簡儒家哲學思想與宋代理學, *Journal of Henan University* 42,1 (2002). Stephen C. Angle, *Sagehood: The Contemporary Significance of Neo-Confucian Philosophy* (New York: Oxford University Press, 2009), 5, 38–41; Hoyt Cleveland Tillman, "A New Direction in Confucian Scholarship: Approaches to Examining the Differences between Neo-Confucianism and Tao-hsüeh" *Philosophy East and West* 42, 3 (July 1992): 455–74; William Theodore de Bary, "The Uses of Neo-Confucianism: A Response to Professor Tillman," *Philosophy East and West* 43, 3 (July 1993): 541–55; Hoyt Cleveland Tillman, "The Uses of Neo-Confucianism, Revisited: A Reply to Professor de Bary," *Philosophy East and West* 44, 1 (January 1994): 135–42.

CHAPTER 2: THE ROLE OF NATURE IN A WORLD OF FRICTION

1. Another unlikely interpretation is that the judgment of excess is being handed down by the higher level of the Dao, a force that is always going to judge human actions as imperfect. Being damned to an existence of imperfection has no support from the text, so while it might be an interesting theory it not a compelling explanation.
2. The question raised is if a transcendent principle is dead, how can it interface with our living vital energy? Naturally, the terminology and other concerns are different in "Xing zi mingchu," but the question of how a transcendent model relates to lived experience is interestingly similar. Berthrong, *Expanding Process*, 105–107.
3. It is possible that this box is something inserted by a later scribe or a reader. Each section is again divisible in half, but the commas do not reflect a notation of any sort in the original.
4. One example of this can be found in Tang Yijie. Tang Yijie, "'Dao shi yu qing' de zhexue quanshi—Wulun chuangjian Zhongguo jieshixue wenti."
5. Wang Ji 王畿 (1498–1583), courtesy name Ruzhong (汝中), nickname Longxi (龍溪).
6. Guoxiang, "Continuity between Classical Confucianism and Neo-Confucianism," 108.
7. Guoxiang, "Continuity between Classical Confucianism and Neo-Confucianism," 108–10.
8. Michael Puett, "Following the Commands of Heaven: The Notion of Ming in Early China," in *The Magnitude of Ming: Command, Allotment and Fate in Chinese Culture*, Christopher Lupke, ed. (Honolulu: University of Hawai'i Press, 2005).
9. A similar quote can be found at the end of section 13: "There are four Daos, only the human Dao can be known." 所為道者四，唯人道為可道也.
10. The chapter of this book on The Rectification of Names will go into detail on another example of a similar phrase that discusses limitations on our ability to comprehend the full Dao that starts the *Daode jing*.
11. The one variation between the two quotes of four techniques versus four Daos seems to be overshadowed by the other similarities between the quotes.
12. Holloway, "An Inquiry into the 'Xing zi mingchu.'"

CHAPTER 3: HAVING FUN WITH THE DAO

1. I would like to thank Barbara Hendrischke for reminding me of this out in her review of my first book. Barbara Hendrischke, "Review of Kenneth W. Holloway 'Guodian: The Newly Discovered Seeds of Chinese Religious and Political Philosophy,'" *Journal of the Royal Asiatic Society*, 3d ser., 21 (2011): 124–26.
2. The first line of section 8 is on the same strip as the end of sections 5–7, so this chapter will analyze them as a group. In fact, this section break is not universally followed; an alternate grouping that places this discussion of the Dao along with the earlier sections is followed by Tu Zongliu and Liu Zuxin. They then start a new section with a discussion of the four books *Odes, Documents, Rites*, and *Music*. Tu Zongliu 涂宗流 and Liu Zuxin 劉祖信, *Guodian chujian xianqin rujia yishu jiaoshi* 郭店楚簡先秦儒家佚書校釋 (Taibei: Wanjuanlou, 2001), 150–56.
3. Jiao Xun 焦循 (1763–1820), *Mengzi zhengyi* 孟子正義, in *Zhuzi jicheng* 諸子集成 (Beijing: Zhonghua, 1996), 6A.2, 433.
4. "I. In the month of Equalizing Rule, Revise the laws and order punishments; Select the knights and sharpen weapons. Inquire about and punish the unrighteous, To embrace those in distant quarters." 夷則之月, 修法飭刑, 選士厲兵, 詰誅不義, 以懷遠方. John Knoblock and Jeffrey Riegel, tr., *The Annals of Lu Buwei* (Stanford: Stanford University Press, 2000), (季夏紀 Almanac for the Third Month of Summer), 159. Another example is in Xunzi's "Strengthening the State" 彊國: "For the state there is also grinding and sharpening, the rites and righteousness, and moral standards." 彼國者亦有砥厲, 禮義、節奏是也. Wang Xianqian 王先謙 (1842–1918), *Xunzi ji jie, kao zheng: ji jie er shi juan kao zheng er juan* 荀子集解·考證: 集解二十卷考証二卷 (Taibei: Shijie, 1967), 194.
5. Roger T. Ames, "The Focus-Field Self in Classical Confucianism," in Ames et al.., *Self As Person in Asian Theory and Practice* (Albany: State University of New York Press, 1994).
6. Holloway, *Guodian*, 107–109.
7. Ibid.
8. Ibid.
9. There are quite a number of examples where humanity and righteousness represent binary opposites. "Yu Cong One" 語叢一 states: "Being thick in humanity and thin in righteousness you are familial but do not elevate [the outstanding]. Being thick in righteousness and thin in humanity you elevate [the outstanding] but are not familial." 7:2 (厚於仁, 薄)於義, 親而不尊. 厚於義, 薄於仁, 尊而不親. Another Guodian text, "Zun de yi," 尊德義 states: "Humanity can be familial, righteousness can elevate [the outstanding]." 3. 仁為可親也, 義為可尊也... Both of these texts show a clear tension between humanity and righteousness.
10. Holloway, *Guodian*, 107–109.
11. They dedicate the third section of the book to this question. It is entitled "Transcendence and Immanence as Cultural Clues." David L. Hall and Roger T. Ames, *Thinking from the Han: Self, Truth, and Transcendence in Chinese and Western Culture* (Albany: State University of New York Press, 1997), 244–46.
12. This second option means that our nature is not simply an entity that is either good or neutral as Mencius and Xunzi believe. Instead, nature is something that must be cultivated in order to stabilize the heart. There are a few passages in Xunzi where the transformation of nature is mentioned. In the "Nature Is Evil" chapter we have "Therefore sages transformed nature and conscious activity arose" 故聖人化性而起偽. The passage continues: "All that was venerated by the noble people Yao Yu, could transform nature and cause conscious activity to arise. Conscious activity

arose and gave birth to the rites and righteousness." 凡所貴堯禹君子者. 能化性能起偽. 偽起而生禮義. In the "Ruxiao" chapter, Xunzi states: "Managing our habits and customs is that by which we transform our nature." 注錯習俗. 所以化性也. This last citation from the "Ruxiao" chapter is also quoted in Ma Chengyuan's Shanghai edition. Aside from Xunzi, the idea of transforming your nature does not appear in the received tradition from the pre-Han period. *Xunzi Jijie*, "Xing e" 性惡, 292, 295 "Ru Xiao" 儒效, 91. Ma Chengyuan et al., *Shanghai Bowuguan cang Zhanguo Chu zhushu* 上海博物館藏戰國楚竹書, vol. 1 (Shanghai: Guji, 2001), 220.

13. One part of this motion is a reaction to *zuo* 作, a term that has been discussed at great length by Michael Puett in his book *The Ambivalence of Creation*. He translates the term "*zuo*" as "creation" and finds that there are some texts where this is a positive attribute and others where it is negative. This mixed reaction of texts to the term "*zuo*" leads him to characterize sources as ambivalent as to the value of creating things. While his analysis is provocative and important, it was completed too early to consider Guodian material. Michael Puett, *The Ambivalence of Creation: Debates Concerning Innovation and Artifice in Early China* (Stanford: Stanford University Press, 2001).

14. In paragraph 5, we have: "Humane thoughts: [they] are essential; being essential ❶❷ you will have keen insight; having keen insight you will be at ease; being at ease you will be gentle; being gentle you will be happy; being happy your demeanor is pleasant; having a pleasant demeanor you can be intimate; being intimate you will be loving; loving your countenance will be jade-like; having a jade-like countenance you will be formed; being formed you will be humane. ■ ❶❸" 5. 仁之思也精. 精❶❷ 則察, 察則安, 安則溫, 溫則悅, 悅則戚, 戚則親, 親則愛, 愛則玉色, 玉色則形. 形則仁. ■ ❶❸.

In paragraph 12 we have: "If you are not open to change you will not be happy; if you are not happy you will not have a pleasant demeanor; if you do not have a pleasant demeanor you will not be intimate; if you are not intimate, you will not love; if you do not love you will not be humane." 12. 不變不悅, 不悅不戚, 不戚不親, 不親不愛, 不愛不仁. ■ Holloway, *Guodian*, 133–34.

15. Holloway, *Guodian*, 131.
16. Holloway, *Guodian*, 138.
17. Holloway, *Guodian*, 136.
18. The final instance of the term "cultivation" is on strip 61. "When living alone, practice what brought joy to your father and brother." 獨處, 則習父兄之所樂. Unfortunately, the terms "father" and "son" do not appear elsewhere in the text, but the appearance of delighting, which is similar to happiness in the first strip of the text, is an indicator of a positive attribute.
19. See chapter 3, "Rhetoric as Self-Cultivation: A Question of Language," of my book. Here is one section that illustrates the issue: "17. Hearing the way of the noble man is having keen hearing; hearing something and knowing it is sagacity. Sages know the way of heaven." 聞君子道, 聰也. 聞而知之, 聖也. 聖人知天道也. Holloway, *Guodian*, 135–36.
20. This is similar to what has already been discussed as the way we are supposed to judge actions in the "Wuxing pian." In this text, the embodiment of virtue is the standard.
21. Please see the "Music and Fun" section of this chapter for further discussion of the inseparability of laughter, music, and ritual.
22. Literally it says "materials," *wu* 物.
23. This character *yong* 咏 (sing) is an equivalent of *yong* 詠 (sing) that is found in the "Xing zi mingchu."

24. *Li ji zhengyi*, "Tangong Xia" 檀弓下, 175.
25. "yun (angry) is like nu (anger)" 慍猶怒也 *Li ji zhengyi*, "Tangong Xia," 175.
26. James Legge, trans (1815-1897). *Li Ki Book of Rites*, vol. 27 (Oxford: Clarendon, 1879–85; repr., Delhi: Motilal Banarsidass, 1966), 177.
27. This ecstatic connotation is admittedly stronger in the note inserted into the Book of Rites, where the character *nu* 怒 is found. What comes to mind is the action of the Peng bird in Zhuangzi who furiously beats his wings in *nu* prior to taking flight.
28. A minor difference is that in section 12, instead of a discussion of music from specific countries and particular types of instruments, vocalizations are the main form being mentioned.
29. Mark Edward Lewis, *The Early Chinese Empires: Qin and Han* (Cambridge, MA: Belknap Press of Harvard University Press, 2007), 43–44; Alan R. Thrasher, *Sizhu Instrumental Music of South China: Ethos, Theory and Practice* (Boston: Brill, 2008), 46–47; Lothar von Falkenhausen, *Chinese Society in the Age of Confucius*, 348–57; Lothar von Falkenhausen, *Suspended Music: Chime-Bells in the Culture of Bronze Age China* (Berkeley: University of California Press, 1993), 52–54.
30. Chen Wei states that music here refers to licentious music. Chen Wei 陳偉 et al., *Chudi chutu Zhanguo jian ce (Shisan zhong)* 楚地出土戰國簡冊（十三種）, (Beijing: Jingji kexue, 2009), 10.

CHAPTER 4: ABSOLUTE VERSUS RELATIVE MORALITY

1. Yan Binggang 顏炳罡, "Guodian Chujian 'Xing zi mingchu' yu Xunzi de qingxing zhexue" 郭店楚簡《性自命出》與荀子的情性哲學, *Zhongguo zhexue shi* 中國哲學史1 (2009): 5–9.
2. This translation is adapted from Burton Watson. Burton Watson, tr., *Hsün Tzu: Basic Writings* (New York: Columbia University Press, 1996), 139–40.
3. *Xunzi Jijie*, "Zhengming" 正名, 274–75.
4. John Knoblock, *Xunzi: A Translation and Study of the Complete Works*, vol. 3. (Stanford: Stanford University Press, 1994), 127.
5. *Xunzi Jijie*, "Xing e," 289.
6. A cautionary note should be taken regarding this analysis; it is largely based on the *Xunzi* chapter "Xing e." There is one contradiction in the "Discourse on Music" where Xunzi states: "The *qing* of music exhausts the root, and is the ultimate transformation. The constant way of ritual is that the clearly sincere eliminates conscious activity" 窮本極變. 樂之情也. 著誠去偽. 禮之經也. *Xunzi Jijie*, "Yue lun" 樂論, 255. For a further discussion, see Paul R. Goldin, *Confucianism* (Berkeley: University of California Press, 2011), 67–98.
7. Paul Goldin has argued for important similarities between Xunzi and "Xing zi mingchu," but he believes the rectification of names is not one of these analogous areas. Paul R. Goldin, "Xunzi in the Light of the Guodian Manuscripts," *Early China* 25 (2000): 113–46. Reprinted in Paul R. Goldin, *After Confucius: Studies in Early Chinese Philosophy* (Honolulu: University of Hawai'i Press, 2005).
8. Ouyang Zhenren feels that "Xing zi mingchu" follows the heavenly way of Confucius, but takes the notion of nature and externalizes it to become an action that animates our lives. Ouyang Zhenren 歐陽禎人, "'Xunzi' zhong 'qing' zi de zhexue yihan" 《荀子》中"情"字的哲學意涵 *Zhongguo qingnian zhengzhi xueyuan xuebao* 中國青年政治學院學報 17, 3 (2008): 41–47.
9. *Xunzi Jijie*, "Xing e," 290.
10. Sato Masayuki, *The Confucian Quest for Order: The Origin and Formation of the Political Thought of Xunzi* (Boston: Brill, 2003), 370–82.

11. He Shanmeng何善蒙, "Zhongguo chuantong yishu zhong 'qing' de zhexue quanshi" 中國傳統藝術中"情"的哲學詮釋, *Wenhua yishu yanjiu*文化藝術研究 1, 2 (2008): 59–74.
12. Halvor Eifring, ed., *Love and Emotions in Traditional Chinese Literature* (Boston: Brill, 2004).
13. *Qing* as a link in the "Xing zi mingchu" has already been covered in detail.
14. Chad Hansen, "A Tao of Tao in Chuang-tzu," in *Experimental Essays on Chuang-tzu*, Victor H. Mair, ed., *Asian Studies at Hawaii* 29 (Honolulu: University of Hawai'i Press, 1983), 24–55; Edward Slingerland, *Effortless Action: Wu-wei as Conceptual Metaphor and Spiritual Ideal in Early China* (New York: Oxford University Press, 2003).
15. Alison Dundes Renteln, "Relativism and the Search for Human Rights," *American Anthropologist, New Series* 90, 1 (March 1988): 56–72.
16. Michael F. Brown, "Cultural Relativism 2.0," *Current Anthropology* 49, 3 (June 2008): 363–83; S. F. Sapontzis, "Moral Relativism: A Causal Interpretation and Defense," *American Philosophical Quarterly* 24, 4 (October 1987): 329–37; Robert M. Stewart and Lynn L. Thomas, "Recent Work on Ethical Relativism," *American Philosophical Quarterly* 28, 2 (April 1991): 85–100; Nicholas Unwin, "Relativism and Moral Complacency," *Philosophy* 60, 232 (April 1985): 205–14.
17. A. C. Graham, *Disputers of the Tao: Philosophical Argument in Ancient China* (Chicago: Open Court, 1999).
18. Paul Goldin also discusses the same issue of the highly specific nature of Confucius's advice in reference to 11.22 where the same question is again answered completely oppositely to two different people. Goldin, *Confucianism*, 8–10.
19. Huang, *Lunyu huijiao jishi*, 121–26.
20. Huang, *Lunyu huijiao jishi*, 127–29.
21. The following is but a small sampling of the multitude of scholarship that has demonstrated the compatibility of Confucianism with egalitarianism, human rights, democracy, and feminism. William Theodore de Bary and Tu Weiming, eds., *Confucianism and Human Rights* (New York: Columbia University Press, 1998); Daniel A. Bell and Hahm Chaibong, eds., *Confucianism for the Modern World* (New York: Cambridge University Press, 2003); Goldin, *Confucius*; Erica Fox Brindley, *Individualism in Early China* (Honolulu: University of Hawai'i Press, 2010); Steven C. Angle, *Human Rights and Chinese Thought: A Cross-Cultural Inquiry* (New York: Cambridge University Press, 2002).
22. Michael Nylan and Thomas Wilson dedicate a chapter to "Kongzi and his critics" wherein they cite *Analects* 18.5. Here Confucius is lampooned by a madman, but much of their discussion centers around the ample source of criticism of Confucius in other sources such as by the Mohists. Michael Nylan and Thomas Wilson, *Lives of Confucius: Civilization's Greatest Sage through the Ages* (New York: Doubleday, 2010), 29–66.
23. Huang, *Lunyu huijiao jishi*, 121–23.
24. For further details on important strengths I find in his book, please see my book review. Kenneth Holloway, "Review of *Envisioning Eternal Empire: Chinese Political Thought of the Warring States Era*, by Yuri Pines," *Sino Platonic Papers*, twenty-fifth anniversary issue 208 (2011): 29–31; Yuri Pines, *Envisioning Eternal Empire: Chinese Political Thought of the Warring States Era* (Honolulu: University of Hawai'i Press, 2009).
25. William Max Knorpp, Jr., "What Relativism Isn't," *Philosophy* 73, 284 (1998): 277–300.

26. Huang, *Lunyu huijiao jishi*, 95.
27. Huang, *Lunyu huijiao jishi*, 316–20.
28. Bryan W. Van Norden, *Virtue Ethics and Consequentialism in Early Chinese Philosophy* (New York: Cambridge University Press, 2007).

CHAPTER 5: THE RECTIFICATION OF NAMES
1. Naming becomes quite important in the post-Han era discussions of Names and Principles. Alan K. L. Chan, *Two Visions of the Way: A study of the Wang Pi and the Ho-Shang Kung Commentaries on the Lao-Tzu*, (Albany: State University of New York Press, 1991), 21–24.
2. For a discussion of whether the rectification of names belongs in the *Analects*, please see Benjamin I. Schwartz, *The World of Thought in Ancient China* (Cambridge, MA: Belknap, 1985), 85–99. Another broad discussion of the issue can be found in Mark Edward Lewis, *Writing and Authority in Early China* (Albany: State University of New York Press, 1999), 28–35.
3. Schaberg is discussing the idea of commanding (*ming* 命) when he states that the character can also be used to assign a name (*ming* 名). Graham states that "command" (*ming* 命) and "name" (*ming* 名) are cognates. In addition, the Shuowen text states: "ming (name) comes from ming (endowment)" 名自命也. David Schaberg, "Command and the Content of Tradition," in *The Magnitude of Ming: Command, Allotment, and Fate in Chinese Culture*, Christopher Lupke, ed. (Honolulu: University of Hawai'i Press, 2005), 31–32; A. C. Graham, *Disputers of the Tao: Philosophical Argument in Ancient China* (La Salle, IL: Open Court, 1989), 23; Jiang Renjie 蔣人傑, *Shuowen Jiezi Jizhu* 說文解字集注, vol.1 (Shanghai: Guji, 1996), 252.
4. Cheng Shude 程樹德 (1877–1944), *Lunyu jishi* (Beijing: Zhonghua, 1990), 885-93.
5. These are 4:5, 8:19, 9:2, 12:11, 13:3, and 15:20.
6. *Lunyu jishi*, 855.
7. This context results in the distinct yet related answers to the same issue of government in 12:11 and 13:3, for example.
8. *Lunyu jishi*, 1212.
9. H. G. Creel, *Confucius and the Chinese Way* (New York: Harper and Row, 1960), 211–21; Goldin, *Confucianism*, 126–27, n. 32.
10. Incidentally these are also concepts that do appear in pairs in the *Analects*, but the connection between rites and music is widespread in early China. A good discussion of this can be found in Scott Cook, "Zhuang Zi and his Carving of the Confucian Ox," *Philosophy East and West* 47, 4 (1997): 521–53.
11. Huang, *Lunyu huijiao jishi*, 104–109.
12. Paul R. Goldin, "Persistent Misconceptions about Chinese 'Legalism,'" *Journal of Chinese Philosophy* 38, 1 (2011): 88–104.
13. E. Bruce Brooks and A. Taeko Brooks, *The Original Analects: Sayings of Confucius and His Successors* (New York: Columbia University Press, 1998), 92, 190.
14. *Way* in the Moss Roberts translation here and the Victor Mair translation below is transliterated as Dao in my translations and analysis. Moss Roberts, *Daode jing: The Book of the Way* (Berkeley: University of California Press, 2001), 27.
15. This passage is not in the Guodian edition; it is present in both editions that were buried in Mawangdui. I do not see this as a problem as far as analysis since my argument is the excavated text "Xing zi mingchu" completes the transition between two texts previously known from the received tradition. In Mawangdui, "common/lasting" (*chang*常) is "common/lasting" (*heng* 恒) because of the taboo of using the

character *heng* that appeared in the emperor's name. The meaning is not changed by the substitution. The other difference is that the clause- or sentence-ending character (*ye* 也) is inserted after the second and third characters for Dao and name. What this does is reinforce the pauses between the second occurrence of these words that Roberts puts in quotes and the common usage of these words. It also supports the period in between the first sentence regarding Dao and the second regarding name. The Chinese characters can be found here: Gao Ming 高明, *Boshu Laozi jiaozhu* 帛書老子校注 (Beijing: Zhonghua, 1996), 221–24.

16. Victor Mair, *Tao Te Ching: The Classic Book of Integrity and the Way* (New York: Bantam, 1990), 59.
17. Ming, *Boshu Laozi jiaozhu*, 221–24.
18. Stanza 32: "The Dao is eternally nameless." 道常無名 *Boshu Laozi jiaozhu*, 397. Stanza 37: "The Dao eternally transcends action and thus nothing is left undone." 道常無為而無不為 Ming, *Boshu Laozi jiaozhu*, 421.
19. Stanza 6: "The valley spirit never dies." 谷神不死 Ming, *Boshu Laozi jiaozhu*, 247.
20. "The five colors cause people to go blind, the five tones cause people to go deaf, the five flavors give people a dull palate." 五色令人目盲, 五音令人耳聾, 五味令人口爽 Ming, *Boshu Laozi jiaozhu*, 273.
21. In the Yi Ben 乙本 Laozi from Mawangdui we have "order" (命 *ming*) instead of "name" (名 *ming*), but as was already discussed, these characters are cognates in early China. Ming, *Boshu Laozi jiaozhu*, 282.
22. In the Shuowen, this character 摶 (*tuan*) means "to turn around" (圜 *huan*). So, this could be to roll around in your hand when examining something. Jiang Renjie, *Shuowen Jiezi Jizhu*, vol. 3, 2575.
23. Mawangdui has "Facing and you do not see its head, following and you do not see its rear." 迎而不見其首, 隨而不見其後. Ming, *Boshu Laozi jiaozhu*, 288.
24. Ming, *Boshu Laozi jiaozhu*, 282–88.
25. Roberts, *Daode jing*, 74.
26. Ming, *Boshu Laozi jiaozhu*, 332.
27. In both Mawangdui versions, stanza 37 reads: "The Dao is eternally nameless." 道恒無名. This is different from the characters in the transmitted version, 道常無爲, but it does not affect the meaning. Ming, *Boshu Laozi jiaozhu*, 421.
28. Guodian does not have *wu* 吾 (I). Also it has the negation *wei* 未 instead of *bu* 不. *Guodian Chujian jiaoshi*, 215. *Wei* is an aspectual negation such as "never," and *bu* is a simple negation. Edwin Pulleyblank, *Outline of Classical Chinese Grammar* (Vancouver: University of British Columbia Press, 1996), 103–11.
29. The Mawangdui version begins this last part with the addition of *wu* 吾 (I). 吾強為之名曰大. However, the *wu* is implied in the second half of the transmitted version since it is present at the sentence beginning where it states: "I do not know its name." 吾不知其名. Ming, *Boshu Laozi jiaozhu*, 350.
29. Ming, *Boshu Laozi jiaozhu*, 24.
30. Mair, *Tao Te Ching*, 7.
31. Ming, *Boshu Laozi jiaozhu*, 20.
32. Guodian has 上士昏道, 堇能行於兀中; 中士昏道, 若昏若亡; 下士昏道大笑之 The first dark (昏 *Hun*) is taken to be hear (聞 *wen*). The second *hun* 昏 (dark) is corrected based on the Mawangdui and received versions that have 存. The phonetic component *jin* 堇 could be barely (僅 *jin*) or cautious (謹 *jin*). The result is that the beginning of the sentence could be changed to "When the superior person hears the Dao, he is barely (or cautiously) able to put it into practice it averagely." Liao Mingchun 廖名春 *Guodian Chujian jiaoshi* 郭店楚簡校釋 (Beijing: Qinghua, 2003), 428–31.

33. In Guodian we see 弗大笑, 不足以爲道矣. *Fu* 弗 (not + the pronoun *zhi* 之) can be different from *bu* 不 (not). Liao feels that the *Fu* 弗 (not + pronoun) fits the grammar better in that the pronoun refers to the Dao. Pulleyblank points out that *Fu* 弗 is sometimes a substitute for *bu* 不 and that there are cases where the *bu* 不 negation has omitted the pronoun *zhi* 之. Edward Shaughnessy has recently called into question the strict variations among negatives by arguing that they are used much more fluidly in excavated manuscripts. Gao, *Boshu Laozi jiaozhu*, 18; Liao, *Guodian Chujian jiaoshi*, 433–34; *Outline of Classical Chinese Grammar*, 104–105; Edward Shaughnessy, *Rewriting Early Chinese Texts* (Albany: State University of New York Press, 2006), 37–42.
34. Ming, *Boshu Laozi jiaozhu*, 29.
35. This idea arose from a private conversation with Moss Roberts.
36. At a minimum, Xunzi's "Jiebi" 解蔽 chapter indicates that the first lines of the *Daode jing* were from an early time understood as referring to our inability to know the Dao. The prospect that the knowable way is distinct from the true Way provides a very different perspective on the text. It significantly shrinks the importance of the role of humans to the point of real insignificance. It is interesting that with the abrupt turn in the statement "that which can be...is not" we have a jarring moment that suddenly negates what has just been established as having a potential.
37. Tang Yijie, "'Dao shi yu qing' de zhexue quanshi—Wulun chuangjian Zhongguo jieshixue wenti."

APPENDIX

1. There is considerable disagreement on the arrangement of sections; this translation follows Li Ling's Guodian numbering system DGDJDJ. Most sources I cite in this translation have slight differences in the arrangement of slips. In fact, Li Ling uses a different order for his Shanghai edition, and Liu Zhao does not use sections at all DSHJDJ; LZ. What I think this means, more than anything, is that the ideas in the text interconnect in a number of ways. These different ways are explored in the preceding chapters of this book.
2. Shanghai has this variant transcription 生 (性) SHGJ, 220; Ding's version has a misprint so it appears oppositely as 性 (生) DSHGJ, 31. Li Ling simply leaves it as 性 *xing*, "nature," DGDJDJ, 18; DSHJDJ, 23.
3. Shanghai has 亡 *wu* in the transcription but explains in a note that it should be read as 無 *wu*, "not having," SHGJ, 221. 奠 *dian* can be transcribed as 定 *ding*, "fixed," 正 *zheng*, "straight," but their meaning in Chinese is quite similar as Ding notes DZLBX, 32.
4. For this and subsequent instances of this character there are different difficult to reproduce descendentless characters (DGDWW, 31 and SHDB, 154. Both agree that these characters represent *dai* 待. Another transcription of this character is 寺(待) DSHGJ, 31.
5. Another transcription of the original character is 乍 (作) SHGJ, 220 and SHDB, 154. Strangely, this is again reversed in Ding's edition so he has作 (乍) DSHGJ, 31.
6. The heart radical could also be placed at the bottom of the character descendentless character. The Wenwu edition has it on the side as shown here.
7. This transcription "丌" is not found in the Guodian edition, but it is in the Shanghai edition. The characters on both strips are similar so in this and subsequent instances I provide the transcription and then the modern equivalent GDWW, 61, 179; SHGJ, 220.

8. Here and in section 7, this character could also be 見(現)*xian*, "appear," SHDB, 154, 160.
9. An alternate transcription is 内 (納) *na*, "receive," SHDB, 154 and DGDWW, 31; Li Ling agrees with the modern equivalent but simply leaves it as 入, so this is what is followed DGDJDJ, 18 and DSHJDJ, 23.
10. This 所 *suo*, a grammatical particle, is missing in the Shanghai edition DSHJDJ, 23 DSHGJ, 32.
11. Shanghai has藝 *yi*, "skill," DSHGJ, 32.
12. This term出 *chu*, "emerge," is an important one to the text, but it has been impossible to find one single translation for it. Below, in this same section, it is translated as "express." Here are the other section numbers and translations: 2 "emanate," 5 and 6 "emit," 8 "inception," 9 two instances of "emanate," 13 "emanate," and 20 "express."
13. This 也 *ye* particle is not present in Li Ling's Guodian transcription, but it is present in his Shanghai version DGDJDJ, 18; DSHJDJ, 23. The reason for this is that the strip is broken in Guodian, but the character is present in Shanghai. After the character 鳴 *ming*, "ring," which ends the third Shanghai strip, the version is missing at least an entire strip DSHGJ, 60.
14. Shanghai Duben lists the following modern equivalents for the character as *gou* 鉤, "hook." The first is 扣 *kou*, "beat," the second is 敂 *kou*, "strike," the author feels that the correct character is *ji* 擊, "strike/beat," but this does not affect my translation SHDB, 158, n. 1.
15. Shanghai and Guodian are broken here; it is possible that these are the missing characters: 人之 *renzhi*, "For people," DGDJDJ, 18; DSHJDJ, 23.
16. After the end of strip 3, Shanghai is missing these bamboo strips; it resumes in section 4 where noted SHGJ, 225.
17. These characters are damaged on both Shanghai and Guodian versions. Based on context alone, text is interpolated as having the characters in parenthesis. The characters outside of the bracket are seen on the Guodian text but are missing from the Shanghai version. The Shanghai Duben has "not [able, the heart's not able to] act alone" 不 [可, 心之不可] 蜀 (獨) 行SHDB, 58. A more likely version is "not [able, the person not able to] act alone" 不[可, 人之不可]獨行 DGDJDJ, 18; Liu Zhao has the same except he places the comma after "person," LZ, 93.
18. This modern equivalent is from DGDJDJ, 18; an alternate character is *yan* 鴈, "goose," but this is just different readings of the Guodian since Shanghai is missing in this section. Either way, the meaning is the same since both characters mean "goose" DSHJDJ, 23; SHDB, 158.
19. Both Shanghai and Guodian versions are broken here, but based on context, Shanghai transcribes it as "its nature, [humans are born] and study" 丌(其)省(性) [也人生]而學 SHDB, 158. Liu Zhao has "its nature, [making it so people] and study" 丌 (其) 眚 (性) [使肰 (然), 人] 而學 LZ, 93. Liu Zhao has the same modern equivalents as Li Ling, but the latter does not provide the alternate transcriptions before the corrected characters DGDJDJ, 18; DSHJDJ, 23.
20. The Shanghai strip is still missing, but based on the Guodian calligraphy, it can also be transcribed "change" 變 or "differentiate" 辨 SHDB, 159. N. 4.
21. Shanghai is missing, but based on Guodian transcribes [其 (期)] SHDB, 158. The literal translation of this part is "nothing lacks a difference," but the double negative does not work well in English so it is translated "everything is different."
22. The Shanghai version resumes here. For the English translation, the term "within" is on the Shanghai strip, but the term "seas" precedes it and is missing. DSHGJ, 70.
23. Or its nature is unity or to unify.

24. Here and in the next instance of the character in section 6, Shanghai has 節 *jie*, "regulate," SHDB, 160. Ding argues that it can be read as 室 *shi*, "house/structure," or 實 *shi*, "solid." Either way, he feels that it should be a framework for nature DZLBX, 77. Ding's conclusion fits the Shanghai transcription, so it could be translated as "regulate." The problem is that the calligraphy in the Guodian version is the same here, and in the next instances of the character in section 16 of the text. The calligraphy is fairly clear in both sections, making the connection unproblematic. In section 16 the character clearly means "interact" because it is something you do to what is above and also below you. It does not make sense to regulate what is above, but interaction is fine. There is an additional parallel between the sections, in that they both include "purpose" 古 (故), *gu*, which I have translated as "special purpose." For images of the calligraphy, see GDWW, 61 and 65.
25. Shanghai has 礪 *li*, "whetstone," SHDB, 160; Liu Zhao has 萬 (礪) *li*, "whetstone," LZ, 94.
26. Here and in section 6, the character 出 *chu*, "emit," is believed to be a substitute for 絀 *chu*, "deficit," DGDJDJ, 18; DSHJDJ, 23–24; Ding argues that it should be 黜 *chu*, "harvest," DZLBX, 76–78. The calligraphy in both the Shanghai and Guodian versions is the same here as other instances of 出 *chu*, "emit." Since the term has an important role in the text, I do not agree with the substitution.
27. This list is not unlike *Daode jing* 51 where we are given a list of attributes that the Dao accomplishes, including nourishing them and growing them (all things).
28. Shanghai has 其 (己) *ji*, "oneself," SHDB, 161.
29. Another transcription is 設 *she*, "set up," DGDJDJ, 19.
30. Shanghai has the addition of the grammatical particle 也 *ye* prior to a break in the strip: 道也[者] DSHGJ, 83.
31. Here and in the previous sentence, this translation takes 群 *qun*, "all/group," as an adjective modifying the noun "materials"; see SHDB, 161. It is also possible that *qun* is a verb: "The Dao is the Dao that brings materials into a group."
32. This 道 *dao*, "Way," can be taken as 導 *dao*, "lead," making the translation "As for the other three techniques, they do no more than guide as an intermediary." SHDB, 164–65. I think it is less problematic to leave this character as 道 *dao* and translate it as "speak" because "no more than" is clearly trying to downplay the importance of *dao* and the previous sentence seems certainly not to be referring to "leading" for *dao*.
33. The character 論 *lun*, "discuss," is followed in most editions DGDJDJ, 19; DSHJDJ, 24; DSHGJ, 90. One unlikely possibility is 倫 *lun*, "categorize," DGDWW, 89.
34. 順 *Shun*, "restraint," is from the following editions: DGDJDJ, 19; DSHJDJ, 24.
35. This character is translated as "regulate," but it could also be translated as "rhythm" as in section 9 below.
36. Liu Zhao has 睾 (興) *xing*, "arise," LZ, 95.
37. *Mencius* 3A.3 explains that 序 *xu* is a term for "school" in the Shang Dynasty. This would change the translation to "prioritizes the school, thus the Dao is righteous." However, in the context of "prioritizing," it is more likely that *xu* means "sequence." For this and the next instance of the character 序·*xu*, "order," Chen Wei has 舍 (敍) *xu*, "order," CW, 222. This provides a further reason for not translating the character as "school."
38. Li Ling has 又 *you*, "again," but Ding follows the Wenwu and Guji editions, which has 或 *huo*, "something," ZLBX, 110–11.
39. The original transcription is 廟, but it is corrected in the notes to 貌 DZLBX, 108. This is also followed in the following DSHJDJ, 24; DGDJDJ, 19.

40. Paul Goldin cautions against unilaterally correcting 安 *an* as 焉 *yan* in excavated manuscripts because this imposes a received-text reading onto the tomb corpus. He argues that both terms have similar usages and are cognates. Paul R. Goldin, "The Old Chinese Particles *yan* 焉 and *an* 安," *Journal of the American Oriental Society* 123 (2003): 169–73; Paul R. Goldin, "A Further Note on *yan* 焉 and *an* 安," *Journal of the American Oriental Society* 124 (2004): 101–102.
41. Both Shanghai and Guodian are broken, but Shanghai has interpolated by Zhou Fengwu 周鳳五 as [為 敬也] *wei jing ye*, "create respect," SHDB, 165; Liao Mingchun 廖明春 has 為服也 *wei fu ye*, "create obedience"; see DZLBX, 117. Chen Wei leaves his transcription 為□也 *wei* □ *ye*, "create □," CW, 226, n. 50.
42. Zhang Guangyu 張光裕 transcribes this as *yu* 諛, "flatter," which should be read as 譽 *yu*, "praise/flatter" DZLBX, 116; SHDB, 173. Zhou Fengwu argues it should be read as 數 *shu*, "skill/technique," SHDB, 173.
43. Another possibility is 敏 *min*, "agile or quick," DGDJDJ, 19, but Ding has the following descendentless character 夏, which in an earlier occurrence he cites Li Tianhong 李天虹 who says it should be 文 *wen*, "embellishment, or language" DZLBX, 101–102. Li's reading is followed here.
44. Chen Wei has 徵 *zheng*, "verify," in his text; he explains in his notes that the compilers have it as 證 *zheng*, "verify," CW, 222 and 226, n. 52.
45. This is based on the Shanghai transcription DSHGJ, 90; Li Ling has 辭 *ci*, "explain." Chen Wei has 詞 *ci*, "word/language," DGDJDJ, 19; DSHJDJ, 24; CW, 222.
46. For this and the next instance of 禮 *li*, "ritual," Shanghai has 喜 *xi*, "happy," and Chen Wei follows Shanghai DSHGJ, 90; DSHJDJ,,24; CW, 222.
47. 人們所說的 "四術", 只有以忠愛為內容的人道可被稱道之外, 其他三術, 只不過說說罷了.

    As for what people call the "four techniques," it is only the Dao of humans, taking the substance of loyalty and love that can be referred to as outside the Dao. The other three techniques are merely to be discussed and that is all. Tu and Liu, *Guodian chujian xianqin rujia yishu jiaoshi*, 153.
48. Instead of a "second usage" of the classics, it could be that their use for instructing is something that happens after the process of formation has been fulfilled. A similar usage of the term is found in the *Analects* where Zhuxi 朱熹 notes that 復 *fu* means 踐言 *jianyan*, "fulfill a promise," DZLBX, 104.
49. This translation is adapted from Paul Goldin's in *After Confucius*: "The sages compared the categories [of the classics] and, expounding on these, assembled [the people]; they observed the sequences [of the classics] and restrained and instructed [the people]; they embodied the morality [of the classics] and ordered [the people]; they organized their *qing* and expressed [what should be expressed] and brought inside [what should be brought inside oneself]." Paul R. Goldin, *After Confucius: Studies in Early Chinese Philosophy* (Honolulu: University of Hawai'i Press, 2005), 41. I see the passage describing a progression leading up to the internalization of the classics by the sage instead of being directly used to instruct the people. I see the process of instructing others only occurring after the sage internalized the classics. This reads the term "again" to mean that once the sage has created them and been transformed by this process, they are once again used for the benefit of others.
50. "Etiquette" is the translation for 節 *jie*, "measure/regulate," because etiquette is related to the way your actions become regulated in a ritual context. The ritual context is seen in two sentences previous to this.
51. In this passage, the change in tense is a product of my English translation; such nuances are not part of classical Chinese. The turning point I selected is the Dao

because of the transition in section 16 that occurs when a person has the wisdom of the Dao.

52. Cook has an important argument relating this passage to the human locus of morality. Scott Cook, "The Debate over Coercive Rulership and the 'Human Way' in Light of Recently Excavated Warring States Texts," *Harvard Journal of Asiatic Studies* 64, 2 (December 2004): 399–440.
53. In this section, *ye* 也 is being taken as an auxiliary particle representing a pause in the thought process. HYDCD, 50.
54. 逍建偉 Xiao Jianwei read this as 撥動 *bodong*, "moved," SHDB, 176.
55. Chen Wei has 厚 *hou*, "thick," CW, 222.
56. This character 斯 *si* is being taken as 而 *er*, "and/or/therefore," DZLBX, 126.
57. Chen Wei has 舀 *yao*, "ladle," but in his note he reads it as 慆 *tao*, "happy," CW 222, 227, n. 57. The character is translated "carefree" in the text to create contrast with 鬱陶 *yutao*, which means "happy but worried." Please see the footnote in section 12 for more information on *yutao*.
58. This character was originally transcribed as 難 *nan*, "difficult," but it should be read as 歎 *tan*, which means "lament" DZLBX, 128.
59. Ding has 齊 *qi*, "even," being read as 憤 *qi*, "angry," DZLBX, 127; in his further interpretation he also offers 齋 *zhai*, "upright or dignified," as a preferred alternative DZLBX, 129
60. This can also be transcribed as 儉 *jian* "frugal" DZLBX, 127, 129; CW, 222.
61. This is from Liu Zhao's version, LZ, 97; Li Ling agrees with the modern equivalent DSHJDJ, 24.
62. Ding explains 節 *jie* as 節拍 *jiepai*, "meter or rhythm"; Li Ling has 次 *ci*, "sequence." Liu Zhao is cited in the SHDB as explaining the phrase as follows: 遵循節奏要持久，重新開始慎重 "Following the rhythm has to be enduring, start anew with caution" DZLBX, 133; DGDJDJ, 19; DSHJDJ, 24; SHDB, 179–80. 節 *jie* can also mean moderation, so this could also be read as "dwelling in moderation" with dwelling being taken as a metaphorical statement.
63. Others take "trustworthy" as a modifier of the way sounds come from the *qing*. "As for sounds generally, if they emerge in a trustworthy manner from the *qing*, then they will enter and stir up people's hearts profoundly." Goldin, "Xunzi in the Light of the Guodian Manuscripts," 46. This is similar to the Shanghai Duben 聲音，能真正地出自人情... "sounds, if they are able to come from a person's *qing* in a genuine manner..." SHDB, 175. I follow Ding's reading that there is no "if" implied in the sentence 凡聲音出自於真實的情感，其感入人心必將深厚. "All sounds that come authentically from our emotions, the feeling enters people's hearts it will inevitably be deep."
64. Ding cites a note in Lin Ling's *Guodian jian jiaoduji* 郭店簡 校讀記, stating: '鮮如' 猶 '粲然.' "Xianru" is like "smiling broadly" DZLBX, 126; SHCJSP,124.
65. This term 悸 *ji* often refers to being moved in an alarmed fashion as in when you are scared. There seems no reason for a negative connotation here, so moved should just mean the way you feel when your heart skips a beat in an excited but positive manner.
66. Another possible reading comes from Ding, who cites Li Tianhong's explanation of 始 *shi*, "start" 滋息, as proliferate. In addition, Ding points out that the starting and ending are assigned important philosophical meaning in section 1 of the text "When you start you are close to *qing*, when you end you are close to righteousness. Those who know *qing* can express it; those who know righteousness are able to internalize it." DZLBX, 133–34.

67. This refers to 淫樂 yinyue, "licentious music," DZLBX, 141–42.
68. For a discussion of the relationship between *Analects* 7:14 where Confucius states that hearing Shao music resulted in not noticing the taste of meat for three months, see Tang Yijie, Brian Bruya, and Hai-ming Wen, "Emotion in Pre-Qin Ruist Moral Theory: An Explanation of 'Dao Begins in Qing'" *Philosophy East and West* 53, 2 (April 2003), 273. A further discussion of music in the "Xing zi ming chu" can be found here: Yao Haiyan 姚海燕 and Sun Wenzhong 孫文鐘, "Zhanguo Chu zhushujian 'Xingqing lun' de yue jiao sixiang yu xiandai yinyue liaofa" 戰國楚竹書簡《性情論》的樂教思想與現代音樂療法, *Zhong yiyao wenhua* 中醫藥文化, 2006.5.
69. This is based on an explanation by Li Xueqin 李學勤 DZLBX, 140–41.
70. Ding cites Li Xueqin who quotes the Book of Odes where 龍 long, "dragon," means 和 he, "harmony," DZLBX, 140; Ding explains 指 zhi, "finger/point," as meaning "intention" in the Book of Documents DZLBX, 142. My sense is that the text is seeing the various positive *and* negative elements of our world as equally capable of assisting us in our quest for self-cultivation.
71. The original Guodian transcription is interchangeable with 浸 jin, "soak," so it does not affect the translation DGDWW, 146.
72. Shanghai has 焊 han, "to dry with fire," thus dry eyes and no tears would be the translation DSHGJ, 146; DSHJDJ, 25. Ding says that 焊 han should be 悍 han, "brave," so "crying bravely" DZLBX, 150; Ding also considers that a character closer to the original transcription 殺 sha, "cut off," would mean "despondent and cut off from others" DZLBX, 151–52. In the end the characters are describing a situation where someone is crying SHDB 185–86.
73. This is the modern equivalent from Li Ling DSHJDJ, 25; DGDJDJ, 19. Liao Mingchun notes that this term *lie* 烈, "intense," here refers to the apprehension of facing the preservation of life dying out 即面對存身絕滅的惶惑 DZLBX, 151–52. In section 18, this intensity is something to be avoided in our interactions with others.
74. Liu Zhao explains 戀戀 lianlian as 依依不舍 yiyibushe, "unable to bear parting" LZ, 98.
75. This is the modern equivalent from Li Ling DSHJDJ, 25; DGDJDJ, 20
76. This translation comes from a discussion of a similar usage in the Book of Odes where 戚 qi is defined as 憂 you, "anguish or worry"; see *Shijing* 詩經《詩•小雅•小明》, 447; DZLBX, 152–53. However, 戚 qi also refers to familial feelings of kinship, so it could be anguish of this sort. Chen Wei has 慼 qi, "anguish," CW, 223.
77. *Yutao* 鬱陶 is somewhat problematic to translate. The two characters are used together in the Book of Documents to refer to a melancholy state. In *Mencius* the characters are said by Emperor Shun's brother Xiang. Xiang wants to kill Shun, so when he enters his bedroom he masks his homicidal intentions by saying "I am thinking of you" 鬱陶思君. The state of Xiang's thoughts are described as *yutao*, which should mean "concern or worry," but it is not a straightforward usage. Independently, the character *yu* means "melancholy" and *tao* means "happy." In the Book of Rites *yutao* means "happy." so a reader of the "Xing zi ming chu" could have taken the characters either as sad or happy. Here the characters could be translated as either "pensive" or "happy but not at ease," which is why "giddy" is used. The idea is that there is a happy mental state but not one free of concern. The transcription of *yutao* is from Zhou Fengwu, CW, 228, n. 75.
78. The characters are 流如 liuru, "flowingly." The context is sad, thus the flowing of tears would be tearful.

79. Li Ling and the original Shanghai transcription have 歎 *tan*, "lamentation," which fits better with the context of the next two sentences that continue to discuss sound and also *yin* 吟, which means "chant or recite," DGDJDJ, 20; DSHJDJ, 25; DSHGJ, 156. In fact, *tan* 歎 is defined as *yin* 吟, "chant/recite," in the *Shuowen*; the problem is that it does not convey the necessary sadness of a lamentation. Jiang, *Shuowen Jiezi Jizhu*, vol. 2, 1844. Ding has 難 *nan*, "difficult," here and in strip 34 below. This would make the sentence "Difficulty provides a method for your thinking" DZLBX, 158.
80. The Guodian strip is broken here, but the Shanghai is not DGDJDJ, 20; DSHJDJ, 25.
81. Shanghai is broken here, so the four characters that start this sentence are from Guodian. Modern equivalents are from Li Ling, original transcriptions from Guodian Wenwu DGDJDJ, 20; DSHJDJ, 25; DGDWW, 156. There is an unlikely transcription in Chen Wei's text; he has 唫 *jin*, "mouth shut" CW, 223.
82. Ding notes that 遊 *you* means 流露 *liulou*, "subconsciously reveal your feelings or thoughts," DZLBX, 160.
83. Modern equivalents are from Li Ling; the original transcription is from Guodian and Shanghai. The end of this sentence is the end of the Shanghai version for section 12 DGDJDJ, 20; DSHJDJ, 25; DGDWW, 156; DSHWW, 156.
84. Li Ling has 嘔 *ou*, "sing," DGDJDJ, 20; DSHJDJ, 25. Ding argues that 謳 *ou*, "sing," is preferable DZLBX, 162.
85. The twelve characters preceding this endnote mark are from the top of Shanghai strip 21.
86. This transcription and equivalent are based on Liu Zhao. Li Ling only provides a modern equivalent, but it is in agreement LZ, 99; DGDJDJ, 20.
87. This character 辟 *pi*, "to slap one's chest," is sometimes transcribed as 拊 *fu*, "clap/pat," or 撫 *fu*, "pat," but the impact on the meaning is negligible DZLBX, 167. The transcription and equivalent are based on Liu Zhao. Li Ling only provides a modern equivalent, but it is in agreement LZ, 99; DGDJDJ, 20.
88. 忻 *Xin*, "happy or joyous," is translated as "delight."
89. "Resonance" is the same word translated as "sound" above; the character is (聖) 聲 *sheng*, which means "sound" but is a cognate for *sagacity*, so sound and moral cultivation are subtly connected.
90. The character 通 *tong* is explained as relating to 踊 *yong*, "leap/hop," or 踴 *yong*, "leap/hop"; the character is translated as "hop" as in "hopping mad" DZLBX, 167.
91. From here to the end of strip 49 come after the characters 谷後 *gu hou* on strip 62 in the Shanghai Duben text SHDB, 191–203; Ding numbers this section as 19 DZLBX, 220.
92. Shanghai has 凡教者求其心有偽也 "Of all who teach, seeking the heart creates" DSHJDJ, 26; SHGJ, 265; Ding argues that 偽 *wei*, "create/false," should be 為*wei*, "to be," DZLBX, 221–26. The Shanghai Duben agrees with Ding SHDB, 204–205. Based on the usage in Xunzi of 偽 *wei* meaning "what is made by people," especially ritual, I follow the SHGJ transcription in my translation.
93. Li Ling transcribes this 為 *wei*, "create," and the one in the next sentence is transcribed as 偽 *wei*, "false." The original Wenwu edition has 為 *wei*, "create"; Chen Wei has 為 (偽) *wei*, "false." DGDJDJ, 20; DGDWW, 220; CW, 229.
94. This 不 is from the Shanghai version, Guodian is broken here DSHJDJ, 26; DSHWW, 220; DSHGJ, 220.
95. This is based on Li Ling. Liu Zhao leaves it 安 *an*, "how," DGDJDJ, 20; LZ, 100.

96. Some scholars argue that this should be 東(柬/簡) jian, "admonish," due to the phrase in the "Five Aspects of Conduct" where we have 簡, 義之方 "admonishing is the method of righteousness," but the characters are very different in "Xing zi ming chu." Liu Zhao has it transcribed as 恕 shu, "reciprocity," except this character is more commonly associated with 仁 ren, "humanity," than with righteousness. Cha 察, "investigate," seems the most reasonable of the proposed characters. It also fits the context of " The Five Aspects of Conduct" where investigation relates to serious crimes that involve capital punishment. DZLBX, 226–28; LZ, 100.

97. Ding's analysis is closest to "Ordered by bliss" for 樂之速. I used the word *bliss* to indicate a deep, spiritual type of happiness. Another acceptable translation of 樂 is "music" and the dual meaning of the term would not have been lost on Warring States readers. This would make the phrase "ordered by music," and with ritual being a common partner with music, the ability of these to produce order is unproblematic. I have followed the translation of 速 *su* as "speed," and in this context it would point to the powerful efficacy of music or bliss in the development of a person's moral cultivation. Of these options, Ding does not agree with 樂 as either simple "joy" or "music" but sees it as a part of our cultivation that brings a deeper type of happiness. He also argues that "order" is preferable to "speed" for 速 *su* DZLBX, 224. Following his reading, the passage would read: "Of all who cultivate, seeking one's heart is difficult, you obtain it by following what you are near, but this is not as good as being ordered by bliss."

98. An alternative translation could be "Do not act excessively."

99. Paul Goldin has demonstrated the problem with this translation of the character 忠 *zhong* since it is the way a minion serves a superior as well as the way that a superior serves those of lower status. Loyalty can only be exhibited from one of lower status to something that it greater, but *zhong* is reciprocal since it works both ways. Despite the problem, it is difficult to find a good substitute. Paul R. Goldin, "When zhong 忠 Does Not Mean 'Loyalty,'" *Dao* 7, 2 (2008): 165–74.

100. Qiu Xigui notes that this might also be *bian* 變, which Ding explains through a *Liji* reference could be 動 *dong*, "move." Ding's preferred explanation, which I follow in my translation, is also based on a *Liji* note where 弁 *bian* is explained as simply meaning 急 *ji*, "urgent," DZLBX, 239–40. Li Ling has 忭 *bian*, "happy," DGDJDJ, 20; DSHJDJ, 27.

101. Here and in the next sentence, Chen Wei has 柬(簡) 柬(簡) *jianjian*, "grand," CW, 230.

102. Li Ling has 始 *shi*, "start," but Liao Mingchun feels it should be 殆 *dai*, "danger." He explains that when you treat people magnanimously but do not have an upright will, your conscience will lack concern, you will not be careful, and then you will be disrespectful. "這是說為人寬大, 但如果沒有常危之志, 沒有憂患意識, 就會輕慢而不上心." DZLBX 244.

103. This character is from Ding's explanation. Li Ling has 縵 *man*, "plain silk," in his Guodian version and 慢 *man*, "slow," in his Shanghai version DZLBX, 24; DGDJDJ, 21; DSHJDJ, 27.

104. Li Ling has 辭, Ding has 詞, which is closer to the Chu character DGDJDJ, 21; DSHJDJ, 27; DZLBX, 244.

105. Shanghai has 慧 *hui*, "intelligent/wise," but there is some similarity with the meaning of 快 *kuai*, "sharp," DZLBX, 247.

106. The Shanghai strip is broken. This character is from Li Ling' see DZLBX, 248.

107. See note 77 in section 11 for an explanation.

108. The literal translation "their restraints are restrained" is too awkward.
109. 采 *Cai*, "false adornment," DZLBX, 243.
110. Section 17 has a similar character 悋, except in section 15 it does not have the heart radical 忄 on the left. Guodian originally explained the character in section 15 as 文 *wen*, "culture." Based on its usage in the Mawangdui *Laozi* where it is a substitute for 鄰 *lin*, "neighbor," Ding feels it could be read as 憐 *lian*, "pitiful." He also explains it as 矜 *jin*, "pity," ZLBX, 252. I believe that Li Ling's transcription of 吝 *lin* works best here and can be understood best as "regret," but the next best meaning would be "stingy" DGDJDJ, 21; DSHJDJ, 27. Chen Wei reads this character as 隱 *yin*, "conceal," CW, 230.
111. In section 20 this becomes a positive term, "consider," but here it is translated "schemers" because section 16 is describing someone who is incorrect.
112. Li Ling has 貪富 *tanfu*, "having wealth," but Ding argues that 貪 *tan* is interchangeable with 含 *han*, "contain/conceal," that it should be 含福 *hanfu* "concealed wealth," explaining that it means the same as 含德 *hande*, "concealed virtue," so the wealth is moral in nature, not material DGDJDJ, 21; DSHJDJ, 25; DZLBX, 178–79. I appreciate the assistance of Dr. John S. Major in retooling my translation of this passage.
113. GDWW, 169, n. 9.
114. See DZLBX, 181.
115. Shanghai has the addition of the character 眾 *zhong*, "many," here: 下交得眾 DSHJDJ, 25; DSHGJ, 174; CW, 230.
116. This is based on the Shanghai version, which is quite clear. The Guodian strip is broken.
117. Ding explains this as 樂逸 *lemian*, "at ease/carefree," Chen Wei has 宛 *wan*, "winding/bent," DZLBX, 191–92; CW, 230.
118. There is a good chance that the rest of this paragraph is describing the characteristics of a leader, either political or religious. The Chinese text does not specify this, but the implication of the context is that the ideal person in question is acting as a leader.
119. Here and in the next sentences the character for "reflecting" is *fan* 反, which can also mean "oppose."
120. The character for body, *shen* 身, can also be translated as "self," but it should not be confused with a physical entity unconnected with a moral project. Guodian texts in particular emphasize the physical changes that occur as a result of moral cultivation, and it is for this reason that the character is not translated merely as "self."
121. This probably refers to family. In other cases, it could be people from the same teacher such as classmates except that regulation for such a group would seem unlikely.
122. Li Ling has 悅 *yue*, "happy." Ding says this should be read as 說服 *shuifu*, "persuade," DGDJDJ, 21; DSHJDJ, 26; DZLBX, 212.
123. Ding explains this as 吝嗇 *linse*, "stingy/miserly," but to me the context seems closer to another meaning of *lin*, which is "regret." Chen Wei reads this character as 隱 *yin*, "conceal," DZLBX, 212; CW, 230.
124. The characters appearing on Shanghai strip 29 are divided between section 17 and 20.
125. Li Ling transcribes this as 烈 *lie*, "intense," but Ding cites Li Ling's notes as saying that the character is the original form of 剌 *la*, "extreme," which is used

in the DGDJDJ, 21; DSHJDJ, 26; DZLBX, 213. In section 11, this intensity is emotional and related to crying.

126. Shanghai has 道路 *daolu*, "road," which could also be translated as "pathways," but consistency with other sections seems more important than sensitivity to one edition.

    Li Ling transcribes 悢 *wei*, "afraid," as 思 *si*, "think," for the Shanghai version. This would make it: "Of all the Dao, do not think, do not speak alone." DSHJDJ, 26.

127. Chen Wei has 納 *na*, "enter," CW, 231. Ding explains this as 容納 *rongna*, "tolerate." DZLBX, 217.

128. The characters from this endnote mark to the start of the section are from Shanghai strip 31.

129. Shanghai and Guodian versions can also be transcribed as 遣 *qian*, "send/dispatch." Ding explains that the character could mean 過 *guo*, "exceed," 感 *gan*, "emotion," or 撼 *han*, "shake/shock," DZLBX 198–200.

130. Shanghai has 異 *yi*, "different," instead of 偽 *wei*, "false." After this, there are the following characters, which are not found in Guodian: "退欲緊而毋輕口欲口而有禮言欲直而毋流;局處欲逸易而毋漫。" Shanghai resumes with the following Guodian characters "君子執志必又" DSHGJ, 197.

131. The Guodian Wenwu edition and Chen Wei have this character as 拔 *ba*, "exceed," DGDWW, 196; CW, 231. Ding explains the meaning of 伐 *fa* as "arrogant" DZLBX, 200.

132. It is possible that the character for heart, 心 *xin*, should appear before this character as follows: 杲(伐), 心谷(欲) DGDJDJ, 22; DZLBX, 200–201.

133. This is taken as 齋 *zhai*, "purify," DZLBX, 201.

134. Li Ling's transcription is 有 *you*, "have." 又有 *Youyou*, "also have," is from the original Guodian transcription DGDJDJ, 22; DGDWW, 196.

135. Another transcription is 斂 *lian*, "hold back/restrain," DGDJDJ, 22; CW, 231.

136. Li Ling has 盈 *ying*, "full," but Ding argues that 湼 *ying*, "full," should be used DGDJDJ, 22; DZLBX, 202.

137. Chen Wei follows Zhou Fengwu in reading this 暴 *bao*, "ferocious," CW, 231, 235, n. 53.

138. Chen Wei Reads this as 文 *wen*, "culture," CW, 231.

139. This can be read as 柬柬 *jianjian*, "big," 簡簡 *jianjian*, "simple/easy," or 謇謇 *jianjian*, "upright/loyal." The only combination that appears in other pre-Han texts is the last 謇謇, so it is followed in my translation DZLBX 207–208.

140. There are an additional four characters after this point at the end of the Shanghai strip 29, but they are moved to section 17.

141. The last sentence is missing from Shanghai.

142. The character 柔 *rou*, "soft," is taken by Liao Mingchun as 務 *wu*, "serve/attend," which would make the phrase "you should want to attend to purity and tranquility" DZLBX, 201.

143. A smoother translation is "words that you say," but I am trying to stay closer to the literal meaning of "emitting words" in keeping with the importance of the term "emit" 出 in the text.

BIBLIOGRAPHY

MODERN SOURCES

Ai Lan 艾蘭, and Xing Wen 邢文, eds. *Xinchu jianbo yanjiu: Xinchu jianbo guoji yantaohui lunwenji* 新出簡帛研究: 新出簡帛國際研討會論文集. *Beijing daxue zhendan gudai wenming yanjiu zhongxin xueshu congshu* 8. Beijing: Wenwu, 2004.

Ames, Roger T. "The Focus-Field Self in Classical Confucianism." In Ames et al. *Self As Person in Asian Theory and Practice*. Albany: State University of New York Press, 1994.

Ames, Roger T., et al. *Self As Person in Asian Theory and Practice*. Albany: State University of New York Press, 1994.

Andreini, Attilio. "The Meaning of *Qing* 情 in Texts from Guodian Tomb No. 1." In *Love, Hatred, and Other Passions: Questions and Themes on Emotions in Chinese Civilization*. Paolo Santangelo and Donatella Guida, eds. Leiden: Brill, 2006.

Angle, Stephen C. *Human Rights and Chinese Thought: A Cross-Cultural Inquiry*. New York: Cambridge University Press, 2002.

———. *Sagehood: The Contemporary Significance of Neo-Confucian Philosophy*. New York: Oxford University Press, 2009.

de Bary, Wm. Theodore. *The Trouble with Confucianism*. Cambridge, MA: Harvard University Press, 1991.

———. "The Uses of Neo-Confucianism: A Response to Professor Tillman." *Philosophy East and West* 43, 3 (July 1993): 541–55.

de Bary, Wm. Theodore, and Tu Weiming, eds. *Confucianism and Human Rights*. New York: Columbia University Press, 1998.

Bell, Daniel A., and Hahm Chaibong, eds. *Confucianism for the Modern World*. New York: Cambridge University Press, 2003.

Berthrong, John. *Expanding Process: Exploring Philosophical and Theological Transformations in China and the West*. Albany: State University of New York Press, 2008.

Brindley, Erica Fox. *Individualism in Early China*. Honolulu: University of Hawai'i Press, 2010.

Brooks, E. Bruce, and A. Taeko Brooks. *The Original Analects: Sayings of Confucius and His Successors*. New York: Columbia University Press, 1998.

Brown, Michael F. "Cultural Relativism 2.0." *Current Anthropology* 49, 3 (June 2008): 363–83.

Chan, Alan K. L. *Two Visions of the Way: a study of the Wang Pi and the Ho-Shang Kung commentaries on the Lao-Tzu*. Albany: State University of New York Press, 1991.

Chan, Shirley. "Human Nature and Moral Cultivation in the Guodian 郭店 Text of the Xing zi mingchu 性自命出 (Nature Derives from Mandate)." *Dao* 8, 4 (2009): 361–82.

Chan, Wing-tsit. *Chu Hsi and Neo-Confucianism*. Honolulu: University of Hawai'i Press, 1986.

Chen, Fubin 陳福濱, ed. *Xinchu Chujian yu Rujia sixiang lunwenji* 新出楚簡與儒家思想論文集. Taipei: Furen Daxue, 2002.

Chen, Guying 陳鼓應. "Taiyi sheng shui yu 'Xing zi mingchu' fawei"《太一生水》與《性自命出》發微. *Dongfang wenhua* 東方文化 5 (1999): 30–36. Reprinted in *Daojia wenhua yanjiu* 道家文化研究 17 (1999): 393–411.

Chen, Lai 陳來. "Guodian Chujian zhi 'Xing zi mingchu' pian chutan" 郭店楚簡之《性自命出》篇初探. *Kongzi yanjiu* 孔子研究 3 (1998): 52–60. Reprinted as "Jingmen chujian zhi 'Xing zhi ming chu' pian chutan" in *Guodian Chujian yanjiu. Zhongguo zhexue* 郭店楚簡研究中國哲學 20 (1999): 293–314.

———. "'Xing zi mingchu': Chenshui le liangqian yu nian de wenxian"《性自命出》：沉睡了兩千餘年的文獻. *Wenshi zhishi* 文史知識 9 (1999): 41–45.

Chen, Ligui 陳麗桂. "'Xing qing lun' shuo 'Dao'"《性情論》說"道." In *Shangboguan cang Zhanguo Chu zhushu yanjiu* 上博館藏戰國楚竹書研究. Zhu Yuanqing and Liao Mingchun, eds. Shanghai: Shudian 2002–2004.

———. "'Xing qing lun' shuo 'xing,' 'qing'"《性情論》說"性"、"情." In *Xin chutu wenxian yu gudai wenming yanjiu* 新出土文獻與古代文明研究. Xie Weiyang and Zhu Yuanqing, eds. Shanghai: Shanghai Daxue, 2004.

Chen, Tongsheng 陳桐生. "Zhexue‧Lixue‧Shixue—tan 'Xing qing lun' yu 'Kongzi shilun' de xueshu lianxi" 哲學‧禮學‧詩學—談《性情論》與《孔子詩論》的學術聯係. *Zhongguo zhexueshi* 中國哲學史 4 (2004): 77–84.

Chen, Wei 陳偉. "Guodianjianshu 'Xingzimingchu' jiaoshi" 郭店簡書《性自命出》校釋. In *Xin chutu wenxian yu gudai wenming yanjiu* 新出土文獻與古代文明研究. Xie Weiyang and Zhu Yuanqing, eds. Shanghai: Shanghai Daxue, 2004.

Chen, Wei 陳偉 et al. *Chudi chutu Zhanguo jian ce (Shisan zhong)* 楚地出土戰國簡冊(十三種). Beijing: Jingji kexue, 2009.

Chen, Zhaoying 陳昭瑛. "Xingqing zhong ren: Shi cong Chu wenhua lun *Guodian Chujian* 'Xing qing pian'" 性情中人：試從楚文化論《郭店楚簡‧性情篇》. *Guodian Chujian guoji xueshu yantaohui lunwenji* 郭店楚簡國際學術研討會論文集. Wuhan: Hubei renmin chubanshe, 2000.

Cook, Scott. "Zhuang Zi and his Carving of the Confucian Ox." *Philosophy East and West* 47, 4 (1997): 521–53.

———. "The Debate over Coercive Rulership and the 'Human Way' in Light of Recently Excavated Warring States Texts." *Harvard Journal of Asiatic Studies* 64, 2 (December 2004): 399–440.

Creel, H. G. *Confucius and the Chinese Way*. New York: Harper and Row, 1960.

Csikszentmihalyi, Mark, and Philip J. Ivanhoe, eds. *Religious and Philosophical Aspects of Laozi*. Albany: State University of New York Press, 1999.

Ding, Sixin 丁四新. "'Xing zi mingchu' yu Gongsun Nizi de guanxi"《性自命出》與公孫尼子的關係. *Wuhan Daxue xuebao (Zheshe ban)* 武漢大學學報 (哲社版) 5 (1999): 38–41.

———. "Lun Kongzi yu Guodian Rujian de tianming, tiandao guan" 論孔子與郭店儒簡的天命、天道觀. *Xiangtan shifan xueyuanbao* 湘潭師範學報 21, 5 (2000): 25–29.

———. "Lun 'Xing zi mingchu' yu Simeng xuepai de guanxi" 論《性自命出》與思孟學派的關係. *Zhongguo zhexue shi* 中國哲學史 4 (2000): 28–35.

———. "Lun Guodian Chujian 'qing' de neihan" 論郭店楚簡"情"的內涵. *Xiandai zhexue* 現代哲學 4 (2003): 61–68.

———. "Lun Guodian Chujian 'qing' de neihan" 論郭店楚簡"情"的內涵. *Chudi jianbo sixiang yanjiu* 楚地簡帛思想研究 2 (2004): 135–66.

Ding, Yuanming 丁原明. "Guodian rujian 'xing,' qing' shuo tanwei" 郭店儒簡"性"、"情"說探微. *Qilu xuekan* 齊魯學刊 1(2002): 35–42.

Ding, Yuanzhi 丁原植. *Chujian Rujia xingqingshuo yanjiu* 楚簡儒家性情說研究. *Chutu wenxian yizhu yanxi congshu* 出土文獻譯注研析叢書 P015. Taipei: Wanjuanlou, 2002.

———. "Chujian Rujia yiji de xingqing shuo" 楚簡儒家佚籍的性情說. In *Xinchu Chujian yu Rujia sixiang lunwenji* 新出楚簡與儒家思想論文集. Chen Fubin, ed. Taipei: Furen Daxue, 2002. Reprinted in *Xin chutu wenxian yu gudai wenming yanjiu* 新出土文獻與古代文明研究. Xie Weiyang and Zhu Yuanqing, eds. Shanghai: Shanghai Daxue, 2004.

Dongfang, Shuo 東方朔. "'Xing zi mingchu' pian de xinxing guannian chutan" 《性自命出》篇的心性觀念初探. *Guodian Chujian guoji xueshu yantaohui lunwenji* 郭店楚簡國際學術研討會論文集. Wuhan: Hubei renmin chubanshe, 2000.

Eifring, Halvor, ed. *Love and Emotions in Traditional Chinese Literature*. Sinica Leidensia 63. Leiden: Brill, 2004.

von Falkenhausen, Lothar. *Suspended Music: Chime-Bells in the Culture of Bronze Age China*. Berkeley: University of California Press, 1993.

———. *Chinese Society in the Age of Confucius (1000–250 BC): The Archaeological Evidence*. Los Angeles: Cotsen Institute of Archaeology, 2006.

Feng, Shengjun 馮勝君. "'Xing qing lun' shouju 'Fan ren sui you sheng' xinjie" 《性情論》首句"凡人雖有生"新解. *Jianbo* 簡帛 2 (2007): 227–29.

Gao, Huaping 高華平. "Lunshu *Guodian Chumu zhujian* 'Xing zi mingchu' de Daojia sixiang" 論述《郭店楚墓竹簡‧性自命出》的道家思想. *Guodian Chujianguoji xueshu yantaohui lunwenji* 郭店楚簡國際學術研討會論文集. Wuhan: Hubei renmin chubanshe, 2000.

Goldin, Paul R. "The Old Chinese Particles yan 焉 and an 安." *Journal of the American Oriental Society* 123 (2003): 169–73.

———. "A Further Note on yan 焉 and an 安." *Journal of the American Oriental Society* 124 (2004): 101–102.

———. "Xunzi in the Light of the Guodian Manuscripts." *Early China* 25 (2000): 113–46. Reprinted in Paul R. Goldin. *After Confucius: Studies in Early Chinese Philosophy*. Honolulu: University of Hawai'i Press, 2005.

———. *After Confucius: Studies in Early Chinese Philosophy*. Honolulu: University of Hawai'i Press, 2005.

———. "When zhong 忠 Does Not Mean 'Loyalty.'" *Dao* 7, 2 (2008): 165–74.

———. *Confucianism*. Berkeley: University of California Press, 2011.

———. "Persistent Misconceptions about Chinese 'Legalism.'" *Journal of Chinese Philosophy* 38, 1 (2011): 88–104.

Graham, A. C. *Disputers of the Tao: Philosophical Argument in Ancient China*. La Salle, IL: Open Court, 1989.

———. "The Background of the Mencian Theory of Human Nature." *Tsing Hua Journal of Chinese Studies* 6 (1967): 215–71. Reprinted in A. C. Graham. *Studies in Chinese Philosophy and Philosophical Literature*. Albany: State University of New York Press, 1990.

Guo, Lihua 郭梨華. "'Xing qing lun' yu 'Xing zi mingchu' zhong guanyu 'qing' de zhexue tansuo" 《性情論》與《性自命出》中關於"情"的哲學探索. In *Xin chutu wenxian yu gudai wenming yanjiu* 新出土文獻與古代文明研究. Xie Weiyang and Zhu Yuanqing, eds. Shanghai: Shanghai Daxue, 2004.

Guo, Qiyong 郭齊勇. "Guodian Chujian 'Xing zi mingchu' de xinshuguan" 郭店楚簡《性自命出》的心術觀. *Anhui Daxue xuebao: Zheshe ban* 安徽大學學報（哲社版）5 (2000): 48–53. Reprinted in *Gumu xinzhi* 古墓新知. Pang Pu et al. *Chutu sixiang wenwu yu wenxian yanjiu congshu* 10. Taipei: Taiwan Guji, 2002.

———. "Guodian Chujian 'Xing zi mingchu,' 'Wuxing' fawei" 郭店楚簡《性自命出》、《五行》發微. *Chudi chutu jianbo wenxian sixiang yanjiu* 楚地出土簡帛文獻思想研究 1 (2002): 1–21.

Graham, A. C. *Disputers of the Tao: Philosophical Argument in Ancient China*. Chicago: Open Court, 1999.

Guo, Yi 郭沂. "'Xing zi mingchu' dui Zisi renxinglun de yangqi" 《性自命出》對子思人性論的揚棄. In *Jianbo kaolun* 簡帛考論. Liu, Dajun 劉大鈞, ed. Shanghai: Guji, 2007.

Guo, Zhenxiang 郭振香. "'Xing zi mingchu' xing qing lun bianxi—Jianlun qi xuepai guishu wenti" 《性自命出》性情論辨析—兼論其學派歸屬問題. *Kongzi yanjiu* 孔子研究 2 (2005): 25–32.

Hall, David L., and Roger T. Ames. *Thinking Through Confucius*. Albany: State University of New York Press, 1987.

———. *Thinking from the Han: Self, Truth, and Transcendence in Chinese and Western Culture*. Albany: State University of New York Press, 1997.

Han, Dongyu 韓東育. "'Xing zi mingchu' yu fajia de 'renqing lun'" 《性自命出》與法家的"人情論." *Shixue jikan* 史學集刊 2 (2002): 9–14.

Hansen, Chad. "A Tao of Tao in Chuang-tzu." In *Experimental Essays on Chuang-tzu*. Victor H. Mair, ed. *Asian Studies at Hawaii* 29. Honolulu: University of Hawai'i Press, 1983.

Harris, William V. *Restraining Rage: The Ideology of Anger Control in Classical Antiquity*. Cambridge, MA: Harvard University Press, 2001.

Hashimoto, Akinori 橋本昭典. "Kakuten Sokan 'Sei ji mei shutsu' ni okeru 'jō' ni tsuite" 郭店楚簡《性自命出》における"情"について. *Chūgoku kenkyū shūkan* 中國研究集刊 36 (2004): 182–99.

He, Shanmeng 何善蒙. "Zhongguo chuantong yishu zhong 'qing' de zhexue quanshi" 中國傳統藝術中"情"的哲學詮釋. *Wenhua yishu yanjiu* 文化藝術研究 1, 2 (2008): 59–74.

Hendrischke, Barbara. "Review of Kenneth W. Holloway 'Guodian: The Newly Discovered Seeds of Chinese Religious and Political Philosophy.'" *Journal of the Royal Asiatic Society*, 3d ser., 21 (2011): 124–26.

Holloway, Kenneth W. *Guodian: Guodian: The Newly Discovered Seeds of Chinese Religious and Political Philosophy*. New York: Oxford University Press, 2009.

———. "Can an Understanding of Guodian Manuscripts Help Bridge Divisions in Chinese Buddhism?" In *Proceedings of the Second World Buddhist Forum* 第二屆世界佛教論壇論文集. Beijing: Preparatory Office of the World Buddhist Forum 世界佛教論壇籌備辦公室, 2009.

———. "An Inquiry into the 'Xing zi mingchu' from the Perspective of the 'Five Aspects of Conduct'" 從《五行篇》的角度探討《性自命出》. *Taiwan Journal of East Asian Studies* 臺灣東亞文明研究學刊 6, 1 (June 2009): 203–10.

———. "Review of *Envisioning Eternal Empire: Chinese Political Thought of the Warring States Era*, by Yuri Pines" *Sino Platonic Papers*, twenty-fifth anniversary issue 208 (2011): 29–31.

Huang, Xiangyang 黃湘陽. "Shangbo jian 'Xing qing lun' yu yuejiao zhuzhang" 上博《性情論》與樂教主張. In *Xinchu Chujian yu Rujia sixiang lunwenji* 新出楚簡與儒家思想論文集. Chen Fubin, ed. Taipei: Furen Daxue, 2002.

Ikeda, Tomohisa 池田知久, ed. *Kakuten Sokan Jukyō kenkyū* 郭店楚簡儒教研究. Tokyo: Kyūko, 2003.

———. "Kakuten Sokan 'Sei ji mei shutsu' ni okeru 'dō no shijutsu'" 郭店楚簡《性自命出》における「道の四術」. In *Kakuten Sokan Jukyō kenkyū*. Ikeda Tomohisa, ed. Tokyo: Kyūko, 2003.

Kanaya, Osamu 金谷治. "Chujian 'Xing zi mingchu' pian kaocha" 楚簡"性自命出"篇考察. Gong Ying, tr. 龔穎. *Jianbo yanjiu* 簡帛研究 (2004): 377–90.

Knoblock, John. *Xunzi: A Translation and Study of the Complete Works*. 3 vols. Stanford: Stanford University Press, 1994.

Knoblock, John, and Jeffrey Riegel, tr. *The Annals of Lu Buwei*. Stanford: Stanford University Press, 2000.

Knorpp, William Max, Jr. "What Relativism Isn't." *Philosophy* 73, 284 (1998): 277–300.

Legge, James, tr. (1815-1897). *Li Ki Book of Rites*, vol. 27. Oxford: Clarendon, 1879–85; repr., Delhi: Motilal Banarsidass, 1966.

Lewis, Mark Edward. *Writing and Authority in Early China*. Albany: State University of New York Press, 1999.

———. *The Early Chinese Empires: Qin and Han*. Cambridge, MA: Belknap Press of Harvard University Press, 2007.

Li, Changchun 李長春. "Xing yu tiandao, ke de yu wen: cong 'Xing zi mingchu' kan xian Qin Ruxue 'xing yu tiandao' sixiang de zhankai" 性與天道，可得與聞：從《性自命出》看先秦儒學"性與天道"思想的展開. *Shehui kexue yanjiu* 社會科學研究 3 (2009): 146–52.

Li, Jinglin 李景林. "Du Shangbo jian 'Xing qing lun' de jidian lianxiang" 讀上博簡《性情論》的幾點聯想. *Jilin Daxue shehui kexue xuebao* 吉林大學社會科學學報 6 (2002): 91–95.

Li, Tianhong 李天虹. *Guodian zhujian "Xing zi ming chu" yanjiu* 郭店竹簡《性自命出》研究. *Xinchu jianbo yanjiu congshu* 新出簡帛研究叢書. Wuhan: Hubei jiaoyu, 2002.

———. "'Xing zi mingchu' 'X,' 'X' erzi bushi" 《性自命出》"X"、"X"二字補釋. *Jianbo* 簡帛 1 (2006): 53–57.

Li, Weiwu 李維武. "'Xing zi mingchu' de zhexue yiyun chutan" 《性自命出》的哲學意蘊初探. *Guodian Chujian guoji xueshu yantaohui lunwenji* 郭店楚簡國際學術研討會論文集. Wuhan: Hubei renmin chubanshe, 2000.

Li, Xueqin 李學勤. "Shi 'Xingqing lun' jian 'yidang'" 釋《性情論》簡"逸蕩." *Gugong Bowuyuan yuankan* 故宮博物院院刊 2 (2002): 25–26.

Li, Youguang 李友廣. "Zhenshi buwei: Qian Meng Xun shidai de renxinglun—Yi 'Xing zi mingchu, ming zi tian jiang' wei jidian" 真實不偽：前孟荀時代的人性論—以"性自命出，命自天降"為基點. *Lanzhou xuekan* 蘭州學刊 11 (2008): 4–8, 59. [Translated by Huang Deyuan as "The true or the artificial: Theories on human nature before Mencius and Xunzi—based on 'Sheng is from Ming, and Ming is from Tian,'" *Frontiers of Philosophy in China* 5, 1 (2010): 31–50.]

Li, Youping 李有兵, et al. "Xin xing ben buer: cong Guodian chujian 'Xing zi mingchu' pian lun Rujia 'xing' lun zhi tezheng" 心性本不二：從《郭店竹簡•性自命出》篇論儒家"性"論之特徵. *Fudan xuebao: Sheke ban* 復旦學報：社科版 4 (2002): 101–104.

Li, Yujie李玉潔. "Guodian Chujian rujia zhexue sixiang yu Songdai Lixue" 郭店楚簡儒家哲學思想與宋代理學. *Journal of Henan University* 42, 1 (2002).

Lian, Shaoming 連劭名. "Lun Guodian Chujian 'Xing zi mingchu' zhong de 'dao'" 論郭店楚簡《性自命出》中的《道》. *Zhongguo zhexue shi*中國哲學史 4 (2000): 36–40.

Liang, Tao 梁濤. "'Xing zi mingchu' yu zaoqi Rujia xinxinglun"《性自命出》與早期儒家心性論. In *Gumu xinzhi* 古墓新知. Pang Pu et al. *Chutu sixiang wenwu yu wenxian yanjiu congshu* 10. Taipei: Taiwan Guji, 2002.

———. "Zhujian 'Xing zi mingchu' yu Mengzi 'tianxi zhi yan xing' zhang" 竹簡《性自命出》與《孟子》"天下之言性" 章. *Zhongguo zhexue shi*中國哲學史 4 (2004): 70–76.

Liao, Mingchun 廖名春. "Guodian Chujian Rujia zhuzuo kao" 郭店楚簡儒家著作考. *Kongzi yanjiu* 孔子研究 3 (1998): 69–83.

———. "Guodian Chujian 'Xing zi mingchu' pian jiaoshi" 郭店楚簡《性自命出》篇校釋. *Qinghua jianbo yanjiu*清華簡帛研究 1 (2000): 28–67.

———. "Guodian jian 'Xing zi mingchu' de bian lian yu fenhe wenti" 郭店簡《性自命出》的編連與分合問題. *Zhongguo zhexue shi*中國哲學史 4 (2000) 14–21.

———. *Guodian Chujian jiaoshi* 郭店楚簡校釋 (Beijing: Qinghua, 2003).

Liu, Dajun劉大鈞, ed. *Jianbo kaolun* 簡帛考論. Shanghai: Guji, 2007.

Liu, Guangsheng 劉光勝. "You 'Zengzi' shipian kan 'Xing zi mingchu' de chengshu ji lilu—jianlun Song ru dui xian Qin ruxue de wudu" 由《曾子》十篇看《性自命出》的成書及理路—兼論宋儒對先秦儒學的誤讀. *Shilin*史林 2 (2009): 100–106.

Liu, Lexian 劉樂賢. "'Xing zi mingchu' yu Huainanzi 'Miucheng' lun 'qing'"《性自命出》與《淮南子•繆稱》論 "情." *Qinghua jianbo yanjiu*清華簡帛研究 1 (2000): 164–72. Reprinted in *Zhongguo zhexue shi*中國哲學史 4 (2000): 22–27.

Liu, Lexian 劉樂賢. "'Xing zi mingchu' de xuepai xingzhi"《性自命出》的學派性 質. In *Gumu xinzhi* 古墓新知. Pang Pu et al. *Chutu sixiang wenwu yu wenxian yanjiu congshu* 10. Taipei: Taiwan Guji, 2002. Liu, Xinlan 劉昕嵐. "Guodian Chujian 'Xing zi mingchu' pian jianshi" 郭店楚簡《性自命出》篇箋釋. *Guodian Chujian guoji xueshu yantaohui lunwenji* 郭店楚簡國際學術研討會論.文集.Wuhan: Hubei renmin chubanshe, 2000.

Lupke, Christopher, ed. *The Magnitude of Ming: Command, Allotment and Fate in Chinese Culture*. Honolulu: University of Hawai'i Press, 2005.

Ma, Chengyuan馬承源, et al. *Shanghai Bowuguan cang Zhanguo Chu zhushu* 上海博物館藏戰國楚竹書. 8 vols. to date. Shanghai: Guji, 2001–.

Mair, Victor H., ed. *Experimental Essays on Chuang-tzu*. Asian Studies at Hawaii 29. Honolulu: University of Hawai'i Press, 1983.

Mair, Victor. *Tao Te Ching: The Classic Book of Integrity and the Way*. New York: Bantam, 1990.

Marks, Joel, and Roger Ames, eds. *Emotions in Asian Thought: A Dialogue in Comparative Philosophy*. Albany: State University of New York Press, 1995.

Mollier, Christine. *Buddhism and Taoism Face to Face*. Honolulu: University of Hawai'i Press, 2008.

Nakajima, Ryuzo 中嶋隆藏. "Guodian Chujian 'Xing zi mingchu' pian xiaokao" 郭店楚簡《性自命出》篇小考. *Chudi jianbo sixiang yanjiu*楚地簡帛思想研究 3 (2007): 416–39.

Nedostup, Rebecca. *Superstitious Regimes, Religion and the Politics of Chinese Modernity*. Cambridge, MA: Harvard University Asia Center, 2009.

Niu, Hongen 牛鴻恩. "Lunyu de shiming xianzai keyi lundingle—Guodian Chujian 'Xing zi mingchu' de 'lunhui' ji Lunyu zhi 'lun' de hanyi"《論語》的釋名現在可以論定了—《郭店竹簡·性自命出》的"侖會"即《論語》之"論"的含義. *Changjiang xueshu* 長江學術 1 (2007): 139–47.

Nylan, Michael, and Thomas Wilson. *Lives of Confucius: Civilization's Greatest Sage through the Ages*. New York: Doubleday, 2010.

Ouyang, Zhenren 歐陽禎人. "'Taiyi shengshui' yu Rujia xingqing lun de guanxi"《太一生水》與儒家性情論的關係. In *Xinchu jianbo yanjiu: Xinchu jianbo guoji yantaohui lunwenji* 新出簡帛研究: 新出簡帛國際研討會論文集. Ai Lan and Xing Wen, eds. *Beijing daxue zhendan gudai wenming yanjiu zhongxin xueshu congshu* 8. Beijing: Wenwu, 2004.

———. "'Xing zi mingchu' de xingqing sixiang yanjiu"《性自命出》的性情思想研究. *Chudi jianbo sixiang yanjiu* 楚地簡帛思想研究 2 (2004): 167–207.

———. *Xian Qin Rujia xingqing sixiang yanjiu* 先秦儒家性情思想研究. Wuhan: Wuhan Daxue, 2005.

———. "'Xunzi' zhong 'qing' zi de zhexue yihan"《荀子》中"情"字的哲學意涵. *Zhongguo qingnian zhengzhi xueyuan xuebao* 中國青年政治學院學報 17, 3 (2008): 41–47.

Pan, Xiaohui 潘小慧. "Shangbo jian yu Guodian jian 'Xing zi mingchu' pian zhong 'qing' de yiyi yu jiazhi" 上博簡與郭店簡《性自命出》篇中"情"的意義與價值. In *Xinchu Chujian yu Rujia sixiang lunwenji* 新出楚簡與儒家思想論文集. Chen Fubin, ed. Taipei: Furen Daxue, 2002.

Pang, Pu 龐樸, et al. *Gumu xinzhi* 古墓新知. *Chutu sixiang wenwu yu wenxian yanjiu congshu* 10. Taipei: Taiwan Guji, 2002.

Peng, Guoxiang 彭國翔. "Continuity between Classical Confucianism and Neo-Confucianism: As Seen through Archeological Finds of Confucian Texts" 從出土文獻看宋明理學與先秦儒學的連貫性—郭店與上博儒家文獻的啟示. *Social Sciences in China* (April 2007).

Peng, Lin 彭林. "Guodian Chujian 'Xing zi mingchu' bushi"《郭店楚簡·性自命出》補釋. *Guodian Chujian yanjiu. Zhongguo zhexue* 郭店楚簡研究中國哲學 20 (1999): 315–20.

———. "Ru, Dao liangjia de xingqing lun yu tiandao guan" 儒、道兩家的性情論與天道觀. *Jianbo yanjiu* 簡帛研究 (2002–2003): 65–73.

Pines, Yuri. *Envisioning Eternal Empire: Chinese Political Thought of the Warring States Era*. Honolulu: University of Hawai'i Press, 2009.

Pollock, Linda A. "Anger and the Negotiation of Relationships in Early Modern England." *The Historical Journal* 47, 3 (September 2004): 567–90.

Puett, Michael. *The Ambivalence of Creation: Debates Concerning Innovation and Artifice in Early China*. Stanford: Stanford University Press, 2001.

———. "The Ethics of Responding Properly: The Notion of *Qíng* 情 in Early Chinese Thought." In *Love and Emotions in Traditional Chinese Literature*. Halvor Eifring, ed. Leiden: Brill, 2004.

———. "Following the Commands of Heaven: The Notion of Ming in Early China." In *The Magnitude of Ming: Command, Allotment and Fate in Chinese Culture*. Christopher Lupke, ed. Honolulu: University of Hawai'i Press, 2005.

Pulleyblank, Edwin. *Outline of Classical Chinese Grammar*. Vancouver: University of British Columbia Press, 1996.

Pye, Michael. *Skilful Means: A Concept in Mahayana Buddhism*. 2d ed. London: Taylor & Francis Routledge, 2003.

Qian, Xun 錢遜. "'Xing zi mingchu' (qian ban bufen) zhaji"《性自命出》(前半 部分) 札記. *Qinghua jianbo yanjiu* 清華簡帛研究 1 (2000): 147–50.

Renteln, Alison Dundes. "Relativism and the Search for Human Rights." *American Anthropologist, New Series*, 90, 1 (March 1988): 56–72.

Roberts, Moss. *Daode jing: The Book of the Way*. Berkeley: University of California Press, 2001.

Rosenwein, Barbara H. "Worrying about Emotions in History." *The American Historical Review* 107, 3 (June 2002): 821–45.

Sapontzis, S. F. "Moral Relativism: A Causal Interpretation and Defense." *American Philosophical Quarterly* 24, 4 (October 1987): 329–37.

Sato, Masayuki. *The Confucian Quest for Order: The Origin and Formation of the Political Thought of Xunzi*. Boston: Brill, 2003.

Schaberg, David. "Command and the Content of Tradition." In *The Magnitude of Ming: Command, Allotment, and Fate in Chinese Culture*. Christopher Lupke, ed. Honolulu: University of Hawai'i Press, 2005.

Schwartz, Benjamin I. *The World of Thought in Ancient China*. Cambridge, MA: Belknap, 1985.

Shaughnessy, Edward. *Rewriting Early Chinese Texts*. Albany: State University of New York Press, 2006.

Shibuya, Yuki 澁谷由紀. "'Sei' to 'shin'—"Sei ji mei shutsu" no bunseki o tsūjite" "性"と"心"—《性自命出》の分析を通じて. *Chūgoku shutsudo shiryō kenkyūkai* 8 (2004): 1–21.

Shun, Kwong-loi. "Mencius on Jen-hsing." *Philosophy East and West*, 47, 1, *Human "Nature" in Chinese Philosophy: A Panel of the 1995 Annual Meeting of the Association for Asian Studies* (January 1997): 1–20.

Slingerland, Edward. *Effortless Action: Wu-wei Aas Conceptual Metaphor and Spiritual Ideal in Early China*. New York: Oxford University Press, 2003.

Stewart, Robert M., and Lynn L. Thomas. "Recent Work on Ethical Relativism." *American Philosophical Quarterly* 28, 2 (April 1991): 85–100.

Sun, Bangjin 孫邦金. "Guodian Chujian 'Xing zi mingchu' de tianmingguan yu xinxinglun" 郭店楚簡《性自命出》的天命觀與心性論. *Changjiang Daxue xuebao: Sheke ban* 長江大學學報：社科版 1 (2004): 13–17.

Tang, Yijie 湯一介. "'Dao shi yu qing' de zhexue quanshi—Wulun chuangjian Zhongguo jieshixue wenti" "道始於情"的哲學詮釋—五論創建中國解失學問題. *Xueshu yuekan* 7 (2001): 40–44. "Emotion in Pre-Qin Ruist Moral Theory: An Explanation of '*Dao* Begins in *Qing*.'" Brian Bruya and Hai-ming Wen, tr. *Philosophy East and West* 53, 2 (2003): 271–81.

Thrasher, Alan R. *Sizhu Instrumental Music of South China: Ethos, Theory and Practice*. Boston: Brill, 2008.

Tillman, Hoyt Cleveland. "A New Direction in Confucian Scholarship: Approaches to Examining the Differences between Neo-Confucianism and Tao-hsüeh." *Philosophy East and West* 42, 3 (July 1992): 455–74.

———. "The Uses of Neo-Confucianism, Revisited: A Reply to Professor de Bary." *Philosophy East and West* 44, 1 (January 1994): 135–42.

Tu, Zongliu 涂宗流, and Liu Zuxin 劉祖信. Guodian chujian xianqin rujia yishu jiaoshi 郭店楚簡先秦儒家佚書校釋. Taibei: Wanjuanlou, 2001.

Unwin, Nicholas. "Relativism and Moral Complacency." *Philosophy* 60, 232 (April 1985): 205–14.

Van Norden, Bryan W. "Method in the Madness of the Laozi," In *Religious and Philosophical Aspects of Laozi*. Mark Csikszentmihalyi and Philip J. Ivanhoe, eds. Albany: State University of New York Press, 1999.

———. *Virtue Ethics and Consequentialism in Early Chinese Philosophy*. New York: Cambridge University Press, 2007.

Wang, Xingping 王幸平. "'Xing zi mingchu' dui Kongzi renxinglun de fazhan" 《性自命出》對孔子人性論的發展. *Jianghan Daxue xuebao: Renwen kexue ban* 江漢大學學報: 人文科學版 3 (2004): 67–69.

Wang, Zhenfu 王振復, and Chen Lijun. 陳立群. "Guodian Chujian 'Xing zi mingchu' de meixue yiyi" 郭店楚簡《性自命出》的美學意義. *Fudan xuebao: Sheke ban* 復旦學報: 社科版 1 (2003): 96–100.

Watson, Burton tr. *Hsün Tzu: Basic Writings*. New York: Columbia University Press, 1996.

Xiang, Shiling 向世陵. "Guodian chujian 'xing' 'qing' shuo" 郭店竹簡"性""情"說. *Kongzi yanjiu* 孔子研究 1 (1999): 70–78, 86.

Xie, Weiyang 謝維揚, and Zhu Yuanqing, eds. *Xin chutu wenxian yu gudai wenming yanjiu* 新出土文獻與古代文明研究. Shanghai: Shanghai Daxue, 2004.

Xu, Kangsheng 許抗生. "'Xing zi mingchu,' 'Zhong yong,' *Mengzi* sixiang de bijiao yanjiu" 《性自命出》、《中庸》、《孟子》思想的比較研究. *Kongzi yanjiu* 孔子研究 1 (2002): 4–13.

Xu, Zaiguo 徐在國. "Shangbo jian 'Xing qing lun' bushi yize" 上博簡《性情論》補釋一則. *Shixue jikan* 史學集刊 1 (2003). Reprinted in *Xin chutu wenxian yu gudai wenming yanjiu* 新出土文獻與古代文明研究. Xie, Weiyang, and Zhu Yuanqing, eds. Shanghai: Shanghai Daxue, 2004.

Xu, Zaiguo, and Huang Dekuan 黃德寬. "Shanghai Bowuguan cang Zhanguo Chu zhushu (yi) 'Ziyi,' 'Xing qing lun,' shiwen buzheng" 《上海博物館藏戰國楚竹書（一）.緇衣、性情論》釋文補正.*Gujizhengli yanjiu xuekan* 古籍整理研究學刊 3 (2002): 1–6.

Yan, Binggang 顏炳罡. "Guodian Chujian 'Xing zi mingchu' yu Xunzi de qingxing zhexue" 郭店楚簡《性自命出》與荀子的情性哲學. *Zhongguo zhexue shi* 中國哲學史 1 (2009): 5–9.

Yan, Zhonghu. "A Study of Xing (Human Nature) in Nature Comes from the Decreed, A Recently Discovered Confucian Text at Guodian." *East Asia Forum* 10 (2005): 1–16.

Yang, Baoshan 楊寶山. "Cong Guodian zhujian 'Xing zi mingchu' kan Yueji de chengshu niandai" 從郭店竹簡《性自命出》看《樂記》的成書年代. *Guoji ruxue yanjiu* 國際儒學研究 11 (2001): 54–70.

Yang, Mayfair Mei-Hui, ed. *Chinese Religiosities, Afflictions of Modernity and State Formation*. Berkeley: University of California Press, 2008.

Yang, Zhaoming 楊朝明. "'Yi Zhoushu' 'Zhouxun' yu rujia de renxing xueshuo—Cong *Yi Zhoushu* 'Duxun' deng pian dao Guodian Chujian 'Xing zi mingchu'" 《逸周書》"周訓"與儒家的人性學說—從《逸周書·度訓》等篇到郭店楚簡《性自命出》. *Guoxue xuekan* 國學學刊 3 (2009): 83–90.

Yao, Haiyan 姚海燕, and Sun Wenzhong 孫文钟. "Zhanguo Chu zhushujian 'Xingqing lun' de yue jiao sixiang yu xiandai yinyue liaofa" 戰國楚竹書簡《性情論》的樂教思想與現代音樂療法. *Zhong yiyao wenhua* 中醫藥文化, 2006.5.

Yu, Chun-fang. *Kuan-yin, The Chinese Transformation of Avalokitesvara*. New York: Columbia University Press, 2001.

Yu, Zhiping 余治平. "Zhexue benti shiye xia de xin, xing, qing, jing tanjiu—Guodian Chujian 'Xing zi mingchu' de ling yi zhong jiedu" 哲學本體視野下的心、性、情、敬探究—郭店楚簡《性自命出》的另一種解讀. *Guodian Chujian guoji xueshu yantaohui lunwenji* 郭店楚簡國際學術研討會論文集. Wuhan: Hubei renmin chubanshe, 2000.

Zhang, Maoze 張茂澤. "Xing zi mingchu pian xinxing lun da butong yu 'zhongyong' shuo" 《性自命出》篇心性論大不同於《中庸》說. *Renwen zazhi* 人文雜誌 3 (2000): 111–15.

Zhao, Jianwei 趙建偉. "Guodian chujian 'Zhongxin zhi dao,' 'Xing zi mingchu' jiaoshi" 郭店楚簡《忠信之道》、《性自命出》校釋. *Zhongguo zhexueshi* 中國哲學史 2 (1999): 34–39.

Zhao, Zhongwei 趙中偉. "Xing zi mingchu, ming zi tian jiang—Shanghai Zhanguo zhujian 'Xing qing lun' yu Guodian zhujian 'Xing zi mingchu' zhi renxinglun pouxi" 性自命出, 命自天降—上海戰國竹簡《性情論》與郭店竹簡《性命出》之人性論剖析. In *Xinchu Chujian yu Rujia sixiang lunwenji* 新出楚簡與儒家思想論文集. Chen, Fubin, ed. Taipei: Furen Daxue, 2002.

Zhou, Fengwu 周鳳五. "Shangbo 'Xing qing lun' xiaojian" 上博《性情論》小箋. *Qilu xuekan* 齊魯學刊 4(2002): 13–16.

———. "Guodian 'Xing zi mingchu' 'nu yu ying er wubao' shuo" 郭店《性自命出》"怒欲盈而毋暴"說. In *Xin chutu wenxian yu gudai wenming yanjiu* 新出土文獻與古代文明研究. Xie Weiyang and Zhu Yuanqing, eds. Shanghai: Shanghai Daxue, 2004.

Zhu, Yuanqing 朱淵清 and Liao Mingchun 廖名春, eds. *Shangboguan cang Zhanguo Chu zhushu yanjiu* 上博館藏戰國楚竹書研究. 2 vols. Shanghai: Shanghai shudian, 2002–2004.

TRADITIONAL SOURCES

Cheng, Shude 程樹德 (1877–1944). *Lunyu jishi* 論語集釋. Beijing: Zhonghua, 1990.

Gao, Ming 高明. *Boshu Laozi jiaozhu* 帛書老子校注. Beijing: Zhonghua, 1996.

Huang, Huaixin 黃懷信. *Lunyu huijiao jishi* 論語彙校集釋. Shanghai: Shanghai Guji, 2008.

Jiang, Renjie 蔣人傑. *Shuowen Jiezi Jizhu* 說文解字集注. 3 vols. Shanghai: Guji, 1996.

Jiao, Xun 焦循 (1763–1820). *Mengzi zhengyi* 孟子正義. In *Zhuzi jicheng* 諸子集成. Beijing: Zhonghua, 1996.

Ruan, Yuan 阮元 (1764–1849). Li ji zhengyi 禮記正義. In *Shisanjing Zhushu* 十三經注書 1815; repr. Taipei: Yiwen, 1960.

Wang, Xianqian 王先謙 (1842–1918). *Xunzi ji jie, kao zheng: ji jie er shi juan kao zheng er juan* 荀子集解‧考證: 集解二十卷考証二卷. Taibei: Shijie, 1967.

EDITIONS OF THE "XING ZI MINGCHU"

Chen, Wei 陳偉, et al. *Chudi chutu Zhanguo jian ce (Shisan zhong)* 楚地出土戰國簡冊 (十三種). Beijing: Jingji kexue, 2009.

Ding, Yuanzhi 丁原植. *Chujian Rujia "Xing qing shuo" yan jiu* 楚簡儒家《性情說研究》. Taibei: Wanjuanlou, May 2002.

Guodian chumu zhujian 郭店楚幕竹簡. Beijing: Wenwu, 1998.

Ji, Xusheng 季旭昇. *Shanghaibowuguan cang Zhanguo Chu zhushu yi duben* 上海博物館藏戰國楚竹書 (一)讀本》. Taibei: Wanjuanlou, 2004.

Li, Ling 李零. *Shanghai Chujian sanpian jiaoduji* 上海楚簡三篇交讀記. Taibei: Wanjuanlou, March 2002.

Liu, Zhao 劉釗. *Guodian chujian jiaoshi* 郭店楚簡校釋. Fujian: Remin, 2003.

Ma, Chengyuan 馬承源, ed. *Shanghaibowuguan cang Zhanguo Chu zhushu (yi)* 上海博物館藏戰國楚竹書 (一) Shanghai: Guji, 2001.

INDEX

abdication, 58–62
Ames, Roger, 58–59, 128n15, 130n5
   and Hall, 6–7, 61, 126n12, 130n11
anger
   as ecstatic response, 1, 12, 23, 27, 119, 132n27
   harmony and, 26, 88
   nu, 27–28, 73, 132n25, 132n27
   qing and, 30
   self-cultivation and, 64
   Western perspective on, 25
   yun, 2, 27, 73, 132n25
Analects
   contextual ethics, 3, 82–85, 87, 95
   criticism of Confucius, 133n22
   dao in, 7, 45, 84, 126n12
   Daode jing and, 39, 78–80, 90, 96–98, 105–108, 110
   heaven in, 2, 127n16
   music in, 74, 91–93, 96, 134n10, 141n68
   naming, 79–80, 87, 90–97, 105–108, 110, 134n2
   North Star in, 85–86
   on the filial, 20, 83
   punishment in, 95–96
   qing and *nature* in, 2
   story of Upright Gong, 27
   Xing zi mingchu and, 2–3, 7, 10, 19–20, 62, 78–80, 84, 86–90, 96, 139n48, 141n68
   Yan Hui in, 19, 128n9
aristocracy, 93

bamboo strips, ix, 1, 65, 137n16
de Bary, Wm. Theodore, 6, 126n13, 128–29n17, 133n21

Berthrong, John, 128n16, 129n2
Book of Documents, 7, 89, 130n2, 141n70, 141n77
Book of Music, 7, 89, 130n2
Book of Odes, 7, 89, 95, 128n8, 130n2, 141n70
Book of Rites, 7, 72–3, 89, 130n2, 132n26, 132n27, 141n77
Buddhism, ix, 4, 5, 61–62, 78, 125n1, 126n7, 127n2

Chan, Alan K.L., 134n1
Chen, Wei, 114, 132n30, 138n37, 139nn41–6, 140n55, 140n57, 141n76, 142n81, 142n93, 143n101, 144n110, 144n117, 144n123, 145n127, 145n131, 145nn137–8
Clergy, 7, 11–13, 18, 20,
Confucius
   corrective measures, 85, 93, 96
   criticized, 132n22
   dao and, 1
   filial action, 82–3
   focus on immanence, 2, 6, 46
   heaven, 2, 6, 132n8
   Laozi and, 79
   music, 74, 141n68
   on morality, 82, 84–86
   on names, 20, 79–80, 90–95, 97, 106–108
   on orthopraxy, 3, 133n18
   Xing zi mingchu and, 2, 6, 10, 20, 84, 86, 88, 89, 109
Cook, Scott, 134n10, 140n52
Creel, H.G., 95, 134n9
Csikszentmihalyi, Mark, 126n12

Dao
- absolute *dao*, 80–81
- conflict with, 3–4
- eternal, 99–100, 104
- feelings and, 67, 109
- filial relation and, 45, 123
- four daos, 5–6, 12, 41–43, 48, 120, 129n9, 129n11
- four techniques, 40–41, 55, 69, 117, 129n11, 139n47
- fun and, 46
- greater and lesser distinction of, 5–7, 22, 24, 25, 28, 38, 44, 46, 56, 59, 61–62, 67–68, 70, 81, 129n1
- harmony and, 12, 26, 75, 86, 88, 111
- heaven and, 2, 73
- human action and, 122, 135n18, 135n32
- morality and, 11–12, 20, 22, 41, 51, 56, 58, 84, 89–90, 117, 119–20, 138n37
- names and, 79–80, 90, 97–106, 108, 129n10, 135n15, 135n18, 135n27
- nature and, 52–54, 58–59, 130n2
- of Yao and Shun, 58–62
- *qing* and, 1–4, 7, 9–10, 14–18, 20, 29–35, 39–41, 43–45, 48–49, 58, 63, 66, 78, 81, 90, 93, 105, 109–11, 114, 127n7
- ineffability of, 80, 136n36
- source of all things, 103–104, 116, 138n27
- transcendent, 45–49, 58, 61, 69, 87, 100–101, 106, 108–10, 126n12
- translation concerns, 134n14, 136n33, 138nn31–32, 139–40n51, 145n126

Daodejing, 2, 39, 78–80, 87–88, 89–90, 96–104, 105–109, 126n12, 129n10, 136n36, 138n27

Daoism, 127n2
Ding, Sixin, 1–2, 125n4
Ding, Yuanzhi, x, 113–14
Duke Ding, 83
Duke Jing, 94–95, 107

Eifring, Halvor, 79, 133n12
Escher, M.C., 48

Falkenhausen, Lothar von, 12–13, 127n4, 132n29

Gaozi, 52
Graham, A.C., 81, 128n15, 133n17, 134n3
Guanzi, 78
Guodian (texts)
- *Analects* and, 20
- attribution to Zisi, 5
- Buddhist influence on, 127n2
- Dao in, 41, 58–61, 81, 111
- dating of, x
- division of, 4, 65, 136n1
- dualist worldview of, 75
- emotions and, 1
- ethics in, 7, 32–33, 66
- individuality, 69
- Mawangdui text and, 134n15
- on crime, 27
- on the physical existence of morals, 15
- politics of, 14, 60–61, 111
- religious culture and, 12–13

Guodian (tomb), 1, 5, 13, 87, 96

heart
- animals and, 47, 109–10, 115
- *dao* and, 40, 47, 55, 69, 117
- emotions, 23–4, 37, 67, 118, 124, 140n65
- honesty and, 120
- instability of, 28, 35, 44, 63–64, 66, 69, 114
- music and, 21, 23, 66, 70–1, 118–19
- nature and, 28, 31, 35–37, 47, 58, 636–4, 66, 68–69, 115, 130n12
- punishment and, 16, 19, 122
- *qing* and, 21, 23, 37, 71, 73, 117, 119, 140n63
- self-cultivation and, 38, 44, 58, 119
- textual issues, 136n6, 137n17, 143n10, 145n132

Hall, David, 6–7, 61, 126n12, 130n11
Han Dynasty, 95
Hansen, Chad, 59, 80
happiness
- equilibrium and, 26
- extreme, 1, 22–23,
- *Five Aspects of Conduct* and, 66–67
- music and ritual and, 7–8, 23, 58, 72–73
- opposition to anger, 27–28
- *qing* and, 10, 16

Xing zi Mingchu and, 22–23, 27–28, 46, 51 table 3.1, 52, 58, 63–65, 67–68, 72, 86, 88, 114, 116, 119, 122, 128n8, 131n18, 143n97
heaven, 1–2, 6, 26, 34, 41, 48, 58, 61, 63, 66–67, 70, 73, 91, 114, 125n1, 126n12, 127n16, 129n8, 131n19, 132n8
He Shanmeng, 78, 133n11
humanity
   loathing and, 16, 19, 31–32, 40, 81, 86, 121–22
   nature and, 31, 38, 119
   punishment and, 14, 27
   righteousness and, 3, 20, 27, 32, 60–62, 66–67, 74, 89, 128n10, 130n9, 143n96
   self-cultivation and, 16–17, 122

jade-like skin, 7, 13–14, 69, 131n14
Ji Kangzi, 84
Ji Xusheng, 114

Knoblock, John, 76, 130n4, 132n4

Laozi, 1, 6, 45, 46, 62, 70, 79, 80, 88, 90, 109, 135n21, 144n110
laughter, 8, 39, 56–58, 70–73, 117–118, 131n21
Legge, James, 73, 132n26
Lewis, Mark Edward, 132n29, 134n2
Li Ling, 113, 136nn1–2, 137n9, 137n13, 137n19, 138n38, 139n45, 140nn61–62, 141n73, 141n75, 142n79, 142n81, 142nn83–84, 142nn86–87, 142n93, 142n95, 143n100, 143nn102–104, 143n106, 144n110, 144n112, 144n122, 144nn125–26, 145n134, 145n136
Li Tianhong, 4, 126n8, 139n43, 140n66
Li Xueqin, 141nn69–70
Liao Mingchun, 1, 5, 125n3, 126n10, 135n32, 139n41, 141n73, 143n102, 145n142
loathing, 9, 13–14, 17, 19, 30–32, 40, 52, 74, 89
Lushi Chunqui, 54, 78

Marks, Joel, 128n15
materials, 33–37, 42–43, 47, 50–52, 54–55, 59, 62–5, 68, 109, 114–16, 119, 131n22, 138n31
Ma Chengyuan, 114, 130–31n12
Mawangdui, 45, 79, 134n15, 135n21, 135n23, 135n27, 135n29, 135n32, 144n10
Mencius
   Dao in, 138n37
   emotions, 26
   Emperor Shun in, 141n77
   on humanity and righteousness, 20, 109, 130n12
   nature in, 31, 52, 68–69, 109, 128n15
   ritual in, 83–85
   Xing zi mingchu and, 48–49, 68–69, 75, 77, 79, 128n11, 130n12
Meng Wubo, 82–83
Meng Yizi, 82–83
Ming Dynasty, 4, 26, 79
Mohism, 133n22
music
   heart and, 23, 39, 66
   Lai and Wu, 70–71, 73–74, 118
   licentious, 71, 74, 118, 132n30, 141n67
   nature and, 47
   ritual and, 2, 8, 22, 56–58, 69, 72, 77, 91–93, 96, 105, 117, 134n10, 143n97
   self-cultivation and, 46, 70, 74, 109, 124, 131n21, 132n6
   Shao and Xia, 70–71, 73–74, 118, 141n68
   vocalization, 132n28
   Zheng and Wei, 70, 74, 118

Nanjing decade, 12
Neo-Confucianism, 4–5, 26, 33–34, 38, 128n17

Ouyang Zheren, 77, 132n8

Peng Guoxiang, 26, 38, 128–29n17
Pines, Yuri, 85, 133n24
pre-Han, 4, 79, 131n12, 145n139
pre-Qin, 26, 78, 125n2, 127n2, 128n15
Puett, Michael, 39, 129n8, 131n13

qing
  Analects and, 2
  bridging immanence and transcendence, 2, 10–11, 14, 22, 29, 39–41, 48–49, 70, 90, 106
  changes in conception of, 26, 128n15
  cultivation of, 14–15, 18, 56–57, 77–78, 109, 111
  dao and, 1–4, 7, 9–10, 14–18, 20, 29–35, 39–41, 43–45, 48–49, 57–59, 63, 66, 69, 78, 81, 88, 90, 93, 105–106, 109–11, 114, 127n7
  emotions and, 1, 2, 10, 23–25, 31, 37, 48, 57, 71–72, 76, 105, 118, 128n15
  error and, 29, 45, 74
  governing and, 9, 11, 14–15, 78
  heart and, 37, 70–71, 118–119
  naming and, 77, 79, 89–91, 93, 96–97, 109, 140n63
  nature and, 30, 32–35, 37–40, 43–44, 45, 49, 52, 66, 75–77, 114, 119
  of the classics, 56, 117
  protection from criticism, 15, 17–18, 32, 80, 122
  ritual and, 7, 14, 39–40, 56–57, 72, 117
Qing Dynasty, 79

religion, 4, 11, 12, 18, 127n2
ritual
  Analects on, 82–83, 92, 96
  clergy and, 7
  dao and, 14, 40, 78
  music and, 2, 8, 22, 39, 56–58, 72, 77, 92–93, 96, 131n21, 134n10
  names and, 106
  qing and, 7, 14, 39–40, 43, 49, 56–57, 105, 117, 132n6
  The Five Aspects of Conduct on, 14, 66–7
  Xing zi mingchu on, 89, 130n4, 139n46, 139n50, 142n92, 143n97
  Xunzi on, 69, 75, 78, 117, 124, 130–31n12

Sato, Masayuki, 78, 132n10
sagacity, 66–67, 70, 131n19, 142n89
sage, 7, 47, 56–57, 59, 61–62, 67, 69–70, 89, 99, 117, 130n12, 131n19, 139n49

Schwartz, Benjamin, 134n2
self-cultivation
  Analects on, 39, 87, 106, 109
  Daode jing on, 39, 79, 87, 97, 106, 108–109
  dao and, 39, 44, 46
  Mencius on, 49
  neo-Confucian view of, 38–39
  qing and, 15, 20–21, 45, 49, 57, 93, 109
  Tang yu zhidao on, 58
  The Five Aspects of Conduct and, 20, 69–70
  Xing zi mingchu and, 3, 8, 15, 20, 44, 46, 49, 57, 64–65, 68, 70, 93, 110, 141n70
  Zuhxi on, 26
Shang Dynasty, 75, 138n37
Shanghai Corpus, x, 1, 65, 113–14, 131n12, 136nn1–3, 136n7, 137nn10–22, 138nn24–26, 138n28, 138n30, 139n41, 139nn45–46, 141n63, 141n72, 142n79, 142nn80–81, 142n83, 142n85, 142nn91–92, 142n94, 143n103, 143nn105–106, 144nn115–116, 144n124, 145n126, 145nn128–30, 145nn140–41
Shun. See Yao and Shun
Slingerland, Edward, 80, 133n14
Song Dynasty, 4, 26
sorites
  double sorites, 49–50
  epanaleptical, 34
  triple sorites, 50, 52, 54–55, 58–59
  in Analects, 92–95
  in Xing zi mingchu, 53

Tang Yijie, 1, 109, 125n2, 129n4, 136n37, 141n68
Tang Yu zhidao
  between Analects and Laozi, 62
  dao in, 58, 60–62
  ethical friction, 14, 60
  sages Yao and Shun in, 58–62
  Xing zi mingchu and, 60, 62
Ten Commandments, 86
The Five Aspects of Conduct
  black square markings, 65

dao in, 41, 59
emotions in, 24
ethical principles cultivated together, 20, 66–67
humanity and righteousness, 20
jade-like skin in, 7, 13–14, 69, 131n14
law and crime in, 13–14, 27, 143n96
moral action, 3
self cultivation, 15, 70
sorites in, 49–50
Tang Yu zhidao and, 59
Xing zi mingchu and, 3, 49–50, 59, 69–70

Universal Declaration of Human Rights, 81
upaya, 4

Van Norden, Bryan, 87, 126n12, 134n28

Wang Ji, 38, 129n5
Warring States period, 45, 78, 85, 96, 110–11, 142n97
Watson, Burton, 76, 132n2
We-Jin period, 78

xing (nature)
neo-Confucianism and, 4
The Five Aspects of Conduct and, 66
translation of, 125n1, 136n2, 138n36
Dao and, 49
Xing zi mingchu
as anarchist, 44
authorship of, 5, 75
black squares, 65
Book of Rites and, 72–73
Buddhism and, 4
Confucianism and, 1–3
dao in, 3, 6, 10, 20, 34, 40–41, 45–46, 48, 56–58, 62, 66, 69–70, 81, 86, 90, 93, 110
division of, 33, 111
emotions in, 1, 24–28, 44, 67, 76, 110
Guodian context, 5, 41, 60, 65, 96
higher and lower truth, 43
Laozi and, 2
link between *Analects* and *Daode jing*, 2, 86–88, 89–91, 97, 105–109

loathing in, 14, 32, 89
Mencius and, 31, 47–49, 52–3, 68–69, 75, 77, 109
morality, 3, 7, 20, 46, 72, 80–82
music and rituals in, 2, 8, 22, 23, 39, 46–47, 55–8, 66, 70–74, 109, 117–19, 124, 131n21, 132n28, 132n30, 141n67, 143n97
nature in, 29, 31, 38, 66–68, 76
Neo-Confucianism and, 4, 33, 38
on error, 9
orthopraxy in, 3, 84, 86
religious context of, 11–12
resemblance to *Zhongyong*, 39
Shanghai version, 65
self-cultivation in, 15, 55, 110
sorites in, 50, 58
The Five Aspects of Conduct and, 27, 69
Xing qing lun as secondary name, 1
Xunxi and, 54, 68–69, 75–79, 89, 130n4, 132n7, 142n92
See also qing
Xunzi
Analects and, 97
Daode jing and, 97, 136n36
Mencius and, 68–69, 130–31n12
music, 68–69, 77, 132n6
Xing zi mingchu and, 54, 68–69, 75–79, 89, 130n4, 132n7, 142n92

Yan Binggang, 75, 77, 132n1
Yan Hui, 19
Yao and Shun, 58pp–62
Youzi and Ziyou, 72
Yu Cong One, 130n9

Zilu, 87, 91–92, 107
Zisi, 1, 5, 75, 126n10,
Zhuangzi, 19, 47, 80, 132n27
Zhou Fengwu, 139n41, 141n77, 145n37
Zhou Dynasty, 75, 127n4
Zhuxi, 26, 139n48
Zhongyong, 26, 39, 78
Zhuangzi, 80
Zun de yi, 130n9
Zuozhuan, 74